HAL HARTLEY: COLLECTED SCREENPLAYS I

by the same author

AMATEUR
FLIRT
HENRY FOOL

HAL HARTLEY
Collected Screenplays

VOLUME I
The Unbelievable Truth
Trust
Simple Men

faber and faber

This collection first published in 2002
by Faber and Faber Limited
3 Queen Square London WC1N 3AU

Typeset by Faber and Faber Ltd
Printed in England by Bookmarque Ltd, Croydon

Simple Men and *Trust* first published in 1992 by Faber and Faber Ltd
© Hal Hartley, 1992
Introduction © Hal Hartley and Graham Fuller, 1992
This collection © Hal Hartley, 2002

Image from *The Unbelievable Truth* © Action Features/Miramax
Images from *Trust* and *Simple Men* © True Fiction/Zenith

A CIP record for this book
is available from the British Library
ISBN 0-571-21007-4

2 4 6 8 10 9 7 5 3 1

CONTENTS

Introduction
Finding the Essential: Hal Hartley in conversation
with Graham Fuller, 1992
vii

The Unbelievable Truth
1

Trust
129

Simple Men
265

INTRODUCTION
Finding the Essential: Hal Hartley in conversation with Graham Fuller, 1992

GRAHAM FULLER: Before you went to film school, you studied art. Can you detect any evolution between the work you were doing then and your films in terms of style and content?

HAL HARTLEY: I think so. I only did one year at art school, and at the end of that year they would have asked me, 'Do you want to study painting, sculpture, or whatever?' I was very undecided. I was intrigued by fine art, but my skills were in graphic design. Anyway, I used to like to draw pictures from copies of *Sight and Sound* that I picked up in the library. The photos always seemed to be so alive and dramatic – and, in fact, they were dramatic, because they were scene stills.

GF: Anything in particular?

HH: Oh, I couldn't tell. I never really read the articles. It's possible I didn't realize I was looking at a film magazine at all. But I'd make drawings and paintings from them. I began making films toward the end of that year at art school. I took to it immediately. They weren't narrative films, but I had a definite inclination to focus on faces and bodies; hugely, imagistically, not story-wise. And that's something I keep coming back to, this far along. In my films, finding what really excites me about an image almost always leads me back to the human body, the human face, hands.

When we were making *Trust*, my cameraman Mike Spiller and I would ask ourselves, 'In every image we make, what does the human body have to do with this picture? How does this picture gain its significance from the body in it?' Even in landscape shots, we were thinking of how to show towns – that particular Middle American kind of town – without having to get away from a human being. We might show someone walking by a bunch of power plant wires and fences and whatnot, simply to convey a sense of the landscape graphically, in juxtaposition to the human form.

GF: You favor tableaux, too. There's a striking interior shot in
  Trust that shows Maria talking to her mother and sister, with
  Matthew hovering behind her left shoulder. You can't see all
  of him but you can feel the weight of his presence.

HH: Yes. The camera is pretty much entirely on Maria. Her
  mother is behind her. Her sister is off camera left. And
  Matthew is pretty much off camera right, but you can still
  see him.

GF: That elliptical treatment of the human body occurs in
  Robert Bresson's films. There's a compositional austerity in
  your work that also reminds me of Bresson.

HH: I am very affected by Bresson and, more and more, I am
  consciously using that knowledge – whatever that means.
  Sometimes it's just an emotional clarity that I sense in his
  films, that I try to bring to mine when I'm writing. When
  I'm shooting too. Bresson cuts right past everything that's
  superfluous and isolates an image that says exactly what it's
  meant to say.

  In *Surviving Desire*, I show Jude's hand reaching across a
  table to almost touch Sofie's hand. My treatment of that
  action struck me as Bressonian. Recognizing that the gesture
  itself was expressive. Nothing else was needed. It's about
  getting rid of the superfluous and the presumptuous – that's
  what keeps coming up in my notebooks. A lot of my experience over the past four or five years as a filmmaker has been
  in finding out what I need and what I'm going to look at in
  order to tell a story. And this approach of getting rid of
  what's unnecessary requires being totally alive at the
  moment of photography. I always thought that this particular shot in *Surviving Desire* would be done in close-up or two
  matching singles. I thought it was their faces that were
  important at that moment. But it wasn't. It was their hands
  and nothing else.

GF: What do you mean when you say 'presumptuous'?

HH: Assuming that there's a certain way things are done. For
  instance, assuming that you have to shoot a love scene in
  close-up. But why not play a love scene in long-shot, from
  two rooms away through the door?

GF: Is that to sustain your own interest in it, or is it because you're bored with the clichés of film grammar?

HH: They are related. I am an audience member as much as anybody. My job on the set is to represent the potential audience, a crowd of people pretty much like me. If it's boring to me, most likely it'll be boring to them.

GF: You seldom bother with establishing shots.

HH: Establishing shots tell me nothing except where we are. 'Where we are' will be elucidated entirely by what the actors are doing and experiencing. When I look at films made even sixty years ago, it seems establishing shots were redundant then too. For instance, when I look at Carl Dreyer's films I see an extreme insistence on the idea, from one frame to the next, of the character's experience to the exclusion of all else, including establishing shots.

It's true, sometimes you *do* need a little relaxation between scenes. You can't always express an idea in a scene and then go right to another that encompasses a new bunch of ideas without a break. You need a rest. That's something I think about a lot, and I often decide to put in something a little less insistent. Five or ten seconds of something a little easier, so that the audience can digest an idea. But it has to be the right thing. Not empty of meaning.

GF: You also dispense with the accretion of plot information that a lot of filmmakers feel obliged to provide.

HH: Well, I think it's always there. For the most part, the feature films I've made, even up to *Simple Men*, have been based on a fairly traditional, classic narrative structure. I used to have it worked out like a map. But it's blurred now. I believe I was taught that a conventional classic American film was to have sixty-four scenes with everything in its place. Introduction, exposition, inciting incident, false climax, true climax, reversal, and denouement. It was math. A way of structuring the raw material.

Trust was built on that structure too. But once I got the story worked out on that schema, I started screwing around with it, doing damage to it, trying to achieve, moment by moment, what it was I wanted. It's emotional from this point on. If I feel something is lagging or moving too fast, I adjust it. I add scenes. Move scenes around. Whatever is needed to make the thing interesting. But I have started from a fairly traditional dramatic structure on all of my features.

GF: How elaborately do you prepare your movies in terms of the visuals? Do you storyboard?

HH: No, but I do diagrams. It's sort of like engineering. By the time we get to the set to shoot, all the technical crew have these diagrams of the proposed setups. It helps everyone know what to expect. And it helps me prepare for the technical implications of my ideas. This was important on *Simple Men*, where Mike [Spiller] and I knew we would shoot the entire film – with the exception of two shots – on the fifty-millimeter lens.

GF: What effect does that give?

HH: Consistency. Consistency of depth-of-field, primarily. Pictorially, it lends a cohesion to a movie that I like a lot. All the hundreds of images that are placed side by side to make up the movie are all seen through the same eye.

But my relationship to a particular lens is really a commitment. The scope of what the fifty-millimeter lens can see in a given situation forces me to wrestle with the physical environment I'm shooting in. If I discover I need to see more of the room, I can solve the problem by either slapping up a wider angle lens or by moving the camera back a few feet. But sometimes there's a wall in the way. So then I have to reimagine my shot or break down the wall.

GF: Do you see a day when you'll move the camera more?

HH: Well, I do in fact have the camera on the dolly about eighty per cent of the time. There is a lot of small movement in *Trust*. But there's larger small movement in *Simple Men*. Whatever's appropriate. That's my rule of thumb. I've never felt that I've lacked the means to achieve what was needed for the story.

GF: Do you move the camera more in *Simple Men* because there's more *travel* in it than in your other films?

HH: I think so. The fifty-millimeter is not a wide-angle lens. Often, if I want to shoot a scene without cutting I have to design the shot to move amongst the actors.

GF: This kind of camera style, though, is happily unobtrusive in your films.

HH: I think that with *Simple Men* the audience might get the feeling of being 'around' the characters more.

GF: Do you write your stories as screenplays? Is that how they get their first exposure?

HH: They start in my notebook. I write about a character, about a situation. I ask myself questions about the characters in particular situations. After a couple of months they begin to flesh themselves out.

GF: Do you surprise yourself with the direction they take?

HH: Never when I'm writing. But they begin to develop in fascinating ways in the rehearsal stage, which, I'm coming to realize, is just the very furthest stages of writing, where each character that I've written on the page actually takes on a life, becomes a real human person on a day-to-day basis. The actor is then putting things into it, and even at that point I'm still bringing in extreme stuff. And then, in the best circumstances, I'm always surprised. We had a very good rehearsal, actually, with Martin [Donovan], on *Simple Men*. His character, who's called Martin, was very sketchily written. But through rehearsal, the character became much more interesting. It became very clear almost immediately that there was a lot more potential there. Before the day was out, I had a totally different idea of who this guy was and what his significance was to the story. This happened without changing hardly any of the dialogue. Martin's significance to the story is that he is *in love* with this woman, Kate, who lives alone, and he is very protective of her. And when the two brothers, Bill and Dennis, come along, he's this kind of wall that they've got to get through, particularly Bill. I didn't see this so clearly when I wrote it.

GF: Do you normally allow the actors to develop their roles beyond the text?

HH: I don't know if I would have given myself that license with *The Unbelievable Truth*, because of the financial constraints. Sometimes the actors would ask questions or bring up ideas, and I'd say, 'Oh, I'm sorry, we just don't have the time to talk about this; just do what I tell you to do.' But, luckily, they did what they thought was right anyway, within the constraints I imposed.

When the whole job of making a film is not just surviving, getting the film in the can, then that line between what's writing and what's rehearsal becomes a lot less difficult to cross.

GF: Do you allow any room for improvisation?

HH: No, because I've never found it to be effective. I allow myself to change some lines if it seems appropriate, otherwise I'd never get it right. But full-fledged out-and-out improvisation has never, for me, yielded anything effective.

GF: Do you rewrite at all during production?

HH: A little bit, out of necessity. Sometimes it's a word or a response that worked fine on the page or in rehearsal. But in a particular kind of daylight beside this particular tree it no longer seems to be right. So I change things. I leave myself open to that possibility more now. Largely because I can afford it.

GF: How do your stories come to you?

HH: I write a lot. I have certain key ideas about situations and characters and they evolve out of each other. Filmmaking for me, like writing, or having a conversation, is a process of thinking. The more I do, the more I think about. Although a lot of *Trust* existed before *The Unbelievable Truth*, there were certain ideas that I felt were half finished in *The Unbelievable Truth*, things I had discovered in the process of making the film, things that I wanted to expand upon.

I was making this film which I thought was about commerce and personal interaction, and how they are kind of corrupted by well-meaning but difficult to assess needs. The actions are those of two people, Josh and Audry, who have been separated in a *Romeo and Juliet* type way, but are finally reconciled. But there's a scene at the end where Josh picks Audry up and says, 'I don't trust anyone,' meaning her as well as anyone else. But then he kisses her, and it's almost as if he should be saying, 'I love you and this is a happy ending.'

So do love and trust necessarily have anything to do with one another?

This is a good example of how things change. It's not how the original script was written. But by the time I got to shooting that scene on location I knew a lot more about these characters and I had this vague dissatisfaction with the scene. I think we even shot it as written, but as we'd do another take I'd change the lines and say, 'No, say this instead of that.' Then I finally stopped for five minutes and wrote down about eight lines of dialogue on the back of an envelope. I gave it to Robert [Burke] and Adrienne [Shelly] and they immediately said, 'Yes, this is definitely it.' We couldn't summarize what this meant. We couldn't para-phrase it and I still can't. It just hit a chord and made sense of everything in the movie; it provided the glue that made the rest of it stick together.

That idea of saying, 'I don't trust you but I love you,' is some kind of ironic dichotomy. Maybe something essential to human nature. The reconciliation of opposites. Whatever it is, it's where *Trust* – which had only existed as a plot out-line with no real emotional connection for me – took off. At that point, though, I could've taken any story and attacked it from this new perspective. There was something about Josh lifting Audry up and effectively saying, 'Now we've gone through this ridiculous charade, this whole movie, and I'm not going to take anything for granted ever again.' That's how Matthew and Maria begin in *Trust*. Maria, particularly, is a full-blown personality at the beginning, and she gets hacked down to zero, and has to start all over again. She learns to read again. She takes nothing for granted. That's why she sleeps on the floor instead of in a bed – she's elimi-nating everything that gets between her and the actual expe-rience of living and breathing, of becoming an aware human being.

GF: Do you feel that dichotomy between loving someone and not being able to trust them is resolved at the end of *Trust*, or do you think it's still being explored in *Simple Men*?

HH: I'm still working it out. But I worked it out as far as I pos-

sibly could in *Trust*. I think of *Trust* as Maria's movie and in
it she manages to define herself and make decisions for herself and, in fact, walk right past all sorts of very real limita-
tions. When everybody runs out of the factory because
Matthew is in there threatening to detonate his hand
grenade, she actually walks right into this no-man's-land, as
it were. She goes where no human being should be expected
to go, and comes back, having saved someone's life. She has
demonstrated a selflessness so complete it obliterates
dichotomies.

   The balance of *Trust* is this sort of yin–yang thing.
Matthew decides he wants to live only for Maria. Maria
wants to live only for Matthew. Two completely different
personality types complementing the best in each other. The
reconciliation of opposites. It surpasses even their being
together physically, because Maria comes to believe that the
only way to be good for herself is to be good for other people and the only way to be good for other people is to forget
the self. I was trying to make a saint's legend.

GF: When her mother contrives to humiliate Maria by getting
   Matthew into bed with her sister, Maria acts as if nothing
   has happened. What's the significance of that?

HH: She's transcended the need for revenge. Her mother's
   obsessive, petty, manipulative behavior is the behavior of a
   desperately disturbed person. Why lower herself to that
   level? On the other hand, why should Maria assume
   Matthew to be impervious to her sister's temptations? It's
   humility. And it takes a saint to maintain it.

GF: Do you think Matthew and Maria are in love at the end of
   the movie?

HH: I think it's charity. In its original sense, charity means the
   highest and most divine form of love; disinterested and seeking no reward. In that sense, yes, I think they are in love.

GF: Your films seem to posit love as a kind of transcendent
   state, but the characters share a kind of knowledge that it's a
   route fraught with danger.

HH: Oh, absolutely. At the end of *The Unbelievable Truth*, love
   may enable Josh and Audry to transcend all the bullshit in a

very physical, immediate sense, but it doesn't make life any easier or any less dangerous. And then with *Trust* I wanted a love story that didn't gloss over the more difficult implications of commitment and intimacy.

GF: Do you think your films are about escape? Both Audry, in *The Unbelievable Truth*, and Maria, in *Trust*, want to break away. Even your early short film, *Kid*, is about the desire to leave.

HH: That was my senior film in college and it is a discussion about wanting to escape. The whole experience of going to college, which was a great experience for me, was about forming dependencies and having to break them; dependencies on ways of thinking and on certain teachers. By the time I came to make my graduation film, I knew that it had to be about forging my own identity, trying to be very deterministic and saying, 'The world is going to be like this because I want it to be like this.' But I realized that this was crazy. Myself and the world are only the result of what has happened before. So *Kid* was about escape, but it was also about the pointlessness of trying to escape. It's not really escape that's important – what's important is recognizing what I'm trying to escape from and who I am.

Trust is about Maria coming to grips with the fact that she can escape, and the fact that what she has to do is make decisions – which is not necessarily escaping – and take responsibility for her own life. In *The Unbelievable Truth*, Audry is someone just too young, too weak, too disappointed, to do anything but be depressed by the state of things. But simply by falling in love, by being engaged in a very personal and direct situation, experiencing a crisis, she begins to have more of a sense of herself as an individual instead of a slab of meat in a world she feels may end at any time. She begins to act. She begins to see that, 'Yeah, maybe the world will blow up, but I can't stop living. That's not going to help.'

GF: It's kind of alarming at the end of *The Unbelievable Truth* that Audry 'hears the bombs' again in her head.

HH: It should be alarming. Audry is too pessimistic and Josh too optimistic. They kind of trade. He gives her some of his optimism and she gives him some of her skepticism. And at the end, sure, she's happy. She has changed. She is able to fall in love, for instance, in a world she suspects may be ultimately doomed, but she is *not* going to turn a blind eye to it as it is. Even now, after the Cold War, it's an extremely dangerous time. It's naive to assume atomic bombs won't destroy the world.

I really like the Audry character. I remember writing Audry and shaking with excitement, saying, 'This is somebody I like, who is all fucked up, definitely, but maybe not all that fucked up.' It was so easy, once I got an image in my head of who she was, to have those words come out of her mouth.

GF: Audry and Josh have a shared interest in George Washington. Where did that motif come from?

HH: Just prior to *The Unbelievable Truth*, I had been writing a script in which this guy who runs a machine shop meets the ghosts of Benjamin Franklin and George Washington. He keeps meeting the fathers of his country on the street, or in bookstores, or in libraries, or in McDonald's. But that story was going nowhere. The juxtaposition of what George Washington popularly represents with this story of emotional commerce seemed appropriate for *The Unbelievable Truth*.

GF: The characters in *Simple Men* have a much stronger arc than those in *The Unbelievable Truth* and *Trust*.

HH: Certainly the film has a much more recognizable point of beginning and conclusion. It's not exactly complete closure, but Bill basically comes back to Kate and is willing to be taken away in chains, which is kind of a variation on the end of *Trust*. *Trust's* ending, in a way, was much more complex because Matthew and Maria didn't decide exactly what that ending would be. They decided how they were going to do things, but then the world at large came in and ended the movie. In *Simple Men*, the ending is the result of Bill's decision.

GF: At the end of each successive movie, you seem to move an inch closer to a resolution. Excepting *Surviving Desire*, the couples seem to be getting closer to forming a relationship.

HH: It's true. *Surviving Desire* was definitely not about the closure, or completeness, of a relationship that's formed. Instead, it's about a relationship blowing apart. A relationship built entirely on the wrong foundations. But I think the Jude character reached an understanding of himself, of his place in the world. It's a little sadder for Sofie somehow. I feel that she hasn't yet recognized the small tragedy that has happened, and that's really what I wanted to end with. She's not a bad person. She's not evil. She hasn't manipulated him in any way consciously. It's just simply that because she's young she can't see certain things. And in *my* life I just have to accept when that happens. I can kick myself all over creation for ever because I made certain mistakes, but I have to accept the fact that I couldn't have known how to avoid them at the time. And I do learn by experience.

GF: Just after Sofie kisses Jude in *Surviving Desire*, he goes into this impromptu deadpan dance with two other guys on the street. There's also a rock band rehearsing. What were you trying to do with these scenes?

HH: I was just curious. I don't like rock videos, but I like to see dance. I like to hear music and play it. I like that live recording, that documentation, that authenticity. That has a lot to do with the dance sequence as well – the documentation of the work and concentration that goes into the execution of a simple spectacle. Here, it's men dancing. It kind of started when I was rehearsing some scenes for *Theory of Achievement*; Jeff Howard, who is an actor I work with often, came over one day with his accordion and played the song for that film. I remember thinking, 'That's how easy it is to make honest cinema.' Just turn the camera on and point it at somebody doing something, and they'll do all the work. They'll feel it – they won't be pretending anything. I find that very pure and fascinating.

When I was writing the script for *Surviving Desire*, I devised this joke of Sofie kissing Jude and then leaving him there, hanging. The script then goes on to say, 'He stumbles out of the bar, falls off the curb, but kind of saves himself by

doing this little shuffling dance.' And then, very unrealisti-
cally, this other man happens by and does the same sort of
funny dance step, and then they go their separate ways.
Somewhere we began talking it and it became more
and more elaborate. It introduces archetypal gestures that
we were very conscious of: the grabbing of the crotch (where
we were deliberately quoting Madonna, who was already
quoting an existing cultural gesture herself), the crucifixion,
West Side Story, etc.

That dance is not disturbing particularly, but it is very
emotionally confusing. By the time they get to the end, I feel
that what started out as a lighthearted dance of joy, because
he's been kissed, is turning into a complex expression of
vague doom.

GF: The elation in that dance is as bitten back as all other emotions in your film. Your characters very seldom smile.

HH: It's an easy win, a smile, you know.

GF: You don't allow actors to emote – which is what most
actors do in most other films. Even when Matthew punches
somebody walking into a bar in *Trust* it's undramatic, almost
contrapuntal.

HH: It's a footnote about violence.

GF: You forbid actors from investing the dialogue or the ideas
they're putting across with any kind of emotional pitch, and
this is something that goes right through your work.

HH: The thing is, none of us are really the work. The work is
the work. The film is the work. I am probably as close to it
as it gets, because the film is, actually, a result of my pre-
occupations. I don't want anybody's contribution to be so
particular as to take away from the guiding aesthetic principle
of the entire piece. The piece itself should have a personality.
There shouldn't be disparate personalities within the piece. I
guess my job, by the time I'm directing it, is one of 'taste'; of
determining balances, judging what seems appropriate and
what doesn't. I don't like to call attention to acting, I don't
like to call attention to photography. I know my films are
extreme in certain ways, like the fact that nobody smiles. But
I like to think that the camera work shows a similar restraint.

I want the photography, the acting, the sound recording, the editing, the music, and the dialogue all to have a perfect understanding of each other, to all be working in concert.

MARTIN DONOVAN: Hal allowed me to smile a couple of times in the café scene in *Surviving Desire*.

HH: Yeah – I thought we were out of control.

GF: When you first worked together on *Trust*, was this something that you discussed? Were there certain qualities you wanted to bring to Matthew, or did Hal say, 'Look, this is how we do it'? And did you find yourself tuning into that minimalist wavelength immediately?

MD: If you had asked me that during the making of or right after *Trust*, I don't know how I would have answered you. I obviously brought something in myself to the role in auditioning for *Trust* that Hal liked and thought was appropriate. In the reading, and then after he told me I was cast and I'd read with other people to cast the other roles, he pretty much let me alone. I don't remember major directorial stuff from Hal during that period. But when we got on the set everything changed, and it was hard to catch on to the idea that, visually, Hal wanted a very basic, simple film technique that was virtually choreographed. In terms of the character's emotional life, smiles, that sort of thing, Hal didn't say much about anything. If he said anything, he would say, 'Faster.' He would say, 'Less,' or, 'Don't use your face.'

HH: Ideally, by the time I get to the set, that's all my direction is: technical. Sometimes I have people going over the top, but they've got to use the appropriate gestures. That's one of the things I think I made a lot of headway on with particular actors in *Simple Men*. I felt like this is the result of four years of steady working with actors I know. When it came down to it, we could use the same terminology on the set to describe appropriate actions and gestures for what is best going to convey an emotional moment. I find it very entertaining when the characters say exactly what a scene seems to be about, but then move on to bigger things. Why try to give an impression of an idea? Why try to illustrate it? Words already exist to express it perfectly. But the words can serve as a foundation for the reality of gestures; gestures which attempt to express things more 'unspeakable.' And words can be gestures too.

What I want the actors to do is not to pretend – just *do it*. Our rehearsal time is an attempt to isolate and specify the appropriate gestures of expression. It's this physical expression that the actors fill up with their understanding of their characters. These physical gestures need to be understood and believed in. And this tends to eliminate pretense. It seems like a blunt, easy way to do it, but it's actually very difficult.

MD: When you're in a relationship with a director that's working there is air pressure. You feel something coming from the director and you feel something coming out of you and it keeps you in balance. As an actor, it has to do with knowing that the director is paying attention to what you're doing, and that that person is there for you. The more I work, the more I want a strong director, who gives me tasks, tells me what to do.

HH: Pressure is a really good image. Because – as a director – if you're not getting any pressure from an actor, there's not a whole lot you can do. You've got to have a force. You've got to have a shape to work against.

GF: Is it harder to work with Hal, where you have to rein yourself in, as opposed to directors who might want some flamboyance?

MD: If you'd asked when we were making *Trust*, I would have said yes. I would have said, 'It's the most difficult thing, it's horrible, I don't like it, Hal's a tyrant.' Now I realize I like it much more than working with a director who doesn't have ideas. But that doesn't make it easier.

HH: The only usable word in the whole process is 'appropriate.' When it seems inappropriate, I know I'm missing the point.

GF: Your films are about real people experiencing real emotions. People do express anger in your films, for example, but there is no hysteria. In life, people do get hysterical . . .

HH: But hysteria is sloppy and art can't be sloppy. In art, you get the chance to do it right. Every moment in my film should be as important as any other, whether it's a pause or whether it's a word. I appreciate precision in art.

GF: You've been compared to Harold Pinter and David Mamet, because there's a similar stylized accent on the words in your films.

HH: I'm flattered by the comparison, though I don't really know a whole lot about either of them. Their work is primarily in theater. Specificity is something I like about Mamet's movie *House of Games*. It's also why I like Bresson. He doesn't waste time on things that don't convey meaning. Every single frame of his films conveys meaning, even if it's an image of someone sitting with nothing to say. Everything Bresson shows you says something. I figure that's what film does best – convey those moments of meaning in action.

GF: Do you feel you're groping for certain philosophical truths in the making of each film, specifically through what the characters are experiencing?

HH: All my films are a desperate attempt to make some philosophic sense out of my own experience. I want to know more. And what the characters go through are little exercises, little experiments; the most effective means with which to make the world and my own experiences understandable to myself.

GF: Is it therapeutic, do you think?

HH: No. If you define 'therapeutic' as something you hope is going to make you better able to deal with life, then no. I'm not entirely sure making films doesn't simply complicate my life. I don't need therapy – I don't think. But then, what do I know? If I can use it now, I could've used it ten years ago. I have the same problems now as I did when I was answering phones for a living. Things may be different now. I have more money and it's easier to meet women now that I have my picture in the paper, and being published with my scripts and all. But the fundamental problems of my life are still the same.

This is all to say that I don't think making films, for me, is therapeutic. But I do think that it is still a process of grappling with philosophical issues every day, which I still have to do whether I need therapy or not. I think it's absolutely necessary. Anybody can live philosophically. I can pack boxes in a department store and still live philosophically. And I might be happy that way.

GF: This relates to the male protagonists in your features. In *The Unbelievable Truth,* Josh is a car mechanic; in *Trust,* Matthew is an electronics whiz; in *Simple Men,* Bill fixes motorbikes. These skills are somehow ennobling.

HH: To Josh in *The Unbelievable Truth,* the simple usefulness of fixing cars, the concreteness of it, is consoling. In this, he has a lot in common with Maria in *Trust.* Likewise, Matthew's insistence on the adequate maintenance of machinery is a kind of respect, an affirmation of human ingenuity. For all his antisocial behavior, his respect for a 'well made thing' is a real gesture of hope.

GF: It's redemptive, isn't it, doing things?

HH: Yes, especially when it's useful. But Josh's priestly skill for fixing cars becomes a commodity and a marketing chip in his love, and this cheapens everything.

In *Simple Men* I was interested in these two brothers: Dennis, a student with few practical skills, and Bill, a man of concrete action. He can fix motorcycles and rob banks, and has all the confidence that comes along with that. I wanted to juxtapose the usefulness of the contemplative life with the life of action. People are attractive when they do what they like and they do it well. You like to be around them. When your car is broken down and you don't know what to do, the first man or woman who comes along and knows how to fix it is suddenly your savior and you want to buy them a drink. You just want to sit down and talk to them. I've always found that to be true. As superficial as it sounds, that actually might be the root of my interest in these skills. As in real life, I have never really been interested in people who are wavering, who don't know what they like, who don't know what they value. *Simple Men* is about some very confused people, but people who still have real strong convictions or feelings and have developed concrete skills based on those convictions.

GF: There are Oedipal relationships in all your films, but particularly in *Simple Men*, where Dennis is sexually attracted to his father's girlfriend. I wondered if you've read Freud?

HH: I've read as much Freud as any college student has read Freud, but not much more. I guess that incident in *Simple Men* denotes an awareness of Freudian analysis. I don't want to take credit for knowing more than I do. But I guess Freudians would have fun, too, with the fact that Maria winds up wearing Matthew's mother's dress in *Trust*. That was very calculated and very prepared.

GF: What about *The Unbelievable Truth*, in which Audry's father has a repressed sexual desire for her?

HH: That was really the whole motor for that story. I had seen a middle-aged construction worker on the subway one evening gazing at a *Penthouse* magazine. I found myself watching this man and asking myself, 'I wonder what would happen if his daughter were the girl in the centerfold? What would he think about that?' That's where it started. I wanted to know where those *Penthouse* girls really came from. What did their moms and dads think about the way in which they made their living? This line of questioning led to a lot of other things.

GF: There is little concession to sensuality in your films, or at least to titillating the audience.

HH: I think my films are very sensual, but you're right, they're not titillating. I'm the first person to say that films are about sex. But I'm bored by seeing other people fuck. I probably resent it. Movies, though, are great about flirtation, about *trying* to get laid. When I see the standard sex scene in a movie I have otherwise been enjoying, I feel like I am viewing a tire gone suddenly flat. Everything that was compelling is gone. I like foreplay. I am much more interested in the *mechanics* of what leads to consummation. A movie should never consummate. I think sometimes that I've avoided explicit sex in my movies because it's embarrassing. It's redundant. Redundancy is embarrassing. And, of course, it always seems beside the point. I don't have any questions to ask about fucking. Whereas I have a lot of questions to ask about the more mundane aspects of life. Attraction, flirtation, disappointment, affection, resentment, contempt – these things make my head spin.

GF: Is it the same with violence? As well as that undercurrent of sex in your films, there's an undercurrent of violence.

HH: I am much easier with people slapping each other, punching each other. It's a different kind of flirting. They rarely ever break out into fighting.

GF: Women slapping men in the face is a regular occurrence in a Hal Hartley film – again in *Simple Men*.

HH: I like the immediacy of a slap. It can be used to mean anything, but at the same time a slap is so specific. I try to treat a slap or a shove in the same way I treat a puff on a cigarette or the delivery of a line. It's almost as if it's expressive because it's so generic. People falling down – I love people falling down. I've always got my eye out for flat spaces to have someone fall down on. Empty highways have this almost narcotic attraction for me.

One day, I'd love to make a film that is entirely constructed of, say, fifteen gestures. These absurd, admittedly arbitrary gestures give a skeleton to which the actor's intelligence applies itself. The best acting I've seen has always been under extreme technical constraints, because that's when you see the actor really working and paying attention, thinking the feelings. The camera has no conscience, it has no psychology, it has no philosophy, it has no history, and no expectations. The camera simply records execution – and the execution becomes expression. That's what I'm trying to get at with small things like Jude's hand almost touching Sofie's hand in *Surviving Desire*. I suspect that this concentration on physical gesture is ultimately where the expression of emotion lies.

GF: In *Simple Men*, characters talk about Madonna. That interested me because there aren't that many references to pop culture in your movies.

HH: There will be more of that. *Simple Men*, I think, is where that begins.

GF: The reason I bring it up is because your films have a certain timeless quality.

HH: But the way to make a film timeless is to time it. In college, my literature professor, Bob Stein, said, 'The thing all classics have in common is that they speak *about* their time, but speak *to* all time.' I learned that from Godard too. For example, he subtitled *A Married Woman*, 'Fragments of a Film Made in 1964.' In effect it conveys that 'this is a film made now, by a person like me, in these circumstances.' You can watch it thirty years later and say, 'Look at what they were wearing then,' and that becomes part of the appreciation of the piece. Godard, in a way, *addressed* the fact that women wore miniskirts in the sixties. In *Don Quixote*, Cervantes addressed the fact that he was writing at a particular time at the end of a generation of Romance literature and 'the way I'm telling you this story has a lot to do with the time in which it was written.' I was brought up thinking an artist should strive to make his work timeless. I'm trying to be an artist, so I'm trying to be timeless. I'm trying to date my films appropriately. It's only inappropriately dated films that become ridiculous and don't say anything about their time and about eternity.

GF: Do you think your films are inherently political?

HH: They're probably consequently political. I don't know if trying to speak about the human condition as honestly as possible *is* a political thing. I know it can be, I know it can be used politically. But it's not my primary intention.

GF: In *Trust*, Matthew's decision to quit his job at a factory where they are knowingly manufacturing faulty computers is a political – or at least a moral – principle.

HH: I think so. It's about dissatisfaction with certain aspects of society. Having a guy grab his boss's head and put it in a vice instead of a meek, mild-mannered guy who doesn't say anything must display an appreciation for a particular moral certitude. But is that necessarily political?

GF: In *Simple Men*, you revive the character of Ned from *Kid*. Is that something you'd like to experiment with further?

HH: Actually, Vic Hugo [Audry's father] and Mike [Josh's fellow mechanic] from *The Unbelievable Truth* are in *Simple Men*, as the same characters. They are the same actors playing the same characters in a different situation, with references to their past lives in the other movie. I was encouraged to use one actor in more than one role in *The Unbelievable Truth* by watching Lindsey Anderson's *O Lucky Man!* Continuing to do it from film to film is an attempt to elicit this feeling of a curiously small world.

GF: You shot *Simple Men* in Texas. How did you make it look like a Long Island coastal suburb?

HH: It was very easy. Long Island looks like most other places. It's flat and nondescript. We avoided photographing indigenous vegetation. And also, whatever was red, that Texan brownish red, we painted white. We put fish up everywhere.

GF: Are you going to shift away from your Long Island locales?

HH: The Long Island era is *done*. I started to make films in Long Island because that was the only place I *could* make films. You don't want to be in a vulnerable position when you're making a film. You always go back to a neighborhood where you know you have the possibility of controlling the environment. As a filmmaker, that's one of the first things I learned. I always knew I could do that back home in Lindenhurst, so it just became kind of logical to write scenes that took place there. Why write a scene that takes place in Sweden when you know you're going to have to shoot it in Lindenhurst?

GF: Audiences are naturally going to conclude that you're saying something about that environment.

HH: *The Unbelievable Truth* and *Trust* are set in variations of the archetypal American suburb: one is safe and pretty, and the other is more menacing and cold. The whole country is covered with suburbs like these. Lindenhurst was incidental. *Simple Men*, which was shot in Texas, is the only film I've made with Long Island being integral.

Simple Men* actually takes the topography of Long Island into question. Bill and Dennis are somewhere like in New Jersey or New York City and they have to get out to the end of Long Island – which is an island that stretches away from the mainland and ends in one of two points. If you're afraid of being trapped, don't run to the corners; in this case,

Montauk Point. There's only the ocean. There's either a boat waiting for you or you're fucked. I always thought that was kind of interesting, this idea of running away to a definite end.

GF: You've used epigrams like 'Knowing is not enough' in *Surviving Desire*, and 'There's only trouble and desire' in *Simple Men*. At what point did they suggest themselves to you?

HH: In my thinking process, when I'm trying to make sense of something, I tend to think things through to a point where there are one or two or three little slogans or phrases that somehow retain more meaning than all the thoughts I've had up to that point. It's an organizing principle at first. But then I start using them in situations because they force the characters to make distinctions. They force distinctions on the situations. I think, maybe, that's why there are slogans and clichés. They don't come around by accident – they come around because they appear to be appropriate. This is not always a good thing, but it's something I can't ignore about human nature. The thing about propaganda, for instance, is that it tries to force black and white explanations on complex realities.

GF: Are you trying to create a perfect film?

HH: I can't imagine going out to make a film and not having an idea of what a perfect film is. But it changes. When I made *The Unbelievable Truth* I thought I knew what a perfect film was. But it's different now. It always is.

GF: Now that you've finished *Simple Men*, what are your feelings about the film? Has it taken any unexpected twists and turns as you've edited it?

HH: All the films do. It's always much easier to talk about what a film might mean a year or two after I've made it. But the excitement I feel right now about *Simple Men* is the excitement of discovering, gradually, over the past three months of editing, that what I thought the film was is not what the film is. I always thought that the film was significantly different from *The Unbelievable Truth* and *Trust*. Maybe not in temperament, but in subject matter. But it's not, really. There's something about the end, of Kate refusing to lie, and Bill

coming back to her and giving himself up to the police. It's
like there is no escape from inequity. One way or the other,
he's got to pay. I'm beginning to see that that's a very consis-
tent world outlook for me. You don't get something for nothing, *ever*.

GF: Is there much of a difference between the script and the
finished film?

HH: There are a few scenes I totally rewrote, based on the
character of the actors I worked with. Karen Sillas, who
plays Kate, is an actress I went to college with, and she was
in a few of my short films. I hadn't seen her in a long time. I
had been thinking of someone else in the role of Kate and
was writing it that way. At the last moment, I got Karen.
There is now something particularly formidable about the
character and, by the same token, a peculiar weak spot in
her, which I hadn't written into the script. She's very lonely.
Much more lonely than I had thought. Karen brought all
this in with her.

GF: Does the film say what you wanted it to say, or has that
changed too?

HH: It says much more than I anticipated it saying. Sometimes
I think a scene is going to be about one thing and I try to
make it as moving as possible, but then I begin to see that its
real meaning is something I didn't necessarily write.

GF: Can you give me an example?

HH: The last moment of *Simple Men*, which I was very excited
about when I was writing it. It felt really appropriate. It felt
poetic. It felt as though I had written it with clarity and
meaning. In the original script, Bill gets out of the car,
throws off the cops, and leans against Kate as the Sheriff
asks, 'Kate, do you know this man?' Then she answers, 'Yes,
I know this man.' End of story.

    I can't paraphrase the number of things that this seemed
to mean. But I thought Kate having the last word like that
was what the whole movie was about. But that's not in the
film any more. When I got to that point in the editing it
seemed beside the point. Now, he gets out of the car, throws
off the cops, and stands before her, with everybody watch-

ing. Nobody says anything. Finally, he leans his head on her shoulder and she accepts him back. The Sheriff then says, 'Don't move.' I can't say exactly what this means either. But it feels right. It seems necessary. Unavoidable, even.

GF: Did you shoot the scene with the original lines?

HH: Yeah.

GF: And did you shoot the scene without the lines?

HH: Well, I cut the lines out. I didn't shoot it without the lines. I cut it the way it was originally written, then had to cut things away to make it work. I had to have a little humility and say, 'All right, that's beautiful, but irrelevant. Get it out.'

Whenever I'm doing anything, the material I'm working with tells me certain things about what is appropriate. By the time I get all the footage back from the shoot, it's like starting from zero again. In a way, the first couple of cuts of the film are just awful, because I haven't flushed out all of my preconceptions yet. I have to imagine I'd just found all this stuff in an attic, and I'm going to try and make meaning out of it.

GF: The key principle of your work seems to be that paring down.

HH: Essential. That's a word I like to use a lot. Finding the essential.

The Unbelievable Truth

CAST AND CREW

MAIN CAST

AUDRY HUGO	Adrienne Shelly
JOSH HUTTON	Robert Burke
VIC HUGO	Chris Cooke
PEARL	Julia McNeal
LIZ HUGO	Katherine Mayfield
EMMET	Gary Sauer
MIKE	Mark Bailey
TODD WHITBRED	David Healy
OTIS	Matt Malloy
JANE	Edie Falco

MAIN CREW

Written and Directed by	Hal Hartley
Produced by	Hal Hartley
	Bruce Weiss
Executive Producer	Jerome Brownstein
Original music by	Jim Coleman
	Kendall Brothers
	Philip Reed
	Wild Blue Yonder
	Hal Hartley
Cinematography by	Michael Spiller
Film Editing by	Hal Hartley
Production Design by	Carla Gerona
Costume Design by	Kelly Reichardt

EXT. HIGHWAY — DAY

Josh, a ruggedly handsome but preoccupied young man dressed entirely in black, is hitching a ride as he walks along the highway's edge. His clothes are old and faded. His shoes are worn out. He carries a black gym bag.

He stops finally and turns out to the road, holding out his thumb.

A car drives past him and pulls over to the side of the road.

The car is smoking and making funny noises. The husband swings out of the car, cursing, while his wife and two children remain in the car.

Josh walks over to the car, while the husband stomps his feet and pulls out his hair.

Josh looks from the crazy man to . . .

The wife and children, who stare out at him from the car, worried.

Josh comes over, sets down his bag, and pops the hood.

The husband stops and watches, alarmed, as Josh leans in over the engine and starts working. The severe-looking, black-clad stranger comes away and opens his bag.

It's filled with tools. He takes out a wrench.

The wife and children crane their necks and watch as . . .

Josh works.

INT. CAR — A LITTLE LATER

The husband is happy. He drives along and smiles back at Josh in the back seat with the children.

                          HUSBAND
Excuse me, but . . . are you a priest?

                          JOSH
No. I'm a mechanic.

                          HUSBAND
Where're you headed?

                          JOSH
Home.

                          HUSBAND
Where're you coming from?

                          JOSH
                        (*honestly*)
Prison.

EXT. HIGHWAY — SAME TIME

The car skids to a halt, then pulls over to the side of the road. Josh gets out. The car speeds away, leaving Josh alone on the shoulder. He looks around and waits patiently.

EXT. HIGHWAY — LATER

Josh is walking along again, turning to hitch when he hears a car approaching.

The car slows down and stops. Josh runs up to it. The driver lowers the window, desperate and hunted.

                    DRIVER (OTIS)
Where're you headed?

                          JOSH
Long Island.

                          DRIVER
I ain't goin' that far!

                          JOSH
New York.

DRIVER

Get in.

EXT. HIGHWAY — DAY

The car whizzes by and off into the distance.

EXT. ROADSIDE — LATER

The driver is leaning against the car, sipping a coffee as Josh works over the engine, checking the oil, and water, and so on . . .

DRIVER

I'm beat. You wanna drive?

JOSH
(closes hood)

I don't drive.

He closes up his bag.

DRIVER
(confused)

What do you mean you don't drive?

JOSH

I don't have a license.

DRIVER
(looks him over)

Hey, are you a priest or something?

JOSH

I'm a mechanic.

DRIVER

Yeah, that's what I thought. So how 'bout it?

JOSH

How 'bout what?

DRIVER

You wanna drive?

JOSH

I don't drive.

The driver is forced to accept this. He finishes his coffee, then slips a flask of bourbon out of his coat. He drinks and holds it out to Josh.

I don't drink.

EXT. ROAD — LATER

The car speeds by and heads toward New York City.

EXT. CITY (WALL STREET) — DAY

The car pulls out of traffic and Josh gets out. He shakes hands with the driver and watches as he drives off.

Josh looks around, overwhelmed. He is particularly struck by . . .

The huge statue of George Washington that towers above him.

He looks up at it in awe.

DISSOLVE TO:

INT. VIC'S HOUSE (AUDRY'S ROOM) — MORNING

A big picture of George Washington.

Camera tilts down to . . .

Audry lying in bed. She is seventeen, very pretty, and lying awake. Beside her on the bed is a book titled The End of the World *by someone called Ned Rifle. Morning light floods the room as . . .*

The alarm clock goes off. It's 7 a.m.

Audry looks over at the clock, weary, and turns it off.

She lies there a moment longer, then sits up in bed. She yawns deeply and it looks like she's about to stretch, but, with her arms, she mimics a huge nuclear explosion, slowly, dramatically, raising her arms up and out in the shape of a mushroom cloud.

> AUDRY
> (*hugely*)

Kaboom!!!!

When, finally, the last low rumblings of the explosion are through, Audry just sits there with her eyes closed, listening to the silence.

INT. KITCHEN — A LITTLE LATER

Liz sits at the table with an unlit cigarette. Her husband, Victor, sits at the table in mechanic's coveralls, reading the paper.

Audry slouches in, apathetic and dressed entirely in black. She sits at the table and starts reading her book. All hell breaks loose.

> VIC
> (*throws down his paper*)

Where the hell were you last night?

> AUDRY

Out.

> VIC

Where!

> AUDRY

Walking.

> LIZ

Audry, the high school called again yesterday.

> AUDRY

Oh, yeah. I forgot to go to school yesterday. Sorry.

> LIZ

Honey, you haven't gone to school all week.

> VIC

How do you forget to go to school!

> AUDRY

Pass the sugar, please.

> VIC
> (*passes it*)

No college in the country is gonna accept you if you keep this up!

> AUDRY

I don't want to go to college anyway.

> VIC

Don't start, Audry!

> LIZ
> (*disappointed*)

But, Audry, I thought you wanted to be a journalist; a TV anchor lady like that woman on the six o'clock news?

> AUDRY

Why are you two so concerned about my college education? The world's going to blow up any day now anyway. It's hopeless. Give my college money to the Coalition for Nuclear Disarmament.

> VIC

Bunch of goddamn anarchists stuffing your head with a bunch of left-wing nonsense! You'll be going to college if I gotta drag you there myself! A person hasn't gotta chance in the world these days without a college education!

Audry just peers at Vic from behind her shades. She turns and looks at Liz.

> LIZ
> (*nods*)

I agree with your father, Audry.

Audry looks back and forth between them, shakes her head hopelessly, and reaches into her jacket pocket. She pulls out an envelope and hands it to Liz.

> AUDRY

I got accepted.

Liz and Vic are taken back. Liz opens the envelope excitedly and reads. She screams happily.

LIZ

Oh, honey! Congratulations! Here, look, Vic!

She hands him the letter and leans over to kiss Audry on the forehead.

Vic looks over the letter and frowns in terror.

VIC

Harvard!

AUDRY
(*dryly*)

It's a college.

VIC

It's expensive!

LIZ

You can't put a price tag on a thing like that, Vic.

VIC

You can put a price tag on anything, Liz!
(*to Audry*)
Didn't you apply anywhere else?

AUDRY

No.

VIC
(*hopeless*)

I'm gonna be paying for this the rest of my life.

LIZ

Victor, aren't you proud of her?

AUDRY

I'm not going. We'll all be lucky if we're alive in September anyway.

Vic pounds the table.

VIC

Shut up, you! Of course you're going to college! It says right here in the paper that the present workforce between the ages of twenty-one and thirty-five are the most educated and highest paid in American history. That's what you have to contend with.

AUDRY

But, Dad, history is coming to an end.

VIC
(*to Liz*)

What's she talking about?

LIZ

The end of the world. By the way, Vic, the washing machine is busted.

VIC

Audry, the world's not gonna end when there are so many people out there making so much money.
(*to Liz*)
What's this about the washing machine?

LIZ

It's busted.

VIC

We just got the damn thing. What's wrong with it?

LIZ

It just shoots water all over the place.

AUDRY

Mom, have you got any valium?

VIC

Hold *on* a minute! I wanna talk about this Harvard thing.

AUDRY
(*sighs*)

Dad, I'm going to be late for school.

VIC

Bullshit!

LIZ

Vic!

VIC
(*points at Audry*)

I hope you're saving the money you make working over there at Burger World.

AUDRY

I quit.

VIC
(*outraged*)

What! When?

AUDRY

Oh, I don't know. A long time ago.

LIZ
(*incredulous*)

But, honey, didn't you *like* working at Burger World?

Audry looks at her mother blankly, then turns and looks at Vic. She lifts her book and reads aloud.

AUDRY
(*reads*)

'Let us consider some of the possible ways a person might die in a nuclear attack. He might be incinerated instantly by the fireball or the thermal pulse. He might be crushed to death by the blast wave. He might receive lethal radiation poisoning from the local fall-out. He might die of starvation because the economy had collapsed and no food was being grown. He might die of cold, for lack of heat or clothing, or of exposure, for lack of shelter. He might be killed by people seeking food or shelter which he had obtained. He might be killed by exposure to the sun, because the damaged ozone layer was no longer filtering out ultra-violet rays . . .'

EXT. STREET — DAY

Audry is walking to school with her boyfriend, Emmet.

Emmet is wearing a dapper, well-cut, gray business suit and tie.

> AUDRY
> What's with the suit, Emmet?

> EMMET
> I just got it. You like it?

> AUDRY
> I think it's gross.

> EMMET
> I like it.

> AUDRY
> I told my parents I quit my job at Burger World.

> EMMET
> (*not listening*)
> You know, things are really looking up for me, Audry.

> AUDRY
> The school psychologist says I'm apathetic.

> EMMET
> The whole world out there in front of me and I'm ready
> for it.

> AUDRY
> I told him about the holes in the ozone layer and he didn't
> believe me.

> EMMET
> A man like me can go far and that's exactly what I plan to
> do.

> AUDRY
> Thousands of people across eastern Europe still experienc-
> ing lung complications because of Chernobyl and he's
> telling me how these should be the happiest years of my life.

EMMET

I'm going to take this world in my teeth, chew it up, and spit it back out again.

AUDRY

Emmet, we're on the brink of global extinction.

EMMET

The wheels of fortune are rolling in my direction.

AUDRY

Every night I go to bed dreaming about suicide. Then I feel ashamed and cry myself to sleep.

EMMET

And my friends all like you a lot. So do my parents. Nothing but opportunity, Audry. Me and you. What do you say?

AUDRY
(*stops*)
Emmet, you're not even listening to me.

EMMET

Oh, yes I am. And I'll tell you quite frankly, Audry, I'm worried.

AUDRY

About what?

EMMET

About you.

AUDRY

Why?

EMMET

Well, because lately you seem so . . . you know, apathetic.

AUDRY
(*moves on*)
Emmet, you're a dick.

EMMET

Oh, come on, Audry, don't be sore! I mean it. I'm worried.

AUDRY

You don't even listen to me when I'm talking!

EMMET

I do so! And you've been talking like a crazy person lately. Everybody says so. I mean, Audry, just look what you're wearing!

AUDRY

Look what *you're* wearing!

EMMET

Hey! This costs a hundred and eighty-five dollars!

AUDRY

Congratulations.

EMMET

Look, Audry, I know you've been a little mixed up lately.

AUDRY

I'm not mixed up. I'm depressed.

EMMET

Whatever . . .

Audry stops and listens.

AUDRY

Shhh!

EMMET
(*stops*)

What?

AUDRY

Listen.

They listen.

EMMET

I don't hear anything.

AUDRY

You hear that?

EMMET
(*strains*)

No.

AUDRY
(*moves on*)

I thought I heard the bombs falling.

EMMET

What I'm trying to say, Audry, is that I don't want to lose
you.

AUDRY

You've never had me, you idiot.

EMMET
(*stops, worried*)

What do you mean?

Audry goes a little further, stops, and looks at the pavement.

AUDRY

I don't know.
(*thinks, then . . .*)
Emmet . . . I don't want to go out with you any more.

EMMET
(*confused*)

What?

AUDRY

You disgust me.

EMMET
(*it's dawning on him*)

You mean . . . You mean you . . . You mean you don't . . .

AUDRY

I don't want you.

Emmet is stunned.

                              EMMET
But, Audry . . .

                              AUDRY
Sorry.

She turns and walks away. Emmet remains standing in the middle of the street, immobilized.

EXT. TRAIN STATION — DAY

The train pulls out of the station.

Josh comes down the stairs to the street. He pauses and looks around. He sees . . .

A woman – Pearl – coming up along the sidewalk. She's about twenty-five years old and kind of shy.

Josh takes out his crushed package of cigarettes and pulls out the last one. He looks in the package to make sure it's really the last one, then crumples it up and shoves it back down in his pocket. He lights it and looks down at . . .

His shoe. The sole is taped to the shoe. His toe is threatening to poke out the front.

He sighs and looks up as . . .

Pearl passes. She is looking at him, but looks down as she goes by. She looks up again and . . .

Josh recognizes her just as . . .

She stops and stares at him. Her mouth falls open. She's speechless.

                              JOSH
How are you, Pearl?

No reaction. Pearl just stares at him.

He waits a moment longer, then turns and starts away.

Pearl passes out and collapses on the sidewalk.

He sees Pearl go down and jumps to her aid.

INT. DINER — MOMENTS LATER

A sort of sleazy, good-looking, young hustler named Todd Whitbred is sitting at the counter. He makes the pretense of being distracted by a young woman sitting two stools away. Finally . . .

TODD

Excuse me for seeming so forward but, you know, you're really quite attractive.

She just looks at him blankly . . .

No really, I mean it. You see, I'm a photographer.

She still just stares . . .

Have you ever thought about going into modeling?

She stares at him a moment longer then, without a word, grabs her things and slides off her stool. Todd curses to himself.

(sotto)
Shit. Too up-front. Gotta relax.

The young woman goes out on to the street just as . . .

Todd slides the girl's half-finished plate of eggs to him and starts to eat.

Josh throws open the door and comes striding into the diner with Pearl in his arms.

People at the counter jump up, alarmed, as . . .

Josh comes right over and lies Pearl out on the counter. Plates, glasses, and silverware crash to the floor. Josh reaches over and takes somebody's glass of water. He splashes it in Pearl's face.

JANE
What happened?

Pearl stirs.

Jane, the waitress behind the counter, approaches cautiously, looking from Josh to Pearl.

JOSH

She passed out.

They all look him over, then return their gazes to Pearl.

Jane leans over Pearl and takes her by the shoulders.

JANE

Pearl? Hey, Pearl!

Pearl snaps awake. Jane waits, then . . .

Pearl leans up on her elbows and looks around.

PEARL

What happened?

JANE

You passed out. This man here brought you in.

Pearl remembers and she looks up at Josh.

He nods but keeps his distance.

Pearl looks him in the eye.

PEARL
(*finally*)

Hello, Josh.

JOSH
(*careful*)

Hello.

Jane takes off her apron and hands it to Pearl, then gives her the check book.

JANE

You're late again.

PEARL
(*snaps out of it*)

Sorry.

JANE
(*rushing away*)

I gotta go. See ya tomorrow.

Pearl slides off the counter and straightens her dress. She steps in behind the counter and puts on the apron, all the while keeping a wary eye on Josh.

PEARL
(*guarded*)

Thanks.

JOSH

Sure.

He rubs his stomach and looks at . . .

Todd's plate of eggs.

He reaches into his pocket and pulls out two dimes and a penny. He swallows hungrily as he contemplates them. He looks up and . . .

Pearl is preparing a cup of coffee before him on the counter.

He looks from it to her and hesitates.

PEARL

How do you like your eggs?

Just then, a big, robust man named Mike, with Josh's bag, dressed in the same type of coveralls as Vic Hugo, comes plowing into the diner.

MIKE
(*to Josh, of bag*)

You belong to this?

He stops, throws out his arms, and bellows expansively . . .

(*to Pearl*)

Pearl! Marry me!

Pearl sighs and shakes her head.

> PEARL
> (*irritated*)

No!

EXT. STREET — DAY

Vic Hugo is driving to work. He turns a corner and slows down when he sees . . .

Emmet standing in the street, frozen to the spot where Audry left him.

> VIC
> (*frowns*)

What's this?

He pulls up beside Emmet and leans out the window.

Hey, Emmet!

No response . . .

Emmet? Emmet, what's the matter?

Emmet turns very slowly from where he is staring at the pavement and looks at Vic. He looks insanely depressed.

Emmet, you look like shit.

> EMMET

She doesn't want me.

> VIC

Who doesn't want you?

> EMMET

Audry.

Vic lets this sink in, then realizes what's going on. He looks away and rolls his eyes. He sighs and turns back to Emmet.

> VIC

Jesus, Emmet, is that all?

EMMET

What do you mean, is that all? Audry is my entire life!

VIC

Relax.

EMMET

I'll never love anybody else. Ever.

Vic steps out of the car and approaches.

VIC
(*sarcastic*)

I'm sorry, I didn't realize it was so serious. Get in the god-damn car.

EMMET
(*jumps away*)

No!

VIC

Emmet, you're over-reacting.

EMMET
(*crazed with grief*)

What's the point! What's a man without the woman he loves! He's nothing! A hollow shell!

Vic looks at him oddly and hesitates, then . . .

VIC

Well, fuck, Emmet.

EMMET

She must love somebody else!

VIC

Come on, ease up. She's going through some kinda phase. It'll pass. She's a girl, Emmet. You know how girls are.

Emmet has been scowling at the pavement through all this. Now he looks back at Vic, pauses, and . . .

EMMET
(*acid*)

She's sleeping with some guy who's gotta bigger cock, I
know it.

*Vic is stunned, speechless. He grabs Emmet and throws him up
against the side of his car.*

VIC
(*wild*)

That's my fucking daughter you're talking about, asshole!

EMMET
(*breathlessly*)

But she's a girl! You said so yourself!

VIC

There's a difference between a girl and a slut!

EMMET

All girls are sluts!

*Vic dives at the kid, but Emmet jumps at Vic too, and they tumble
around, wrestling in the street. They are evenly matched and they
fight hard and dirty.*

*Finally, Vic gets the better of Emmet and flips him on his back. He
starts slapping him silly. Emmet gives up.*

*Vic stands and drags him over to the car. He picks Emmet up and
throws him against it.*

VIC
(*fierce*)

Have you and Audry been having sex?

EMMET

Of course we have!

*Vic falls back, overwhelmed. Emmet pushes him away and steps
aside.*

VIC

You bastard. I trusted you!

EMMET

Trusted me! Get real, Mr Hugo! This is 1988. Me and Audry have been having sex for a long time!

VIC

You fuck!

He starts after him again, but Emmet runs around the end of the car, keeping his distance. Vic stops and they glare at each other over the top of the car.

You're lying!

EMMET

It's the truth!

Vic all but climbs up on the car and leers over at Emmet, crazed.

VIC

I'm warning you, you little pecker-head, you come near Audry again and I'll break your goddamn neck!

Emmet steps back away from the car, real proud and tough. He spits on the ground and thrusts out his chest.

EMMET

Mr Hugo, I wouldn't dirty my hands on that promiscuous little bitch if you gave me money to do it!

Vic, infuriated, shoves Emmet, who shoves back.

INT. THRIFT SHOP — DAY

We see Audry reading while she sits in the aisle of the store.

She looks up as she sees . . .

Josh standing looking around. Both he and Audry are dressed in black.

Josh begins at the bookshelf, hesitantly. Before long, he is tapped on the shoulder. He turns to see . . .

Audry smiling politely up at him. She's attracted to him.

                         AUDRY
Hi.

                         JOSH
Hello.

                         AUDRY
Can I help you find something?

He's a little uneasy; out of his element, but dignified.

                         JOSH
I'm looking for a book about Washington. George Washington. The President.

                         AUDRY
                    (*adds with a smile*)
The first president.

                         JOSH
Right.

                         AUDRY
There aren't any.

                         JOSH
At all?

                         AUDRY
Here.

                         JOSH
Right.

                         AUDRY
You need new shoes.

                         JOSH
Do you work here?

                         AUDRY
No, I go to high school. My name is Audry.

                         JOSH
Josh.

AUDRY

I happen to be a big fan of George Washington myself.

JOSH

Really?

AUDRY

He represents a lot of things I admire. For instance . . .
(*takes out a dollar bill*)
He's singular. One. He's the one-dollar bill. And just look
at the man; he's not very attractive. But he's got dignity.
And he was a farmer.

JOSH

Close to the soil.

AUDRY

Down to earth. And I can't help thinking that were he
alive today, doing the job he did then, leading that particular revolution, he'd be locked up. Or worse. All of them.
Jefferson. Paine. Franklin. They'd be executed.

JOSH

Well, maybe not executed.

AUDRY

Don't put it past people. I don't trust anyone.

*Suddenly, Audry is a little embarrassed by how much she's talking.
She puts away her dollar bill.*

What do you do?

JOSH

I'm a mechanic.

AUDRY

Do you work around here?

JOSH

I don't work anywhere, just yet.

AUDRY

Do you need a job?

                              JOSH
Yeah.

She takes out a pen and writes an address on a dollar bill.

                              AUDRY
Go to this place . . .

INT./EXT. GARAGE — DAY

Victor Hugo's Auto Repair is an aging place that sees a lot of activity. His one mechanic is Mike, the big guy who asked Pearl to marry him in the diner.

Mike is standing in front of a Mercedes wailing on an electric guitar, as Vic pulls into the garage lot and gets out to approach Mike.

                              MIKE
Hi, Vic.

                              VIC
                         (*of Mercedes*)
What's that still doing here?

                              MIKE
Man, Vic, this car is twisted.

                              VIC
This was supposed to be done by Wednesday.

                              MIKE
Tuesday.

                              VIC
What's wrong with it?

                              MIKE
Got me. I thought I fixed it last time.

                              VIC
Last time?

                              MIKE
He had it in here last month too.

VIC

What you're saying is that we didn't do the job right the first time.

MIKE

You got it, chief.

VIC
(*turns away*)

Jesus Christ!

MIKE

Gee, Vic, is something bothering you?

VIC

Well, what did you do to it last time?

MIKE

Hey, back off, I didn't do nothing to it.

They look up and see Josh.

VIC

Yeah? Can I help you?

JOSH

I'm a mechanic. I'm looking for work.

VIC

No. No work here. I'm sorry.

He exits.

MIKE
(*to Josh*)

You know anything about foreign cars?

JOSH

What's wrong with it?

MIKE

Clutch, I think.

JOSH

Worn out?

MIKE

Could be. Sticks bad.

JOSH

Two hours.

MIKE

What?

JOSH

I'll fix it in two hours.

MIKE

Hey, don't I know you?

Vic re-enters the scene.

VIC

What are you still doing here? I said I ain't hiring.

MIKE

He says he'll fix this beast in two hours.

VIC

Where'd you work before?

JOSH

Upstate New York.

VIC

Upstate New York where?

JOSH

Ossining.

VIC

Where in Ossining?

JOSH

In prison. I fixed cars in prison.

Mike and Vic digest this.

EXT. GARAGE YARD — TWO HOURS LATER

Mike and Vic peek out from behind a truck, watching Josh at work in the garage.

> VIC
>
> So what do you think?

> MIKE
>
> It's him. It's him for sure.

> VIC
>
> It's been a long time.

> MIKE
>
> I wasn't so sure before, but now I'm positive. It's him. We gotta fucking mass murderer in the garage.

> VIC
>
> He's not a mass murderer!

> MIKE
>
> That's what I heard!

> VIC
>
> Mike, you're so fucking simple!

> MIKE
>
> I heard him and the girl shot her parents and went on the road and then he shot her too.

> VIC
>
> If he killed all those people he'd be in prison for life!

> MIKE
>
> Well, that's what I heard.

> VIC
>
> Don't Pearl know what happened?

> MIKE
>
> Pearl don't talk about it.

> VIC
>
> Well, what happened, as far as I know, is that he killed the

father because of something like the girl wanted him to.
But then she flipped out and killed herself.

MIKE

What about the mother?

VIC

I never heard about a mother.

Vic turns back and continues watching Josh.

MIKE

What's he doing in there now?

VIC

He's fixing the goddamn Mercedes, you knucklehead!
Why aren't you helping him?

MIKE

He just needed me for the beginning part. You should see
'im work, Vic. Fucking amazing. Knows exactly what he's
doing. Doesn't even hardly make any sound.

VIC

Yeah?

MIKE

Yeah.

VIC

He's good?

MIKE

Oh, so good.

Vic looks away, thinks a moment, then . . .

VIC
(*gets up*)

Come on.

He goes out into the garage. Mike hesitates, then follows.

INT. GARAGE — SAME TIME

Josh is done. He's wiping his hands on a rag as Vic and Mike approach.

Mike comes over and squeezes himself into the Mercedes. He starts it up and it purrs nicely. He backs it out of the garage.

Vic takes out a cigarette for himself and offers one to Josh.

> JOSH
> (*takes it*)

Thanks.

> VIC

So what brings you back to town, Josh?

> JOSH
> (*after a while*)

It's the only place I know really. Outside of prison.

> VIC

Your family's all gone, ain't they?

> JOSH

The house is still there.

> VIC

How long have you been out?

> JOSH

Two days.

He finishes cleaning his hands and puts his jacket back on. He tosses a wrench into his tool bag.

> VIC

What are you going to do now?

> JOSH
> (*disappointed*)

I'm gonna find myself a job.

He picks up his bag, gives Vic a dark look, and starts walking out.

                              VIC
    Hold on.

Josh stops. He waits a moment, simmers down, and looks back.

                             JOSH
    Yeah?

He makes it tough for Vic. He waits and listens.

                              VIC
    Look, I can't pay you much.

                             JOSH
    I don't need much.

                              VIC
    Yeah, well . . .

                             JOSH
    I can start right away.

*Vic is undecided. He walks to the garage door and looks out into the
parking lot. He sees . . .*

*Mike fumbling around over the engine of a car. He drops his
wrench, stoops to get it, hits his head, and knocks over his tool box.*

Vic just shakes his head and turns away.

                              VIC
    There's a pair of coveralls back in the office.

*Josh nods, puts down his tool bag, and takes off his jacket. He's
ready to go to work.*

*Vic starts back to the office, still uncertain. He keeps looking back at
Josh suspiciously.*

INT. DINER — DAY

*Jane, the waitress, brings Todd a plate of food. Todd looks a little dis-
tressed. He sees the food and frowns.*

TODD

What's this?

JANE

What kinda question is that?

TODD

Just asking.

JANE

Fish.

TODD

Really.

JANE

Look, you said the special, right.

TODD

OK! OK! It's fine. Look, I . . .
(looks up at her and gets an idea)
Hey, you know . . . I suppose guys ask you this all the
time, but . . . have you ever been a model?

Jane is blank, then . . .

JANE

What?

TODD

I can swear I saw you in a magazine or an ad or something . . .

JANE

What the hell are you tryin' to pull? Have you got money
to pay for this fish?

TODD
(lies)
Of course I do! I'm a professional photographer. See.
Here's my camera.

JANE
(*skeptical*)

Photographer, huh?
(*calls back to grill*)
Hey, Eddie! We gotta troublemaker up here!

TODD
(*panics*)

No! No! Here! I'll pay now. I have money.

He tumbles out a mass of coins from his pocket and they splash on to the counter. Jane watches as he counts them out. She shakes her head and moves down the counter to where Mike is sitting.

JANE

So are you sure it's him?

MIKE
(*to Jane*)

It's him. Josh Hutton. He's come back to town.

JANE

Ain't you scared to be working with 'im?

MIKE
(*bravely*)

Yeah, well, I'll tell ya. Sometimes he gets this real strange glint in his eye . . .

Emmet is sitting down the counter. He hears, is intrigued, and slides closer to hear more . . .

Like he's remembering something really horrible, you know.

JANE

I'd be terrified.

EMMET

What did he do?

JANE

He raped and murdered Pearl's older sister, then shot her

father, and they never did find the mother.

MIKE

He *did* not!

JANE

He did so!

MIKE

Him and Pearl's sister had this deal, see. She wanted to kill her father, but couldn't do it herself. So she had Josh do it.

JANE

Why did she want to kill her father?

MIKE
(*shrugs*)

I don't know.

EMMET

There was probably some kinda sick, incestuous relationship going on and it was driving her crazy.

JANE

Oh, gross!

MIKE

Maybe, because she killed *herself* right after it all.

Todd leans over and sets them all straight . . .

TODD

The girl killed herself first.

JANE

What the hell do you know about it?

TODD

She killed herself because her old man wouldn't let her marry Josh Hutton. Josh then went out after the old man and shot him. Then he went back and shot his *own* goddamn father!

EMMET

Bullshit! That don't sound right at all.

JANE

Hey! Watch your mouth, kid!

EMMET

Don't call me kid.

MIKE
(*wondering*)

Josh's father got shot too?

EMMET

Well, don't Pearl know anything about all this?

MIKE

Pearl never talks about it. And I'm warning you, kid, don't
you ever ask her.

EMMET

Don't call me kid!

JANE

That's why Pearl's the way she is. She was just a child.
Messed her up good.

MIKE
(*angry*)

There ain't nothin' *wrong* with Pearl!

TODD

You got it all fouled up!

EMMET

Mr Hugo must be crazy hiring a man like that.

MIKE

He's a damn good mechanic.

JANE

He was so nice to Pearl though. Carried her right in off
the highway.

EMMET
(*smug*)

I don't believe the criminal element can ever be completely rehabilitated.

MIKE
(*irritated*)

If you hurry, I think you can catch *Romper Room*.

INT. GARAGE — DAY

Josh is working on a car. Audry comes riding up on her bike. She stops just outside, takes a book from her basket, and comes in toward Josh.

He looks up and smiles.

She plants the book in front of him on the engine.

AUDRY

The life of George Washington. The father of our country.

JOSH
(*looks through it*)

Thanks.

He sees she has another book too.

What's this one?

AUDRY

The Misanthrope. Molière? It's a play.

He doesn't know it. He looks it over and seems intrigued. She watches him admiringly.

JOSH

What's a misanthrope?

AUDRY

Somebody who doesn't like people. I star in it. I mean, in class. We read it in class.

JOSH
Are you the misanthrope?

AUDRY
No. I wanted to, but they wouldn't let me be a man. So, instead, I play flirt.

They are flirting in earnest now, moving closer and closer. Audry is holding his hand, tracing the lines in his palm.

JOSH
Is it an interesting role?

AUDRY
Being a flirt?

JOSH
Hmm.

AUDRY
Sometimes. But the thing about flirting is that it leads to harder things.

JOSH
Is that bad?

AUDRY
No. That's not bad. But it turns out pretty badly for the woman I play.

JOSH
What happens to her?

AUDRY
She can't stop flirting.

JOSH
Ever?

AUDRY
It's just the way some people are. She flirts herself to death.

JOSH

It's a sad play.

AUDRY

Well, she doesn't die actually. It's just that the only man who really loves her has impossible standards.

JOSH

That's too bad.

AUDRY

Yes, it is.

They're very close now, almost kissing.

JOSH

Does it turn out happy in the end?

She moves her lips up to his slowly . . .

AUDRY

Nobody gets what they want and they all go away frustrated and sad.

JOSH
(*whispers*)

A tragedy . . .

Then, BAM!!! They jump.

Vic is standing there in the office doorway, pissed, the door almost thrown off its hinges.

Josh steps back and starts gathering up his tools.

VIC

Audry! What are you doing here?

INT. OFFICE — SAME TIME

Josh's clothes are draped across a chair. The gym bag is nearby. Audry enters and steals his wrench.

She then sits with her arms folded, her face turned away, and her foot tapping, full of attitude.

Vic enters, runs his hand through his hair, and stares at the floor, calming himself.

                    AUDRY
                  (*looks up*)

What?

                    VIC

You know what!

                    AUDRY

What?

                    VIC

What the hell happened with you and Emmet! I'm driving to work this morning and I find the kid standing in the middle of the street immobilized by grief!

                    AUDRY

Emmet wears boxer shorts with dollar signs all over them.

                    VIC
                (*pounds the desk*)

I don't wanna *hear* about Emmet's goddamn *underwear*!

Audry keeps looking out the window into the garage at Josh, smiling.

Hey, I'm talking to you!

                    AUDRY

Excuse me?

                    VIC
                  (*sarcastic*)

What the hell are you so *dreamy* about! The world's gonna blow up tomorrow, remember!

Audry sighs and looks back out at Josh. She smiles again and looks back at her father.

                    AUDRY
                    (*flip*)

But right now it's today. Not tomorrow.

He cocks his head and glares at her.

> VIC

Did you go to school today?

> AUDRY
> (*hesitates*)

No.

Vic shakes his head and sits at his desk. She watches him as he hangs his head. He looks back up at her.

> VIC
> (*finally*)

Audry, listen to me. I've been thinking about this Harvard thing.
> (*hems and haws, then . . .*)

Let's make a . . . a deal.

> AUDRY

A what?

> VIC

A deal! Look, if I give a thousand dollars to this nuke-head commie charity organization of yours, will you forget about Harvard and go to the community college?

Audry regards him carefully, pauses, then approaches.

> AUDRY

Are you serious?

> VIC

Yeah, I'm serious!

> AUDRY
> (*pauses*)

But I don't want to go to college. Any college.

> VIC

Will you just give it a try?

She sits across the desk and considers this.

                                     AUDRY
Would I have to study communications?

                                      VIC
What else would you study?

                                     AUDRY
Literature.

                                      VIC
Literature! What the hell are you gonna do with literature?

                                     AUDRY
Read.

                                      VIC
                                 (*uncertain*)
I don't know.

                                     AUDRY
Would this be a yearly arrangement? Or would I be obli-
gated to a full four years in return for the one donation?

                                      VIC
It would depend.

                                     AUDRY
On what?

                                      VIC
On how well you do each year.

                                     AUDRY
A thousand a year if I pass all my classes.

                                      VIC
If your grade-point average is high.

                                     AUDRY
Medium.

                                      VIC
High.

                              AUDRY
Only for literature. I won't do that for communications.

                               VIC
No deal. Communications or nothing.

Audry scowls and thinks this over. Finally, she shrugs . . .

                              AUDRY
OK, but I have the option to drop out after the first year.

                               VIC
Only if your grade-point average is high.

                              AUDRY
You have to write the check today.

                               VIC
Five hundred now, and the remainder after first semester.

She looks at him sideways and frowns.

    It's only fair, Audry. Normal business procedure.

                              AUDRY
                          (*reluctantly*)
OK.

They shake hands and Audry resumes looking back out at Josh.

                               VIC
Then it's a deal?

                              AUDRY
                           (*far away*)
Yeah, sure.

INT. GARAGE — SAME TIME

*Josh flips through the book she gave him. He stops when he comes
across a flyer between the pages. On it is written: 'Come to my
father's birthday party tonight.'*

    DISSOLVE TO:

EXT. AUDRY'S BACK YARD — NIGHT

Vic's birthday party. People in the pool, patio lights, the whole thing . . .

Audry is keeping an anxious look-out for Josh.

Behind her, Vic is talking with Todd.

> TODD
> Assets. Any kind of assets. You gotta have 'em.

> VIC
> (*shaking his head*)
> The whole fucking country's run on credit. I hate that.

> TODD
> It works out for guys like me and you, though.

> VIC
> I don't trust that speculation crap. I like to see money. I like to put my hands on it.

> TODD
> But you've got to be leveraged.

> VIC
> What?

> TODD
> Leveraged.

Audry moves away and sits on a bench beside Liz, still looking at her watch and scanning the crowd.

> LIZ
> (*notices*)
> Who are you waiting for, Audry?

> AUDRY
> Oh, no one.

> LIZ
> You look beautiful in that dress.

                              AUDRY
Really?

                              LIZ
Wonderful.

                              AUDRY
                           (*relieved*)
Great.

                              LIZ
So, who are you waiting for?

                              AUDRY
Oh, no one.

                              VIC
                            (*off*)
Audry. Come over here a minute.

She looks up and goes over.

Audry, this is Mr Todd Whitbred. I know him from years
and years ago. Well, Todd here, he's a commercial photographer.

                              AUDRY
Hi, I'm Audry. My favorite word is despair. What's yours?

                              TODD
                          (*leering*)
Fine thanks.

                              VIC
So, Todd, go ahead, tell her what we were talking about.
Listen to *this*, Audry.

Vic is a little drunk. He pops open another beer.

                              TODD
Well, like your dad was saying there, Audry, I'm a commercial photographer. I do a lotta weddings and christen-
ings most of the time, but I gotta couple a' spreads in
some magazines and stuff. You know that kinda thing.

But, like I was telling your father here, you really, you know, have a *look*.

Audry frowns, suspicious.

You have what they call poise. A real presence. Poise. That's what you have. Poise. And that's a valuable thing.

                              VIC
                            (*nods*)
Poise.

                             TODD
Oh, everybody thinks so. And, you know, in my profes-sional opinion, I mean, I would say, you could, if you wanted to . . . be a . . . you know, a model.

Todd gulps down some beer and burps. Audry looks back at Vic, skeptical.

                              VIC
Listen to what he says, though.

                            AUDRY
                           (*aside*)
Dad, what's he getting at?

                              VIC
He's talking about *work*, Audry.

                             TODD
There's a lotta money in modeling. Especially for a girl like you who's got great . . . you know, poise.

                              VIC
What Todd's saying here, Audry, is that maybe you can be a model.

                            AUDRY
But I'm going to college . . .

                              VIC
I *know* you're goin' to college! But if you make some money maybe you can help *pay* for college.

AUDRY

If I weren't going to college, I'd like to be a carpenter.

VIC
(*steps back*)

Since when?

AUDRY

Since always.
(*to Todd*)
Jesus was a carpenter. He was a radical. I *like* radicals.

VIC

Audry, knock it off.

AUDRY
(*serious, to Vic*)
If I'm going to help pay for college, then I have to study literature.

VIC

That wasn't the deal.

AUDRY

Well, the deal's different now.

VIC

How 'bout the charity donation?

AUDRY

That still holds.

VIC
(*frowns*)
You drive a hard bargain, Audry.

TODD

You can make a lotta money fast if you make the right connections.

VIC

There, Audry, see.

AUDRY
(*skeptical*)
Oh, yeah? How do you make these connections?

Todd now slips into his sales pitch . . .

TODD
First you need a portfolio.

VIC
A what?

TODD
A portfolio. A group of pictures of Audry here in different
clothes. Different kinds of make-up and hair styles and
stuff. You know, a bunch of pictures to show like . . . what
she can do . . . as a model.

VIC
Where the hell do you get one of them?

TODD
Well, I mean it's up to you, but I can give you a pretty
good deal on the shots myself. And I can introduce Audry
around. Help her make some connections.

VIC
How much?

TODD
Well, it's hard to say right off the bat, but . . . let's say . . .
seven hundred and fifty bucks.

VIC
What!

TODD
Six-fifty.

VIC
For photographs!

TODD

It's a necessary and important investment in a modeling career.

VIC

But I hardly know you! How'd you get in here?

Audry walks away, bored. She bumps into Emmet. He looks desperate, hiding from Vic. She is preoccupied, keeping an anxious lookout for Josh.

AUDRY

What are you doing here?

EMMET

I deserve some kinda explanation, I mean, really, after all we've been through.

AUDRY

What have *we* been through?

EMMET
(*stuck*)

Well, everything. It's another guy, right?

AUDRY

Did you really punch my father in the nose?

EMMET

It's Bill, isn't it?

AUDRY

Emmet, please.

EMMET

I knew it.

Vic and Todd are still bargaining. Vic drinks and thinks and scratches his jaw, then . . .

VIC
(*skeptical*)

Shit. You said five-fifty?

                                 TODD
Six-fifty.

                                  VIC
                            (*shakes his head*)
I don't know.

                                 TODD
Look, Mr Hugo, you stand to make a fortune off the girl. I
mean, she's a good-lookin' kid. Take my word for it. Get
her into this modeling thing. You'll make your money back
in no time.

                                  VIC
Six hundred or nothing.

                                 TODD
It's a deal.

They shake and drink their beer.

Audry looks at her wrist watch. It's late.

*She looks up from it and sighs, disappointed. She leans back against
the car. Emmet is next to her. She's apathetic. He is kissing her neck
and trying to feel her up as she speaks.*

                                 AUDRY
It all just seems so empty to me.

                                 EMMET
What does?

                                 AUDRY
Everything. All of this. This house. These clothes. This
party.

She gets up and walks away toward the pool. She passes . . .

*Bill and Bob, two easy-going high-school guys. They watch Audry
go past and sigh as one, smitten.*

                                 BOB
She's beautiful.

BILL

I'd cut off my left arm for her.

BOB

Really?

BILL
(*reconsiders*)

Well, at least a few fingers.

Emmet suddenly appears beside them.

EMMET

What was that?

BILL

Excuse me?

EMMET
(*belligerent*)

Did you say something?

BILL

Yeah, I said something. What's it to you?

EMMET

I'm not so sure I like what you said.

BILL

You don't even know *what* I said!

EMMET
(*shoves him*)

Oh, yes I do.

BILL
(*to Bob*)

I don't know. Does he?

BOB

Got me.

> BILL
> (*to Emmet*)

What did I say?

> EMMET

I don't *care* what you said! I think it's about time you guys
left this party.

> BOB
> (*disappointed*)

We just got here.

> BILL

Listen, bud, what's your problem?

> EMMET

You wanna go out in the street and settle this?

> BILL

No, I don't.

> EMMET

I think we oughta go out in the street and settle this thing.

> BOB

What thing?

Bill and Emmet are nose to nose . . .

> BILL

Listen, pal, you're buggin' me!

> EMMET

No, you're buggin' me!

> BOB

Bill, come on, let's get outta here.

> BILL

No way! We ain't done nothing!

> EMMET

You're starting trouble, man!

                         BILL
I ain't starting anything!

                        EMMET
Come on, let's go outside.

                          BOB
                       (*terrified*)
Oh, shit!

                         BILL
You wanna go outside?

                        EMMET
Yeah, I wanna go outside

                         BILL
Let's go outside and settle this thing once and for all!

They storm off into the street. Bob is left there holding his head.

EXT. AT THE POOL — SAME TIME

Mike is standing in the pool, and Pearl is on the deck holding a watch.

                         MIKE
Ready?

                        PEARL
OK. Hold on. Get ready. Go!

Mike takes a huge breath and goes under water.

Pearl watches the clock. Audry comes up beside her and they look down at Mike under water. Audry looks around again, accepting that Josh won't show.

                        AUDRY
Let's get out of here.

                        PEARL
Yeah. OK.

She puts the watch in her pocket and they walk off the deck.

EXT. AUDRY'S FRONT YARD — SAME TIME

Emmet and Bill are wrestling savagely on the front lawn. A couple are making out by the fence a few feet away.

Audry and Pearl come out from around the house and find Audry's bike leaning against a tree. They hop on, within feet of Emmet and Bill, and ride off. They only casually notice the brawl.

EXT. STREETS — SAME TIME

Audry and Pearl riding along on the bike. They ride off into the distance.

EXT. SOME FIELD — DAWN

The girls sip their beers, watching the daylight come up, listening intently.

AUDRY

There.

Pearl looks at Audry and listens.

PEARL

What is it?

AUDRY

Do you hear it?

PEARL

Bombs?

AUDRY

Could be.

PEARL

Nearby?

AUDRY
(relaxes)

No. Must not be anything.

PEARL

They wouldn't drop the bomb on the weekend, would
they?

AUDRY

Who knows. Could be some freak accident happens and
BOOM!!! The history of human endeavor is flushed down
the toilet.

PEARL

It makes you think. You know, what kind of people would
let something like that happen?

AUDRY
(*scanning the sky*)
Could be anybody. Everybody's got nuclear capability
now. Even the Pakistanis. You know, they've got this new
bomb now – a nuclear bomb – that fits inside a suitcase.

PEARL

I don't want to think about it.

AUDRY

No. Let's not think about it right now. Let's just lie here.

*They lie there a while, then Audry rolls up on her elbows and comes
closer to Pearl.*

Pearl, do you like older men?

PEARL

Sometimes.

AUDRY

I met a man yesterday.

PEARL

An older man?

AUDRY

I think so. He looks older. I mean, he was older than me.

PEARL

What was he like?

                              AUDRY
He had a history. You could tell just by looking at him.

                              PEARL
Be careful of men with histories.

                              AUDRY
He was . . . poor.

Pearl moans . . .

And hungry.

She moans again . . .

He had no possessions.

And again . . .

Nowhere even to live.

*They fall over and start rolling around on the ground, giggling
uncontrollably. Then . . .*

He was like dressed entirely in black.

*Pearl knows now that Audry is describing Josh, and she sits up,
unsettled.*

                              PEARL
Who is it?

                              AUDRY
His name is Joshua. Joshua Hutton.

This hits Pearl hard. She shivers.

Pearl? What is it?

                              PEARL
I have to go home now.

                              AUDRY
Pearl?

PEARL

No, really. I have to work this afternoon. I should really get some sleep.

She leans over and kisses Audry on the forehead. Audry is a little confused. Pearl is clearly disturbed.

Bye.

She turns and walks off. Audry looks on after her, confused.

EXT. STREET — MORNING

Emmet lies unconscious on the pavement. He comes to, leans up on an elbow, and looks around.

EMMET

Fucking cowards.

He starts to get up, but then sees . . .

Audry riding down the block toward him.

He lies back down and groans, faking.

Audry approaches and looks at him, concerned. She skids her bike to a stop and jumps off. She kneels over him.

AUDRY

Emmet! What happened?

EMMET

Is that you, Audry?

AUDRY

Knock it off! What happened?

EMMET
(*smiles*)

I kicked ass.

AUDRY
(*pauses*)

But . . . why?

EMMET

Well, uhm . . . because I love you, Audry.

Audry stands slowly, looking down at him sadly.

AUDRY
(*with difficulty*)

That's too bad, Emmet.

She gets on her bike, shaking her head, and rides into her yard.

Emmet watches, amazed, as she goes on into her house.

DISSOLVE TO:

EXT. HUGO BACK YARD — DAY

Liz is folding clothes. Audry helps her.

AUDRY

Mom, what do you know about Josh Hutton?

LIZ

Josh Hutton? What do you want to know about Josh Hutton?

AUDRY

Dad just hired him.

LIZ

Really?

AUDRY

Yeah. What do you know about him?

LIZ

He killed some people.

AUDRY

Who did he kill?

LIZ

Pearl's sister.

                         AUDRY
When was this?

                          LIZ
This was a few years before he killed her father.

                         AUDRY
I don't remember any of this.

                          LIZ
It was a long time ago. You were only two years old. Pearl
never talks about it.

Audry mulls this over with a frown.

EXT. AUDRY'S BACK YARD (POOL) — DAY

*Audry and Pearl are submerged up to about their chins. They seem
very pensive and speak in hushed tones.*

                         PEARL
                      (*at length*)
He seems like a nice man.

                         AUDRY
You think so? I mean, after he's killed your father. And
your sister.

                         PEARL
                    (*thinks, shrugs*)
Things happen. People make mistakes.

                         AUDRY
I can see how your sister was a mistake. But . . . he threw
your father down a flight of stairs.

Pearl doesn't know what to say. She looks away and sighs, then . . .

                         PEARL
I think . . . I think he seems like a nice man. And you like
him. Right?

                         AUDRY
He doesn't *seem* like a killer.

                              PEARL
Maybe he isn't.

                              AUDRY
He hasn't killed anybody recently, has he?

                              PEARL
I don't think so.

                              AUDRY
I knew he had a history.

                              PEARL
He seems like a nice man.

                              AUDRY
                             (*hurt*)
I knew it was too good to be true.

                              PEARL
What was?

                              AUDRY
                            (*bitter*)
He seemed so different. Innocent. But I guess nobody's
innocent.

EXT. GARAGE — EVENING

*Vic is not around. Josh and Mike are working under the hood of a
car.*

                              JOSH
Fundamental scientific laws govern the ability of an
engine to convert energy in the fuel to an energy form that
can make a car move.

                              MIKE
Scientific principles, huh?

                              JOSH
Yeah. It's what they call the first and second laws of thermo-
dynamics.

MIKE

Where'd you learn this stuff?

JOSH

In prison. I read this book.

They work in silence for a while, then . . .

MIKE
(*hesitates, then . . .*)

Why'd you kill her father?

Josh looks at him blankly a moment, then . . .

JOSH

I suppose because I was angry.

MIKE

You suppose? I mean, don't you know? Christ, you killed a man.

JOSH

We were both pretty angry. I don't think either of us wanted to kill the other when we started. We just kinda lost control.

MIKE

Why'd you go over to his place, anyway?

JOSH

To apologize for killing his daughter in a car crash.

MIKE

And you threw him down a flight of stairs.

JOSH

Something like that, yeah.

MIKE

Why'd you run?

JOSH

I was scared.

MIKE

It sounds like it was an accident.

JOSH

Killing a man is killing a man.

MIKE

Yeah, I suppose.

Josh stops working and looks up at Mike.

JOSH
(*sincerely*)

How is Pearl?

MIKE

OK, I guess. She's a difficult woman.

JOSH
(*intrigued*)

How's that?

MIKE

Well, I don't know. I mean, the other night we're at this party, right. I go in the pool. I have her time me while I hold my breath under water. I come up and she's gone. Nowhere to be seen. Normally, that wouldn't bug me. But it makes a guy wonder.
     (*leans back in over the engine . . .*)
How 'bout you? You gotta main squeeze?

JOSH

No.

Mike looks over at him, thinks, then . . .

MIKE
(*tentatively*)

Ever?

JOSH

No.

Mike leans back, amazed.

                                MIKE

You're a . . . virgin?

                                JOSH

Yeah.

                                MIKE

Ouch.

Josh looks right up at him and we can tell he's not kidding.

Mike is thunderstruck.

INT. GARAGE — LATER

Mike and Josh are hanging around.

Mike jams on guitar.

                                MIKE

The thing you first notice about having a girlfriend . . . I
mean, right off the bat, when you start staying over her
house and everything, is that you clean yourself a lot better.

                                JOSH

Really.

                                MIKE

No shit. You just sort've pay more attention to everything.
You brush your teeth like every single night before going
to bed. You start worrying about washing your back.

                                JOSH

Your back?

                                MIKE

Your fucking back. Right down the middle. It's almost
impossible and who the hell thinks about it anyway. Girls
do.

                                JOSH

I suppose it must get kinda dirty back there. All that
sweat, you know.

MIKE

And you never see the goddamn thing. Underwear. Suddenly you're buying new underwear all the time.

JOSH

It must be really different when somebody else is seeing you without your clothes on all the time.

MIKE
(*plays a riff*)
Damn straight! So how do you stand this celibacy shit?

JOSH

How does anybody stand anything? Being in prison for all those years helps.

MIKE

You never got any before the car crash?

JOSH

My friends were always making fun of me because I'd never been laid. I was seventeen. So one night I was taking Pearl's sister to the movies. And I was determined. I knew she liked me, and she was as pretty as Pearl is . . . Well, we saw the movie and kissed and all that. Then we decided to drive out to this place I knew.

He trails off. Silence. There's nothing to say. Mike fidgets, then . . .

MIKE

You sure you don't want a beer?

JOSH

No. I'm fine.

MIKE

Aren't you curious?

JOSH

Most of the time.
(*pause, then . . .*)
But, you know, I killed a man. And I never thought I'd be able to do that. I mean, I never even imagined it.

(*looks down and thinks, then . . .*)
When you've done something . . . unimaginable . . . I
mean, when you've done it even before you ever thought
about it. When you see how easy it is. Well, then everything is put into this new perspective. Suddenly things you
had always thought were the most important things in the
world are no more significant than anything else. Because,
you see, you've done the unimaginable. You've done what
you thought was impossible. And then you see . . . you see
that you can do anything.

Mike eyes him sideways and squints.

MIKE

You ain't a homo, are you?

JOSH

No.

MIKE

I don't have anything against guys liking other guys as
long as they don't like me. You know what I'm saying?

JOSH

Sure.

MIKE
(*pops open a beer*)
I thought I was a homo once.

JOSH

Really?

MIKE

Yeah. Fucking unbelievable.

JOSH

What happened?

MIKE

I joined the Marines. They straightened my shit right out.
Look, see my tattoo?

INT. AUDRY'S HOUSE — A FEW DAYS LATER

*Liz and Audry are moving around, looking at her portfolio. Vic is
trying to eat.*

LIZ

My, Audry, you look so elegant in this one!

AUDRY

You should've seen some of the awful clothes they had
there.

LIZ

Well, I *like* this one.

AUDRY
(*looks*)

Oh, yeah, that one's OK. Kinda tight, though.

LIZ

It shows off your breasts well.

VIC
(*eating*)

Will you two shut up!

They pay him no attention.

LIZ

I think Mr Whitbred did a really nice job. Very profes-
sional.

VIC

He better have. I paid seven hundred and fifty bucks for
those. Audry! Don't get your dirty hands all over 'em!

AUDRY
(*of her hands*)

They're clean.

LIZ
(*another photo*)

Wow! Audry, you really do have some figure.

> AUDRY
> (*embarrassed*)

Mom, cut it out.

> LIZ

Don't be silly, Audry. Flaunt it while you have it. I'm just about losing mine.

> AUDRY

You look OK.

> LIZ

Liar.

> AUDRY
> (*stands her up*)

You look great. Don't she, Dad? Look.

> VIC
> (*eating*)

Can't you two see I'm trying to eat!

> AUDRY

Here, Mom, straighten your back. I learned this today.

> LIZ

What, like this?

EXT. GARAGE — DAY

Vic flips through the pages of a newspaper and finally finds what he's looking for. He proudly shoves the newspaper in front of Mike.

> VIC

Look, right here, in the raincoat with the umbrella.

> MIKE
> (*looks*)

Holy shit! Look at that!

> VIC

Ain't that something?

MIKE

Audry right there in the goddamn newspaper.

VIC

She made three hundred dollars for one day's work.

MIKE

No shit?

VIC

Damn straight.

Josh walks by, doing something.

MIKE

Hey, Josh, look at this!

Vic turns away and frowns as Josh takes the paper and looks.

You know Audry, right? Vic's daughter.

Josh recognizes her and looks up at Vic before handing the paper back to Mike.

JOSH
(*politely*)

Pretty girl.

VIC

Yeah, right. OK, let's get back to work. You almost through with that Mustang, Josh?

JOSH

Just gotta set the points and I'll get started on the Firebird.

VIC
(*moves off*)

Right, let's get 'em all finished up today.

JOSH
(*moves off*)

Right.

Mike looks off after both of them, then follows Vic.

MIKE

You ride him pretty hard, don't you think?

VIC

He can take it.

EXT. BUS STOP — DAY

Audry is all dressed up for a modeling job. Emmet sits on the bench beside her, washed out and dejected.

AUDRY

Emmet, you look terrible.

EMMET

I'm telling you, Audry, I'm a wreck.
                    (*looks her over . . .*)
You look really good in that dress.

AUDRY

I'm sorry.

EMMET

I'm gonna kill myself.

AUDRY

Don't be maudlin, Emmet.

EMMET

Well, then I'll kill somebody else. Where are you going, anyway?

AUDRY

To work.

EMMET

Modeling.

AUDRY

Sweaters.

EMMET

I hate seeing you in advertisements where other men can pore over you.

AUDRY

I make a lot of money.

EMMET

Since when are you so interested in money?

AUDRY

Since I started earning it. Isn't it a lovely day?

EMMET

Why are you so happy lately? Don't you know the world's fucked? Did you read the paper today?

AUDRY

Emmet, I know the world's fucked. I don't read the papers any more. And, by the way, have you bathed lately? Emmet, really, you smell.

EMMET

You're in love with that homicidal auto mechanic, aren't you?

AUDRY

Emmet, I'm gonna hit you.

EMMET

It won't last. I know it won't last.

AUDRY

Well, anyway, Emmet, you know what the ancient Greeks said about happiness.

EMMET

Fuck the ancient Greeks.

AUDRY

Here's my ride.

She gets up and starts for the curb. Todd pulls up in a new fancy car.

EMMET
(*pleads*)

Don't go!

AUDRY
(*looks back*)

Emmet, tie your shoe.

A guy passing by on the sidewalk looks Audry up and down and whistles. She just keeps on going, but Emmet spins around . . .

EMMET

Hey!

They jump at each other and wrestle one another to the sidewalk.

Audry looks around, panicked, then hops in the car.

INT. AUDRY'S HOUSE — EVENING

The Hugos are having supper. They're in the middle of a conversation and everything is a little tense. Audry looks back and forth between her parents. Vic scowls down into his food, thinking.

LIZ
(*to Vic*)

Well, I think that maybe it's a good thing. If she's not sure what she wants to study, maybe it would be worthwhile for her to just work for a year. Make some money.

Vic shrugs.

AUDRY

Dad, I promise. It'll just be a year. At the end of a year, I'll have so much money saved up, maybe I can pay for college all by myself.

Vic nods. He sees the sense in it, but he wants to be careful. He points at Audry.

VIC

We had a deal, remember.

AUDRY

I remember.

VIC

I held up my end.

                                  AUDRY

I appreciate that.

                                   VIC
                                 (*eats*)

Shit.

                                   LIZ

Audry, eat your vegetables.

EXT./INT. GARAGE — DAY

Audry rides up on her bike and finds Josh working. There is no one else around. When he looks up from what he is doing and sees her, he smiles and attempts to neaten his appearance.

She comes into the garage. She's angry, contemptuous, hard-boiled.

                                  JOSH

Hi.

                                  AUDRY

Good afternoon, Mr Hutton.

                                  JOSH

You don't have to call me mister.

                                  AUDRY

What am I supposed to call you?

                                  JOSH

You can call me anything you like, but you don't have to call me mister.

                                  AUDRY

I think I'll call you . . . Reverend.

                                  JOSH

Like a priest?

                                  AUDRY

Don't you like it?

JOSH

I admire people who are dedicated to things.

AUDRY

Why didn't you come to the party?

JOSH

I had no money, no clothes.

AUDRY
(*realizes*)

Oh.

JOSH

I'm sorry.

AUDRY

It's OK.
                    (*thinks, then . . .*)
Do you have any money now?

JOSH

I have what I need.

AUDRY

You're saving my father from financial ruin. I hope he
pays you well.

JOSH

He's a good man. He gave me a job when he knew no one
else would.

AUDRY
(*shows him a magazine*)

Look. That's my foot.

JOSH

No kidding?

AUDRY

They paid me almost a thousand dollars to put this shoe
on and let them photograph my foot.

                         JOSH

It's a pretty foot.

                        AUDRY

Thanks.

                         JOSH

Listen, do you want take a walk somewhere?

                        AUDRY
                      (*guarded*)

Where to?

                         JOSH

Anywhere.

                        AUDRY

Why?

                         JOSH

I've got something to tell you about me.

                        AUDRY

I don't want to hear it.

                         JOSH

It's important.

                        AUDRY

What good will it do?

                         JOSH

I think you should know.

Audry stares at him, pauses, then . . .

                        AUDRY

I already know.

Josh isn't surprised, but he's hurt by her fierceness. She's acting like she hates him. But she seems to be working at seeming this way. As they stare at one another, she starts to give in a little, wanting him.

> JOSH
> (*carefully*)

Does it make a difference?

*Audry is trying not to lose control. She fights giving in, but then,
finally . . .*

> AUDRY
> (*gasps*)

No.

And she runs into his arms. They kiss passionately.

Then . . .

> VIC
> (*off*)

Audry!

They look up, stung.

*Vic is just outside the garage, glaring at them, pissed. Audry stands
there looking at her father, with Josh right there over her shoulder.*

Go home.

She hesitates.

Josh stays there staring at Vic.

CUT TO:

INT. AUDRY'S ROOM — LATER

Audry is lying on the bed, furious. Vic stands at the foot of the bed.

> VIC

Audry, listen to me, it's for your own good! I don't want
you to associate with that man.

> AUDRY

But why?

VIC
(*explodes*)

He's a mass murderer!

AUDRY

Dad, cut it out!

VIC

He's a loaded pistol! No tellin' when he'll go off!

AUDRY

If he's so horrible and dangerous, why'd you hire him?

VIC
(*stuck*)

Well, I ah . . . I'm a . . . I'm letting him go tomorrow.

Audry jumps up and glares at him. Vic flinches.

AUDRY

You wouldn't dare.

VIC

Oh yes I would.

AUDRY

Without Josh your whole business would fall down around
your ears!

VIC

Look, Audry, don't tell me about my business, OK!

AUDRY
(*hounds him*)

You know you need a good mechanic! And he's a good
mechanic!

VIC

Since when do *you* know so much about auto repair?
Huh?

Audry hushes up. She doesn't know anything about auto repair.

Look, Audry, what do you want getting involved with

some mechanic from around here for? You'll be going to
college next year and . . .

> AUDRY
> (*crafty*)

Maybe I won't go to college.

> VIC
> (*pissed*)

Don't start, Audry! You promised! We had a deal!

Audry winces.

> (*pressing*)

Right? We had a deal. You can't go back on it now!

> AUDRY

If you don't fire him . . . If you don't fire him, I won't see
him again!

> VIC
> (*suspicious*)

What are you up to?

> AUDRY

I'm not up to anything!

> VIC

If I keep him on, you'll keep away from him?

> AUDRY

Yeah.

> VIC

You promise?

She turns and glares at him.

You're making a bargain, Audry. You gotta stick to it.

> AUDRY
> (*silence, then*)

I see him once more. I have his wrench.

VIC

What the hell are you doing with his wrench?

AUDRY

Once more.

VIC

You promise?

AUDRY
(*sadly*)

Promise.

Vic is pleased. But Audry comes back at him . . .

VIC

And you've got to go to college. This fall!

AUDRY

For literature.

VIC

No! For communications! Broadcasting!

Audry turns away and kicks the wall. She thinks, then spins around.

AUDRY

OK. But it's got to be Harvard.

Vic receives this like a knife in the chest. He sits at the end of the bed and hangs his head.

(*presses*)

OK?

VIC
(*thinks, then . . .*)

All right, but you've gotta model full-time till you get in college and pay back the money I gave that bomb squad charity of yours!

Audry thinks it over, then decides. She shrugs.

> AUDRY

OK . . . It's a deal.

She goes out and Vic hangs his head, beat.

INT. GARAGE — EVENING

Josh is getting ready to go. Vic locks the office door as Josh closes up the garage. He looks over at his boss and stops.

Vic is studying him.

> JOSH

Something else?

> VIC

You know, Josh . . . You make a difference around here.

> JOSH
> *(pauses, then)*

I'm just doing my job.

> VIC
> *(nods)*

Right.
> *(scratches his head and considers, then . . .)*

I think I'll give you a raise.

> JOSH

Well, whatever you think is fair.

> VIC

An extra fifty each week? What do you say?

> JOSH

Thanks.

> VIC

OK.

They shake hands. Vic holds on to Josh's hand, though, and looks him straight in the eye.

(*hard*)
I don't want you coming anywhere near Audry.

Josh is frozen . . .

Got it?

They stare at each other a few moments longer, their hands still gripped together.

EXT. BEACH — A LITTLE LATER

Josh is sitting on a bench, reading. He sees . . .

Pearl walking up from the beach. She sits at the next bench.

Josh hesitates, then approaches her and sits down.

Pearl looks up.

There is an uneasy silence for a moment, then . . .

JOSH
Hello, Pearl.

PEARL
(*guarded*)
Hello.

They sit.

JOSH
(*slowly*)
I just wanted to apologize.

Pearl stares hard at the pavement.

PEARL
Don't.

Josh is at a loss.

She turns and looks at him . . .

Just let's not talk about it.

He is stung by her fierce glare. He just nods . . .

I believe people get what they deserve in the end.

She watches him a moment longer, then turns and continues on her way.

Josh stays there alone in the street.

EXT. AUDRY'S HOUSE — DAY

Vic exits through the front door with a magazine. He sees Liz and goes down the steps.

                              VIC
I can't believe you let her do this!

                              LIZ
Victor, it's only an underwear advertisement!

                              VIC
She's half nude!

                              LIZ
She's wearing underwear and a bra! Girls at the beach wear as little as this! Less!

                              VIC
There's a difference between underwear and a bathing suit! Underwear is not supposed to be seen!

                              LIZ
Calm down. Anyway, she was paid good money for this and you were the one who urged her to go into modeling in the first place!

Vic is stumped. He grits his teeth and stares at the floor.

EXT. JOSH'S PLACE — AFTERNOON

Audry comes walking down the street and stops before the house. It's a little house that he rents. She's a little nervous and it's clear that she's dressed for the occasion. She looks great.

She pushes in through the gate.

Josh is outside the garage, painting. He looks out as he hears knocking.

Audry comes into the yard and approaches the front door. After she knocks, she pauses and looks at herself in the panes of glass of the door.

Josh moves to the side of the house, sees Audry . . .

She puts on lipstick while . . .

Josh calls to her.

Audry jolts and draws a line of lipstick across her cheek. She doesn't see this and quickly closes up her bag. She tousles her hair, smoothes out her skirt, turns and . . .

Trips over the George Washington biography that is there on the steps. She falls to the ground.

Josh starts toward her and . . .

She sees him coming, so slips on her shades and acts like it was nothing.

                              AUDRY
                            (standing)

    Hi!

Josh helps her up. Once she's up, we see her shades are broken.

                            (embarrassed)
    Thanks. I have your wrench.

                              JOSH

    Are you OK?

                              AUDRY
                            (realizing)

    This is a nice house.

                              JOSH

    Your knee!

Her knee is cut.

                              AUDRY
    Oh, it's nothing. Do you live here alone?

JOSH

Here, sit down.

AUDRY

Thanks.

He sits her down on the steps and she inspects her cut knee.

JOSH
(going)
I've got some band-aids in the house . . .

AUDRY
(stops him)
No. It's OK.

JOSH

It belonged to my father. It's been vacant for years.

He stops. She sees the book he's reading . . .

AUDRY

Do you like the book?

JOSH

Oh, yeah. Thanks.
(sees the wrench)
I have others.

AUDRY

Books?

JOSH

Wrenches. There are plenty at work.

AUDRY

But this one is yours, right? Your own personal wrench.

JOSH

Yes.

AUDRY

I thought so. So I'm returning it.

                                JOSH

Why?

                               AUDRY

I thought you'd need it.

                                JOSH

That's true. I mean, I might, but . . . if you need it, you can
keep it.

                               AUDRY

Really?

                                JOSH

Sure.

                               AUDRY
                     (*slips it into her bag*)

Thanks.

An awkward silence, then she spots a piece of machinery off to the side.

What's that?

                                JOSH

Those are planetary gears.

                               AUDRY

What do they do?

                                JOSH

It's part of an automatic transmission. In a car.

                               AUDRY

Right. How's it work?

*Josh is a little surprised that she'd want to hear about this. He fum-
bles a little, then . . .*

                                JOSH

Well, it's . . . I think maybe it's a little complicated.

                               AUDRY
                         (*leans back*)

I have plenty of time.

JOSH
(*smiles*)

You really want to know?

AUDRY
(*sincerely*)

I think it's really interesting what people do. I mean, when
they do something that they love. Because when you do
something that you love, no matter what it is, when you
do something that you love, you do it well. And when you
do something well, you feel useful. And it's important to
feel useful, I think. Because . . .
          (*tries desperately to reach a conclusion*)
Because when you feel useful, well, not so much . . . you
know, there's so much of life that seems . . . pointless.

*She heaves a big breath. Josh watches her a moment, impressed. He
relaxes a little. He lifts the planetary gear set-up on to the little
makeshift table between them.*

JOSH

Well, OK. An automatic transmission . . . There are manual transmissions too. They do the same thing, just differ-
ently. Well, anyway, transmissions work by changing which
gears transmit power from the engine to the wheels of the
car. Follow?

AUDRY
(*nods*)

Uh-huh.

JOSH

Automatic transmissions use planetary gears to do this.
You see here . . .
          (*points things out*)
This is what you call the 'sun' gear in the middle. The
'ring' gear around the circumference. And the 'planet'
gears here in between.

*Josh knows this stuff like the back of his hand. He's completely
relaxed now and totally focused on what he's explaining.*

Audry is staring at him, utterly in love.

The sun gear is attached to the input shaft while the out-
put shaft is attached to the planet gears. Two gear ratios
are available by either clamping the ring gear with a belt
so it can't move or else releasing the clamp and engaging a
clutch that locks the planets to the ring. When the gear set
is locked with the clutch the whole thing revolves as a
unit, providing a one-to-one gear ratio.

                              AUDRY
Will you make love to me?

                              JOSH
                          (*speechless*)
Wait here.

*She watches as he walks into the house. She drops her head in her
hands and screams sotto.*

                              AUDRY
                          (*tormented*)
   ARRRGGGHHHH!!!

She sits up straight, all smiles as . . .

*Josh comes back out with a band-aid. He comes over and kneels
down before her. She watches him silently as he puts the band-aid
over her cut knee.*

*Once he's finished, he leans back. He won't look at her. He's got a
dark, angry expression on his face.*

Audry bites her lip, waiting.

Finally, Josh stands and turns away, looking off across the yard.

                              JOSH
                          (*pauses*)
   Get out of here, Audry.

She is blank. Perfectly still.

   Go on.

Eventually, she starts to fold up inside. She looks like she's about to throw up. But she keeps it together.

Josh walks toward the back yard.

She looks at it a moment, feeling a little dizzy.

EXT. HAND-BALL COURT — DAY

Audry rides her bike around in a wide arc, speeds up, and . . .

BAM!!!! smashes into the hand-ball court wall. She falls to the ground, lifts herself up, and gets back up on the bike. She rides back out away from the wall, starting another wide arc. She starts back around, builds up speed, and . . .

BAM!!!! smashes into the wall again. She climbs out from under the bike, looks at her knee which is bleeding, and gets back up on the bike.

The bike creaks and moans as she forces it out into another pass. She throws her weight down on to the peddles, gritting her teeth, and . . .

BAM!!!! plows back into the wall.

The bike is pretty much demolished at this point, but she tries to make it move anyway. It won't ride, so she gets off it, drags it back, and starts smashing it against the wall.

EXT. POOL — DAY

Audry is floating around on a raft in the pool. Vic and Liz stand on the deck looking down at her.

                          VIC
                       (*furious*)
          What do you mean, you wanna move out?

                         AUDRY
        I know an apartment in New York City I can sublet for six
        months.

                          VIC
          No way!

LIZ

But, Victor, she works in the city all the time. She spends
almost a hundred dollars a month just on train fare.

VIC

So what! She can afford it! Christ, the damn kid makes
more than me!

EXT. MOVIE THEATER — EVENING

*Audry is standing outside the theater, leaning up against the wall,
reading Molière's* The Misanthrope.

Someone comes out of the theater and she looks up.

*It's Jane, the waitress from the diner. She stands there looking at
Audry, uneasy. Momentarily, Emmet comes out behind her and
takes her hand. Then he sees Audry and freezes. It's tense all
around, but finally . . .*

*Audry goes back to her reading. Emmet sees this, then grabs Jane
around the waist and kisses her ferociously on the mouth. They suck
at each other's tongues as Audry tries not to notice.*

*Finally they part. Audry turns a page in her book and yawns. She
checks her watch, looks up, smiles, and goes back to reading.*

Emmet and Jane walk away, but . . .

Emmet sees . . .

Bruce, a young guy, pass by and check out Audry.

Emmet swings around . . .

*He jumps at Bruce and they drag each other to the sidewalk, punch-
ing and kicking.*

*Audry and Jane look around, then at each other, then run off in
opposite directions.*

EXT. AROUND THE CORNER — SAME TIME

Audry comes around into the side street and almost runs right into . . .

Josh. She stops and they stand there, startled, looking at each other.

INT. DINER — A LITTLE LATER

Audry is tight-lipped, embarrassed, and angry. Josh just wants to explain.

>   AUDRY
> This isn't good. I made a deal with my father.

>   JOSH
> I just want to explain . . .

>   AUDRY
> I don't want to hear anything.

They sit a moment, looking off in different directions, then Josh slides the George Washington book toward her.

>   JOSH
> Thanks for lending me the book. I have a library card of
> my own now.

>   AUDRY
>   (*curt*)
> What are you reading?

>   JOSH
> History. I like history.

>   AUDRY
>   (*nasty*)
> History is going to come to an end. Soon.

>   JOSH
>   (*sighs*)
> Yeah, right.

He gets up to go. But she panics and grabs his hand.

> Why are you so sure the human race is going to kill itself?

> AUDRY

Because it can.

> JOSH

That doesn't mean it will.

> AUDRY

The human race has never invented anything it didn't use.

> JOSH

That's a fact. But it's not the last word.

> AUDRY

What is the last word?

> JOSH
> *(looks away, then . . .)*

I don't know. Faith maybe.

> AUDRY

Which one: faith or maybe?

> JOSH

I'd like to see you again.

> AUDRY

Too late. You had your chance.

> JOSH

Let me explain.

> AUDRY

I have a deal to keep.

> JOSH

Fuck the deal!

Jane looks over. Audry is silenced. Josh calms down and stares at the table top. Audry watches him, then . . .

> AUDRY

There are rules.

> JOSH

Break them.

                    AUDRY
I can't. I won't. My father has made good on his end of
the agreement.

                    JOSH
What agreement?

                    AUDRY
Everything in life is just deals. Nobody gets anything for
nothing.

                    JOSH
Unless you have nothing to begin with.

                    AUDRY
Are you telling me I should feel sorry for you?

                    JOSH
I'm not talking about me at all.

                    AUDRY
                 (indignant)
I've got nothing to feel sorry about, Mr hot-shot philoso-
pher auto mechanic! And I know exactly what I'm doing,
so just drop dead.
                 (gets up, but adds . . .)
You can't have faith in people. Only the deals you make
with them. People are only as good as the deals they make
and keep!

*She gets up and storms out. She takes the George Washington biog-
raphy, but forgets* The Misanthrope.

*Josh sits there for a moment, frowning, then picks up the book and
leafs through it.*

EXT. STREET — SAME TIME

*Audry walks unsteadily up the street away from the diner, confused
and angry. She gradually slows and comes to a complete stop. She
stands there staring at the pavement.*

INT. DINER — A LITTLE LATER

*Josh is still sitting there. He looks up from the book as Jane sits
down with him, pauses, then smiles.*

> JANE
>
> I know what you need.

> JOSH
>
> Excuse me?

> JANE
>
> You need a woman.

> JOSH
>
> Oh.

> JANE
>
> That girl's crazy.

> JOSH
>
> I know, but I like her.

> JANE
>
> She's leaving town.

> JOSH
>
> I heard.

> JANE
>
> So come on. I know what you need. What do you say?

> JOSH
>
> Excuse me?

> JANE
>
> You need a woman.

> JOSH
>
> Oh.

> JANE
>
> That girl's crazy.

JOSH

I know, but I like her.

JANE

She's leaving town.

JOSH

I heard.

JANE

So come on. I know what you need. What do you say?

JOSH

Excuse me?

JANE

You need a woman.

JOSH

Oh.

EXT. VIC'S BACK YARD — DAY

Emmet and Vic talk in front of a boat being refurbished. Mike passes by with a sander and gets up on top, ready to attack the job.

EMMET

You double-crossed me.

VIC

Lay off, Emmet.

EMMET

We had a deal.

VIC

We did not.

EMMET

We had an understanding.

VIC

I never said I understood anything.

EMMET

We have a common interest.

VIC

Audry makes up her own mind. If she wants to live in the
city and earn her own keep, what's that got to do with me?
She's eighteen now. She can do what she wants.

EMMET

I can't stand it. Every magazine I open I see her!

VIC

Emmet, you gotta pull yourself together.

EMMET

How can you stand it: all those strangers ogling her?!

VIC

It's better than you ogling her in the flesh. And besides,
she's only gonna do it for a year. Then she's going to Harvard to study journalism. That's what she really wants to
do, you know. This modeling stuff, this is just a phase.
(*to Mike*)
Mike! What the hell are you doing?

EXT. GARAGE — DAY

Liz comes walking up to the garage and leans in the door.

LIZ

Hi, Josh.

Josh comes out of the garage. He is in his work coveralls.

JOSH

How are you, Mrs Hugo? I heard about Audry's picture in
the *Sunday Times*.

LIZ
(*excited*)
Yes. Three pictures. It's a whole, you know, spread.

JOSH

You must be very proud of her.

LIZ

We are. We're going to church now, then we'll go buy the
paper. Then we're having a few people to the house.

JOSH

That's really nice.

*They both seem a little uneasy. Josh smiles awkwardly, nods, and
moves back to his work. Liz comes forward, anxiously, but trying to
hide it.*

LIZ

Josh?

He stops and turns . . .

Josh, you go into the city occasionally, don't you?

JOSH

Every once in a while.

LIZ

(*rushes forward*)

Oh, good! How about tomorrow? Well, when you go will
you take these ear-rings in to Audry for me? She's out of
the country right now but she'll be back tomorrow.

Vic comes out.

VIC

Let's go, Liz. Josh, if you get to it, can you take a look at
that hydraulic jack. It's been sticking all week.

Vic and Liz start walking away. They get in Vic's car.

Josh looks on as they go, unsettled.

DISSOLVE TO:

EXT. CHURCH — DAY

Liz slips out the front door of the church, followed by Vic.

They come down the steps and hurry along the sidewalk. They cross the street to the news-stand and stop when they see . . .

EXT. NEWS-STAND — DAY

Mike, Pearl, Emmet, Jane, and a host of others, all dressed in their Sunday best, are standing around, looking down at their feet, awkwardly.

Vic and Liz approach.

> VIC
> (*nodding*)
>
> Hey, Mike. Pearl.

> LIZ
>
> Hi, Pearl.

> PEARL
>
> Hi.

> VIC
> (*to vendor*)
>
> One *Sunday Times*.

> LIZ
>
> Look, everyone's here. This is so exciting.

No one says anything as Vic hands over the money and takes a paper. Liz pulls it apart, excitedly.

> MIKE
>
> It's killing me.

She and Vic go blank. They stare into the magazine and go pale.

Jane and Emmet look at each other and try to stifle a rising burst of laughter.

> LIZ
>
> She's got nothing on. Not in this one either.

                              PEARL
                            (*carefully*)
        Well, I think it's an ad for jewelry, I think.

Vic is completely red and trembling. He looks at Mike. Mike looks away. He looks at Pearl and she shrugs. He looks around at the others (a small crowd) and sees them all watching him and Liz.

Liz is a little faint.

                              LIZ
                            (*amazed*)
        She's absolutely naked.

                              PEARL
        Well, you don't see much.

                              LIZ
                            (*breathless*)
        You see enough.

Vic explodes and rips the magazine from her hands. He throws it in the street and turns back to glare at the crowd. They just watch him.

He is seething. He picks the magazine up again and tears it to shreds maniacally.

Liz, overwhelmed, puts her hand to her chest and takes Pearl's hand.

        Pearl, let's go back and put some charcoal on the barbe-
        cue.

They start away, but . . .

                              VIC
        Hold it!

This is what the crowd has been waiting for. They edge closer to get a better view. Liz and Pearl stop and look back over their shoulders. Victor Hugo paces back and forth like a preacher hell bent on scaring the shit out of his congregation. He's red in the face, his fists are clenched, and his jaw is set like a vice.

I know what you slobs are thinking. You're thinking, what a fucking slut! Well, let me tell ya', you people make me wanna throw up! Do you think this is easy what she does! This is hard work! You think she just gets up there and takes her clothes off? Huh? What she does is a skill! And she gets paid damn well for it too! Does anybody here make a thousand dollars a day? Huh! Huh! Why, she's in Europe right now! You all want to go to Europe! You all wanna take vacations and drive nice cars! Why hold it against her when she gets it?

MIKE

Vic, come on man, we don't hold nothing against her.

VIC
(*insane*)

I can see it in your eyes! You're all saying how can he let her do that! Doesn't he have any shame? Well, I tell ya' the only thing I'm ashamed of is not having thought of it sooner! There's money to be made out there and if you gotta get your goddamn hands dirty to make it well then so what!

He says nothing more, but looks through the crowd at all the faces.

LIZ

Vic, come on.

She and Pearl turn and walk away. Mike waits for Vic and tugs on his sleeve, urging him to come along. The crowd watch as they go.

EXT. AUDRY'S BACK YARD — AFTERNOON

Vic is getting drunk. Mike sits beside him at the picnic table, uncomfortable.

Liz and Pearl stand at the barbecue, a little further off. Liz stares into space, sadly thinking. Pearl flips through the magazine.

PEARL

I mean, it's not like it's pornography, Mrs Hugo. It's just sort of . . . sexy.

LIZ

I wish she would've warned us. Don't you think that pose
is a little perverse?

PEARL
(*shrugs*)

I don't know . . .

LIZ
(*points*)

They touched up *this* photograph. She has a birthmark
there on her thigh. And up here, beneath her left breast,
she has a scar from when she fell out of that tree back
there behind the pool when she was seven.

She looks a moment longer, then just turns away and sighs.

PEARL

Can I get you something?

LIZ

Thanks, Pearl. A beer.

Pearl gets up and goes into the house.

Liz sulks, but then looks up and smiles when she sees . . .

*Josh standing at the corner of the house, having just arrived. He
approaches.*

JOSH

Vic. Mike.

Vic and Mike wave back.

VIC
(*grumbles*)

And then there's that one.

MIKE

Who? Josh? He's OK.

VIC

A goddamn mass murderer always making eyes at my

daughter. I had to send her away to live in the city! I had
no choice.

                              MIKE
I don't think you gotta worry about Josh.

                              VIC
And why not? Gimme that bottle.

                              MIKE
                          (*passes bottle*)
Well, I mean, he's not, you know, very interested in girls.

                              VIC
                          (*stunned*)
You mean . . . you mean, he's . . . a fag?

                              MIKE
No! It's just, you know, he's like a priest or something.

                              VIC
                          (*laughs*)
Hah! No man is like a priest, Mike. Priests aren't even like
priests when it comes to women.

                              MIKE
It's different with Josh, though. I mean, Vic, all he ever
thinks about is engines. He was telling me this stuff the
other day you wouldn't believe it. All this scientific shit.
Amazing. He don't have time to think about anything. I'm
telling you, Vic, Audry's safer around Josh than she is
around anybody.

                              VIC
You think so?

                              MIKE
For sure.

*Liz pulls her sweater around her and moves up closer to Josh. Josh
presses the ear-rings back into her hand.*

JOSH

Mrs Hugo, I just wanted to say I don't really think this is, well, right. I mean it's right, but . . . I don't think it's what Audry wants.

LIZ

But, well, isn't it what you want? It's what I want. Maybe Audry doesn't know what she wants.

Josh hesitates. He doesn't know how to answer. Then Vic approaches and lays a friendly hand on his shoulder.

JOSH

That's what I mean.

VIC

How are you, Josh? Glad you could stop by!

Vic leads Josh away, shaking hands. Liz looks on.

(*off*)

Come over here a minute, Josh. I wanna talk to you.

They walk away. Pearl returns with two beers. She and Liz sit and look out at Vic and Josh.

LIZ
(*carefully*)

Pearl, what do you think of Josh?

PEARL
(*troubled, but . . .*)

I think . . . Audry is in love with him.

LIZ

Yes, but, under the circumstances . . . What do *you* think of him?

PEARL
(*hesitates again*)

I think he's in love with her too.

Liz sighs, thinks, then . . .

                                    LIZ
Do you hate him?

                                    PEARL
No.

                                    LIZ
Are you afraid of him?

                                    PEARL
Yes.

EXT. HUGO HOUSE — DAY

Vic and Josh sit in an old car by the side of the Hugo house.

                                    VIC
Take a seat. Well, look, Josh. This ain't easy for me to say.
I know you like Audry and . . . well, to be absolutely out in
the open and up front about everything . . . Audry's crazy
about you.

Josh is a little overwhelmed . . .

You look surprised. But listen to me, Josh, I ain't kiddin'
you. The girl sleeps with your crescent wrench.

                                    JOSH
                                 (*at a loss*)
Well, I . . . appreciate you saying this. I think.

                                    VIC
Look, take tomorrow off. She's flying in from Europe
tomorrow afternoon some time. I think it'd be a great surprise for her to find you waiting on her doorstep when she
got home. Here's the address where she's living. She lives
with a friend.
                         (*gives a little slip of paper . . .*)
And here . . . here's five hundred bucks.

                                    JOSH
                                 (*protests*)
No, Mr Hugo, really. I couldn't . . .

VIC

Shut up and take the money! Here, take it! Don't be so goddamn polite. Jesus. Take her out to a play, dinner, a movie, take all the freakin' cabs you want! Show her a good time! That's the way girls are. You gotta spend some money on them. They eat it up!

Josh looks at all the money, overwhelmed. Vic pulls him even further aside and speaks more confidentially.

(*ultra-confidential*)

Look, come here . . . Look, I'm not a real, you know, what you'd call the romantic type, but . . . you know, I think this could be a really beautiful thing.

Moments later . . .

Mike sidesteps over to the lounge chairs and picks up the magazine. He looks to make sure no one is watching, then opens up to the photographs of Audry. He stares at the pictures and his mouth gradually falls open. He's breathing heavily.

(*off, wildly*)

Mike! You son of a bitch!!!

DISSOLVE TO:

INT. JOSH'S PLACE — MORNING

The five hundred bucks and Audry's copy of The Misanthrope *are sitting on the floor beside Josh's bed.*

Josh has just gotten up and is shaving in the bathroom.

He dresses, putting on a new suit of black clothes. He is happy and anxious. He checks himself in the mirror and throws on his jacket. He pockets the money and slips the small book into his inside breast pocket.

He leaves the house.

DISSOLVE TO:

INT./EXT. TRAIN — DAY

Josh stands at the front of the train looking out at the tracks up ahead.

EXT. CITY — DAY

Josh finds his way through the city to . . .

EXT. EAST VILLAGE STREET — DAY

He comes walking up the sidewalk, checking the little piece of paper with Audry's address on it. He finds the building and checks the buzzers.

He finds the apartment number. Beside it is the name WHITBRED.

This name means nothing to Josh. He rings it and waits. No response. He tries again and still no answer. He decides he's too early. Looking around, he figures he'll kill some time walking around the neighborhood.

He crosses the street and comes across a hungry-looking street musician, Otis. Josh stops and drops a dollar in Otis's hat. Then he remembers him as the guy who gave him the ride and dropped him off at the statue of George Washington.

                    JOSH
Hey, aren't you . . .

                    OTIS
                  (*flares up*)
Back off man! It wasn't me! I wasn't even there!

Josh backs off, obligingly. Otis settles down and stares at the sidewalk. Josh waits a minute, then . . .

                    JOSH
Aren't you going to play a song?

                    OTIS
Maybe.

JOSH

Want a cigarette?

OTIS

No! I don't want a cigarette! I ain't a beggar, you know!
I'm an entertainer! I'm an artist, man!

*Josh just waves him away and sits on the steps, looking across at
Audry's building. Otis shuffles around, grumbling to himself. He
slips out a hip flask and takes a hit, then offers it to Josh.*

JOSH

Thanks. I don't drink.

OTIS
(*stunned*)

What!

JOSH

I don't drink.

OTIS

Bullshit! Everybody drinks.

JOSH

Not me.

OTIS

Why the hell not? Hey, are you a priest?

JOSH

No. I'm a mechanic.

OTIS

Really?

JOSH

Yeah.

OTIS

Mechanics drink. My ex-wife's new husband's a mechanic
and he drinks.

JOSH

Well, I don't.

OTIS

I don't believe you.

JOSH

You don't believe I don't drink.

OTIS

No, I don't believe you're a mechanic.

JOSH

But I am!

OTIS

I think you're a man of God!

JOSH

I'm a mechanic.

OTIS

Why don't you have a drink with me? What, am I not good enough for ya?

Josh tells him, sincere, but not heavy.

JOSH
(*smokes*)

The last time I drank I got in a car crash and killed a girl.

OTIS
(*silent, then*)

No.

JOSH

Yes.

Otis looks away and thinks about this, deeply impressed.

OTIS

That's enough to drive you to drink.

JOSH

I've been in prison.

OTIS

They put you in jail for a car accident!

JOSH

No, not for that. But a few years later I got in an argument with the girl's father and I killed him too.

OTIS

No shit?

JOSH

Yeah.

OTIS

How?

JOSH

I pushed him down a flight of stairs.

OTIS

Wow! Why?

JOSH

He was hammering away at my face pretty bad and I just kept laying in to his chest with all my might, you know . . . Next thing I knew . . .

OTIS

Dead?

JOSH

Broken neck. Smashed skull. I didn't even see it happen.

OTIS
(sits)

Man . . . You got a cigarette?

JOSH

Yeah, here.

They sit and smoke for a moment. After a while, Otis just shakes his head, lifts his harmonica, and starts playing.

Josh listens.

A fancy sports car turns the corner and comes up the street.

Josh and Otis watch as it pulls up.

It stops across the street in front of Audry's building. Audry steps out. She's got dark sunglasses on, is all dressed up, but looks bored and anxious to get inside.

But then Josh looks up, sees her, and rises slowly, anxious and startled.

Otis plays away . . .

Josh moves slowly forward, stepping off the curb, staring at . . .

Audry waiting at the door as . . .

Todd Whitbred climbs out of the car and carries some bags over to the door.

Josh is confused. He stops.

Audry turns away from Todd as he comes up and throws his arm around her waist.

Otis howls as he plays, lost in the song.

Audry pushes in through the door, followed in by Todd, who slides . . .

. . . his hand down over her ass. The door swings closed. BAM.

Josh wanders into the middle of the street, staring at the door, utterly disappointed. Crestfallen. Behind him Otis plays on, oblivious to everything.

    CUT TO:

INT. TODD'S APARTMENT — SAME TIME

The chic spacious apartment is on the second floor overlooking the street. Otis's music can be heard outside.

Audry and Todd enter. She drops her bags in the middle of the floor, crosses to the windows, and throws them open.

> TODD
> (*annoyed*)
>
> Do we have to listen to that bum making all that racket?

> AUDRY
> (*unconcerned*)
>
> I like it.

She falls across the couch and lies there a moment, looking at The End of the World.

She lies there thinking.

Todd comes over and starts putting the moves on her. She slaps him briskly.

He rolls down on to the couch and sighs angrily.

> TODD
>
> Come on, Audry!

> AUDRY
>
> You disgust me.

> TODD
>
> Why do you live here with me then if you won't let me touch you?

> AUDRY
>
> Because I *can*. It's free. And I'm greedy.

> TODD
> (*sits up*)
>
> Nothing is *free*, Audry. Greedy people know that.

She breaks away and throws open another window.

> I could throw you out!

> AUDRY
>
> But you won't.

> TODD
>
> Don't count on it.

AUDRY

Here's money then for rent.

TODD
(*turns away*)

I don't want your money.

AUDRY
(*coy*)

Money is all I have.

He goes over and slams the windows shut. Audry moves right along after him, throwing them open again.

TODD

You wouldn't be living like this if it wasn't for me.

AUDRY

You've made a lot of money off of me too, pal.

TODD

You're getting a damn good deal having me as your personal manager!

AUDRY
(*coy*)

But you're not still *satisfied*, are you?

He jumps her again. She struggles. He holds her by the shoulders and forces her to the couch. She swings the wrench and hits him in the ribs.

TODD

OWWW!!! Shit!

He falls back and Audry jumps away. She discovers her copy of The End of the World, *picks it up, and starts reading aloud.*

AUDRY

'The immediate effects of a twenty-megaton bomb are not different in kind from those of a twelve-and-a-half kiloton bomb; they are just more extensive.'

TODD

You gotta play the game, Audry. Life ain't pretty. You gotta make compromises. Life is all compromises.

AUDRY
(*reading*)

'The thermal pulse emitted from both bombs can ignite newspapers fifteen miles away.'

TODD

You don't get something for nothing! You could do a lot worse than me. I'm not a rich man, but I'm doing OK for a guy my age.

AUDRY

'A barren plain of ashes is the image of what our world is always poised to become.'

TODD

I'm leveraged. I've got money in real estate. I own art. I own two Andy Warhol prints! Valuable stuff!

AUDRY

'A barely imaginable horror lies just beneath the surface of our normal life . . .'

TODD

That car outside. You know how much that baby costs?

AUDRY

'. . . and threatens to break through into our normal life at any time.'

TODD

This vase here alone is worth over six thousand dollars. You see, I've been smart. Assets. Tons of assets. And I'm in great shape. I go to the most expensive gym in town . . .

AUDRY

'It is an inescapable truth about our lives today that at any given moment each and every one of us could

become a broken and confused animal scratching the surface of the earth for some small sign of life.'

*Todd grabs her, spins her around by the arm, and throws her to the
floor.*

EXT. STREET — DAY

*Otis wails on the harmonica. Josh stands staring at the pavement,
clutching Audry's little book like a rock.*

INT. APARTMENT — DAY

Todd grips Audry by the arms and lifts her right off the floor.

> AUDRY
> I have nothing.

> TODD
> I don't want anything. I want you.

> AUDRY
> Is that all?

> TODD
> You owe me. We had a deal.

> AUDRY
> We made no deal.

> TODD
> We had an understanding.

> AUDRY
> I never said I understood anything.

> TODD
> (*pulls her close*)
> Do you really think I let you live here out of the goodness
> of my heart?

She doesn't respond.

EXT. STREET — SAME TIME

Josh winds up and throws the book up at the window of the apartment.

INT. APARTMENT — DAY

CRASH! They jump back and see the expensive vase has been shattered by the book.

EXT. STREET — MOMENTS LATER

Josh stuffs the five hundred bucks into Otis's hat and Otis stops playing, looking on curiously as Josh stomps away up the street.

INT. APARTMENT — SAME TIME

Todd falls to his knees above the remains of the vase.

> TODD
> Oh my God! My fucking vase! This isn't even insured!

Audry comes over and picks up the book, looking at it wonder. Todd has forgotten about her.

She gathers her wits and rushes over to the window and looks down into the street.

EXT. STREET — SAME TIME

Audry sees . . .

Otis clutching the five hundred bucks with his mouth hanging open. He looks up and sees Audry, then flees.

Audry looks up and down the block, but Josh is gone.

INT. APARTMENT — SAME TIME

Audry jumps back away from the window, grabs her bag, her wrench, and runs from the apartment.

Todd kneels sobbing over his busted vase.

DISSOLVE TO:

EXT. SUBURBAN TRAIN STATION — DAY

The train pulls out of the station as Josh comes down the steps to the street. He pauses on the sidewalk to light a cigarette. He looks hard and mean and dangerous. He looks up and down the street and stalks off.

INT. GARAGE — DAY

The garage door flies open and Josh is revealed standing there, tall, determined, and reckless. He strides in and approaches . . .

The company car. VICTOR HUGO AUTO REPAIR *is written across the side. Josh gets in.*

Twists the key in the ignition.

The headlights go on.

The exhaust pipe rumbles as the engine revs up.

Josh clenches his cigarette in his teeth and . . .

Jams the stick-shift into drive.

The wheels peel out and he's on his way.

EXT. ROAD — DAY

Josh speeds off into the evening.

EXT. BEER STORE — DAY

Josh exits store with a six-pack of beer. He hops into the Hugo mobile and takes off.

EXT. ROAD — DAY

Josh roars down the highway, drinking a beer. Music blares from the radio.

EXT. BEACH — DAY

Josh skids to a stop in the empty parking lot. He gets out of the car with a beer in the one hand and the rest of the six-pack dangling from the other.

He strides across the flat expanse, grim, single-minded, and scary.

EXT. BEACH HOUSE — SAME TIME

Emmet and Jane are making out up against the closed-up beach house and don't notice as . . .

Josh stalks past on his way to the water. He stops, though, and watches their uninterrupted tongue kiss. He watches from a distance, but frankly and unashamed. He takes a swig of beer and continues on, brooding.

He reaches the sand and starts out for the ocean, but then sees . . .

Pearl sitting all by herself on the ledge that runs along the back of the beach house. She looks real pretty and, when she sees him, she looks down shyly.

He stands there a moment, wondering if he should move to her. She glances up at him again, and smiles nervously.

Josh just nods, stone-faced. After a pause, he starts out for the shore again. But . . .

                          PEARL
     Josh.

He stops.

She hesitates, then . . .

He stays where he is, watching her, then looks out at the water and thinks.

She waits.

He looks back at her, right in the eye, and looks handsome and formidable. Scary, but attractive.

Pearl trembles and heaves a sigh.

He starts toward her.

She slides off the ledge and leans back against it, girlish and uncertain. He comes up before her and stops.

                    JOSH
    How are you, Pearl?

                    PEARL
    Can I talk to you?

                    JOSH
    I'm not much in the mood for talking right now.

                    PEARL
    It's important.

He looks back out at the water, sighs, and . . .

    Would you like to go down to the water?

She does not respond.

He turns and looks right back at Pearl.

                    JOSH
                (*a command*)
    Let's go to my house.

EXT. BEACH HOUSE — MOMENTS LATER

Josh and Pearl walk past . . .

Emmet and Jane. Emmet pulls out of the kiss to watch, baffled, as Josh and Pearl walk out to the car. Jane looks on too.

EXT. PARKING LOT — SAME TIME

Josh opens the door for Pearl. She looks at the car, then at Josh, hesitating. Josh holds the door open and says nothing.

She looks at the six-pack in his hand, then down at the ground.

PEARL

Can we walk?

Josh waits a moment longer, then throws the door closed and turns. He starts walking away. Pearl hesitates, but then follows.

EXT. SUBURBAN TRAIN STATION – DAY

Audry comes down the steps to the street. She runs over to the taxi stand.

EXT. VIC'S BACKYARD – DAY

Vic is sitting in a lawn chair watching a small portable TV. He seems preoccupied. He looks at his watch, then gets up and turns off the set.

EXT. BEACH HOUSE – DAY

Mike is walking around the beach house, looking for Pearl. He looks at the car in the lot, which Josh left there, and which he recognizes from the garage. He comes over to . . .

Emmet and Jane, who are still kissing passionately.

MIKE

You guys seen Pearl?

They part and look at him, dazed.

EMMET

She just left.

JANE

With Josh Hutton.

Mike just looks at him oddly, turns away, and considers this.

INT. JOSH'S PLACE – DAY

Pearl is in the bathroom. Josh waits in the hallway, drinking a beer. He goes to the door and knocks.

JOSH

Pearl? You OK?

PEARL (O.S.)

You didn't kill him.

JOSH
(*lost*)

What?

PEARL (O.S.)

You didn't kill him.

He just stares at the door.

JOSH

Kill who?

PEARL (O.S.)

My father.

JOSH
(*careful*)

What do you mean?

PEARL (O.S.)
(*pauses, then . . .*)

He hit you real hard and you fell in through the bathroom
door. You hit the floor and you didn't move again. He
stepped back into the hall, at the top of the stairs . . . And
then he saw me. I startled him. He stepped back. And fell.

Josh moves a little forward and slides down the wall into a crouch.

So when they asked me . . . They asked me if you had
shoved him. And I just nodded.

Josh hesitates, then moves even closer.

I hated you. Everybody did. All I ever knew was that you
killed my sister and that I was supposed to hate you.

Josh thinks this over.

I've hated you even more since then. I made myself hate

you more and more. Then I tried not to think about it.
And I forgot. I forgot you didn't kill him. You didn't kill
him.

Josh is motionless, staring at the floor.

*Pearl opens the bathroom door and kneels next to a shell-shocked
Josh.*

I read in the papers recently how there had been this big
miscarriage of justice somewhere. A man had spent five
years in prison before everything was sorted out. He went
to court and sued the state and got a whole lot of money.
Maybe you could do something like that.

*He doesn't respond. But after a while, he gets up slowly and sits
there beside Pearl, leaning against her, intimate and trusting. She
takes his hand. He stares off, thinking, then shrugs . . .*

JOSH

I don't need the money.

They sit together in silence a while longer.

INT. BEDROOM — MOMENTS LATER

*Pearl knocks her shoes off and lays her head down on the pillow.
Josh pulls a blanket up over her.*

EXT. GARAGE — DAY

*Vic walks up and looks around. The garage door is wide open. The
car is gone. There is no one around.*

VIC

Mike?

(*no answer . . .*)

Josh?

INT. JOSH'S HOUSE — DAY

*Josh is sitting across the bedroom, sipping a beer, watching Pearl
sleep. Finally, he gets up and steps out into the hall. He realizes he's*

a little drunk, giggles, and goes into the bathroom.

Meanwhile, Vic sneaks in the back door. He gently closes the door, then stops and listens. He hears nothing. He moves on into the house.

Then, Audry appears at the front door. She hesitates, then opens the door and comes quietly in. But she freezes when she sees . . .

Vic down the hall in the kitchen. He doesn't see her and she jumps into a room off the front parlor.

Vic creeps up the hall from the kitchen toward the front parlor. The bedroom door is on his left and the bathroom is on his right.

He is about to turn the knob and peek into the bedroom when he hears Josh running the water in the bathroom.

Josh is washing his face.

Vic listens and smiles just outside the door.

Now, Mike slips quietly in through the back door. He closes it behind him and listens, suspiciously.

Vic hears the door close and moves over to jump into the bedroom, but then thinks better of it. He scrambles up the hall to the parlor.

Meanwhile, Audry peeks in through the front window.

Vic dives behind a chair.

Mike stalks slowly through the kitchen and turns up into the hall. He stops outside the bathroom and listens as . . .

Josh washes his hands.

Mike steps back, looking at the door suspiciously, then reaches out to open the bedroom door. He opens it wide and looks in at . . .

Pearl sleeping.

Mike goes white, devastated. He trembles with anger, but controls himself. He pulls the door closed again and closes it with a short, sharp little slam.

Pearl sleeps.

The bathroom door opens and . . .

Josh steps out.

JOSH

Mike.

MIKE

Fuck you!

And he hauls off and shoves Josh against the wall, but . . .

Vic jumps forward with the solution.

VIC

It's all right, Mike. I know all about it! I wanted him to.

MIKE

Well, nice touch, Vic.

Mike deals Vic a savage shove to the gut and exits through the nearest door. Josh follows.

JOSH
(*running out the door*)

Mike, let me explain.

Audry rounds the corner, smack into a stunned Vic.

AUDRY
(*giving him a good shove*)

Dad! What are you doing here?

And still Pearl sleeps. Audry comes into the room, looking for a phone, and stops dead in her tracks when she sees her friend in Josh's bed. She holds her breath a moment, then comes over and sits on the edge of the bed.

She picks up the phone which is beside the bed and dials, glancing curiously over at Pearl the whole time. Then . . .

(*into phone*)

Hello, Mom? It's me. I'm at Josh Hutton's house. Yeah.

Oh, everybody's here. You should probably come on over.
Dad's hurt himself. OK. See you.

She hangs up hard.

Pearl stirs and wakes. She sees Audry watching her and sits up.

>   PEARL
>
> Audry.

>   AUDRY
>   (*dryly*)
>
> Did you make love to Josh?

>   PEARL
>
> No. Did you?

>   AUDRY
>
> No.

>   PEARL
>
> Why not?

>   AUDRY
>
> I just got here.

Vic stumbles into the bedroom.

He falls on the bed, then looks up at Pearl.

>   VIC
>
> Pearl. What are you doing here?

>   PEARL
>
> Sleeping.

>   VIC
>   (*to Audry*)
>
> Didn't *you* sleep here?

>   AUDRY
>
> I just came from the city.

Vic is amazed. He jumps up off the bed, furious.

VIC

That bastard!

AUDRY

Dad!

VIC

That thief! He owes me five hundred bucks!

EXT. BEACH PARKING LOT — DAY

Mike is marching across the asphalt toward the ocean, pissed.

Josh is hurrying along after him, limping.

JOSH
(*yells*)

Mike! Hold on! Come on! Calm down!

Mike keeps going, but calls out over his shoulder . . .

MIKE

I go out of my way to convince Vic that you're OK for
Audry and what do you do? You fucking put the moves on
Pearl!

JOSH

Don't be an idiot, Mike! I wouldn't do that to you! Slow
down!

*Mike stomps on past the car Josh left parked there in the lot. Josh
stops.*

Where are you going?

MIKE

I'm gonna drown myself!

Vic comes running up and shoves Josh.

Mike looks back and slows down as . . .

JOSH

Now what the hell is your problem!

VIC

Where's my money!

JOSH

I don't have it any more!

Vic jumps up and tries to tackle him again. They wrestle violently.

Mike has stopped. He looks on, curious. He's forgotten that he wants to drown himself. He approaches.

VIC
(*stumbles back*)
I gave him five hundred bucks to get Audry and bring her back! He didn't do it and he kept the money!

JOSH

I didn't even *want* the money!

VIC

You didn't hold up your end of the deal!

JOSH

We didn't make any deal!

VIC

We had an understanding!

JOSH

You don't understand anything!

Vic turns away, disgusted.

VIC

You just can't trust anybody.

Audry, Pearl, and Liz come walking up. Pearl heads straight for Mike, furious.

PEARL

Where were you?

MIKE

Where were *you*?

PEARL

I waited at the beach house till six o'clock. You said you'd meet me there at five!

MIKE
(*remembers*)

Oh, yeah. Well, I got hung up.

PEARL

Why didn't you call me?

MIKE

Well, I ahh . . . you know . . . I didn't have a quarter.

Pearl storms off toward the water and Mike runs after her.

LIZ

Victor, what's wrong with you?

VIC

Nothing is wrong with me. I want my money!

AUDRY
(*to Josh*)

Pearl says you're innocent.

VIC
(*to Liz*)

Innocent of what?

LIZ

He didn't kill Pearl's father.

VIC

What!

AUDRY

Dad, since Josh is not a murderer, all the deals I've made with you are now null and void.

VIC
(*outraged*)

Oh, no! No way! You still gotta go to college!

Audry takes out her check book and leans on the car.

> AUDRY
> (*writing*)

I'll go to college when I feel like it. I'm going to travel. See the world.

> VIC

What about the money I gave that insane charity thing?

Audry rips out the check and hands it to him.

> AUDRY

Eleven thousand dollars. All the money I have in the world. It's all yours.

She throws down her bag and goes back to Josh.

I've decided I can't have faith in what I can't see.

> JOSH
> (*looks at her*)

What do you want to see?

> AUDRY

The world.

> JOSH

What about this guy Whitbred?

> AUDRY

He means nothing to me.

> JOSH

How do I know that?

> AUDRY

You have to trust me.

Josh just stares at her a moment, hard, then turns and takes a few steps away. She watches as he stares a hole in the asphalt at his feet. Finally, he turns back to her, decided. He lifts up and gives her a shake.

JOSH
(*nods*)

I don't trust anyone.

She smiles and moves into his arms. They kiss.

EXT. BEACH — LATER

Audry is riding on Josh's back. He walks around to the passenger side of the van.

JOSH

Do you have any money?

AUDRY
(*looks*)

Twelve dollars. You?

JOSH

No. I don't have my tools either.

AUDRY

I have your wrench.

JOSH

OK, that'll do. Come on, get in.

He opens the door for her and an empty beer can falls out on to the asphalt. They look up from it to each other, uneasily. Then . . .

AUDRY

I suppose we're car thieves now?

JOSH

You just gave your father eleven thousand dollars.

AUDRY

But there was no agreement, no deal.

JOSH

Just money.

AUDRY

Hold it!

She looks up at the sky and listens.

> JOSH
> (*looks up*)

What?

> AUDRY

Do you hear that?

> JOSH
> (*listens*)

No. What is it?

> AUDRY

Listen.

They stand there beside the car, listening intently. The camera rises up and into the evening sky.

CUT TO BLACK.

Trust

CAST AND CREW

MAIN CAST

MARIA COUGHLIN	Adrienne Shelly
MATTHEW SLAUGHTER	Martin Donovan
JEAN COUGHLIN	Rebecca Nelson
JIM SLAUGHTER	John Mackay
PEG COUGHLIN	Edie Falco
ANTHONY	Gary Sauer
ED	Matt Malloy
RACHEL	Suzanne Costollos
ROBERT	Jeff Howard
NURSE PAINE	Karen Sillas
DELI MAN	Tom Thon
BRUCE	M. C. Bailey
RUARK BOSS	Patricia Sullivan
JOHN COUGHLIN	Marko Hunt

MAIN CREW

Written and Directed by	Hal Hartley
Cinematographer	Michael Spiller
Production Designer	Dan Ouellette
Editor	Nick Gomez
Original Music by	Phil Reed
Executive Producer	Jerome Brownstein
Producer	Bruce Weiss

INT. MARIA'S KITCHEN — MORNING

Maria is a spunky, well-intentioned, but troublesome and thoughtless seventeen-year-old with big hair, supermarket clothes, and a mouthful of chewing gum. She's arguing with her father, John, while she puts on her lipstick. Her mother, Jean, watches.

                    MARIA
Dad, gimme five dollars.

                    JOHN
Listen to me, young lady. I've had just about all I'm gonna take!

                    MARIA
Mom, what's he talking about? Gimme five dollars.

                    JEAN
Listen to your father when he's talking to you!

                    MARIA
Well, what's he talking about?

                    JOHN
You know damn well what I'm talking about!

                    JEAN
Maria, you've been thrown outta school!

                    MARIA
I was not thrown out. I quit. Now gimme five dollars!

John moves forward.

                    JOHN
You little . . .

                    JEAN
John, stop it!

MARIA

You wouldn't *dare.*

JOHN

If I had my way around this house, I'd . . .

JEAN

John, shut up!

JOHN

What's gonna happen to her? What is she gonna do with her life?

MARIA

I'm gonna get married.

John and Jean are surprised. They look at each other, then back at Maria.

JEAN

To who?

MARIA

To Anthony.

JOHN

Oh, terrific!

JEAN

Maria, don't be silly. Anthony's going to college.

MARIA
(*lighting a cigarette*)
Only to play football. When he gets out, he'll go to work with his father doing construction and he'll be pullin' in a really bitchin' salary and we'll be like totally hooked . . .

JOHN

Don't smoke in the house!

MARIA
(*blows out smoke*)
And besides, he's gotta marry me. I'm gonna have a baby!

Maria gets up from the table. John snaps straight and tall and frightening, glaring at Maria, who stands confronting him.

JOHN

That's it!

MARIA

That's what?

JOHN

I will not have a goddamn *tramp* living in my house!

MARIA
(*appalled*)

Mom! Did you hear what he *called* me?

Jean is isolated within herself, so Maria turns back to John, furious.

Bastard.

JOHN

Slut.

MARIA
(*truly shocked*)

Daddy!

JOHN

Get out!

Maria hauls off and slaps him hard across the face. Everything goes quiet. John is shocked. Jean is shocked. Maria looks back and forth between them, worried, then proudly throws her head back.

MARIA

So there.

Maria leaves, slamming the door behind her. John just stares into space, mortified. Jean slowly rises from the table, watching him.

JEAN

John?

John falls to the floor, his hand clutching his chest. Peg, Maria's older sister, enters.

                              PEG
    Mom, I'm home!

Peg stops when she sees Jean kneeling over John on the floor. He's lying there, staring lifelessly up at the ceiling.

    Mom?

                             JEAN
    John!

                              PEG
    What happened?

Peg kneels down beside her father and touches his body. She looks at Jean.

He's . . . dead.

    CUT TO BLACK.

TITLE APPEARS . . . 'TRUST' . . . *Then the titles appear over black.*

INT. RUARK COMPUTER FACTORY — DAY

It is a clean and orderly assembly line for the fabrication of computer parts.

Matthew Slaughter is working along the line. He is an absolutely possessed young man of thirty. His face is always twisted into an impatient scowl, his fists are always clenched, and he stalks wildly from bench to bench, overseeing the work. He stops and knocks over an empty carton. Matthew approaches one of the benches. A worker backs away, scared, as Matthew looks down at a particular portion of an exposed circuit board. There's a cigarette gripped in the edge of his mouth and his hair is totally unkempt. This is one mean, abusive, but dedicated human being. Matthew's superior, Ed, comes rushing over. He's all excited and itching for a fight. He's a jerk.

                              ED
    Slaughter! What'd I tell you about smoking on the premises?

MATTHEW

Lay off, Ed!

ED

What's this vice doing here?

MATTHEW

Drop dead. Hand me those pliers.

ED

What's this?

MATTHEW

This is a lost cause, Ed.

ED

What is?

MATTHEW

This!

He puts down his pliers, picks up the piece of high-tech machinery he's working on, and throws it to the floor. It smashes into a million pieces.

Everyone looks on, startled. Ed is outraged.

ED

You'll pay for that!

MATTHEW

This *crap* isn't worth the *time* we put into it!

ED

What's wrong with it?

MATTHEW

It's cheap.

ED

So?

MATTHEW

Cheap!

                              ED
    Can't you fix it?

                           MATTHEW
    No!

                              ED
    Why not?

                           MATTHEW
                    (*lights a new cigarette*)
    Some things shouldn't be fixed.

                              ED
    Well, you don't have a choice, do you? The company
    employs you to oversee the fabrication of . . .

                           MATTHEW
    Ed.

                              ED
    Let me finish. The company . . .

Matthew grabs Ed, forces his head into the vice, and tightens it.

INT. RUARK COMPUTER FACTORY — DAY

*Matthew takes off his lab coat, throws it to the ground, and walks
away, throwing his cigarette away as he goes.*

EXT. RUARK COMPUTER FACTORY PARKING LOT — DAY

*Matthew slams out a door and finds himself in the parking lot. He
walks away.*

INT. HIGH SCHOOL — DAY — A LITTLE LATER

*Maria stands at the bottom of a flight of stairs. A group of guys in
football uniform pass her on their way down. Her boyfriend,
Anthony, brings up the rear.*

                            MARIA
    Hi.

ANTHONY
(*annoyed*)
What the fuck you doing here?

MARIA
I've got to tell you something.

ANTHONY
You get tossed outta school again?

MARIA
Yeah.

ANTHONY
What the hell did you do now?

MARIA
Come upstairs.

ANTHONY
(*obstinate*)
No.

MARIA
Oh, ease up.

ANTHONY
Listen, Maria, this isn't the time to be bugging me right now, OK? I've got a game tonight, and I've gotta take my college entrance exams tomorrow . . .

MARIA
This is important.

ANTHONY
Yeah, well so's this.

MARIA
This is more important. This is more important than football.

ANTHONY
Really.

                            MARIA
I'm gonna have a baby.

                           ANTHONY
What?

                            MARIA
A baby, stupid.

                           ANTHONY
Whose baby?

                            MARIA
                        (*hitting him*)
Yours, you jerk!

Anthony is horrified. He walks away and collapses to the floor.

                           ANTHONY
How could you be so stupid?

                            MARIA
Oh, thanks a lot!

                           ANTHONY
What are my parents gonna say! I've got a scholarship on
the line!

                            MARIA
What about me?

                           ANTHONY
What about you? How could you let this happen?

                            MARIA
I didn't just let this happen all by myself, you know!

                           ANTHONY
Don't try and pin the blame on me!

                            MARIA
I'm not blaming you! It's just that . . .

                           ANTHONY
You did this on purpose!

MARIA

I did not!

ANTHONY

You did this to keep me from going away to college!

MARIA

Anthony . . . You said we'd get married!

ANTHONY

What?

MARIA

You did. You said we'd get married!

ANTHONY

You think I'd marry you now? Why would I marry you now? A high-school drop-out! Pregnant!

Maria starts walking away. Anthony walks along beside her, screaming into her ear.

You know, you squeeze that brat out and you sit around watching television all day long and you know what you're gonna look like by the time you're twenty-one? Huh? Urgh! You think I need that!

Maria forges ahead, but he continues harping on at her . . .

I don't need that. These are the most important years in my life as a football player. This arm! This arm is gonna make me famous! It's gonna take me straight through college and into the NFL! And people say that I'm a smart player. They say I'm good with strategy. That's why I gotta be devoted. I wake up at six o'clock every morning and I run three miles. Then I do eighty push-ups. Then sixty sit-ups. Then I drink this mix of one raw egg, brewer's yeast, soybean extract, wheat germ . . .

Finally, Maria can't stand it any more and she runs off as Anthony carries on shouting.

EXT. MATTHEW'S STREET — DAY

Matthew walks down the street, a beer can in hand, cigarette clenched viciously in his teeth, and his eyes darting around looking for trouble.

INT. MATTHEW'S HOUSE — DAY

Matthew closes the door behind himself.

> DAD
> (*off*)

Matthew!

Matthew starts. With the sound of his dad's voice he becomes an intensely soft-spoken and indecisive person.

Matthew! Is that you?

> MATTHEW

It's me.

> DAD

What?

Matthew passes through the hall and enters the TV room.

INT. TV ROOM — DAY

Dad is some kind of retired blue-collar worker sitting on the sofa with his trucker's cap on. He wears a flannel shirt and work boots. He's big, robust, and clear-eyed. He glares at Matthew.

> DAD

Why aren't you at work?

> MATTHEW

Well, I . . .

> DAD

Speak up, for Christ's sake!

> MATTHEW

I quit.

DAD

You what?

MATTHEW

I quit.

DAD

You quit?

MATTHEW

I got fired.

DAD

Well, which is it, Matthew? You quit or you got fired?

MATTHEW
(*flustered*)

It's not that simple.

DAD

Yes, it is. You quit or you got fired? Which one?

MATTHEW

I quit.

DAD

You're sure about that?

MATTHEW

Yes. I quit.

Dad stands up and hits Matthew across the face.

DAD

You got a lot of fucking nerve, you know that? You go through jobs like most people go through underwear.

MATTHEW

I'll get another job!

DAD

You expect me to support you your whole goddamn life, is that it?

MATTHEW

No.

DAD

What was that?

MATTHEW

I said no.

DAD

When are you gonna wake up and stand up on your own
two feet, huh? You're a grown man! When I was your age I
was on my own and making a damn good living!

MATTHEW

I'll move out then.

DAD

What was that?

Matthew doesn't answer.

Tell me what you said.

MATTHEW

You heard what I said.

DAD

Tell me what you said, coward! Come on!

MATTHEW

I said I'll move out then.

Dad sits down.

DAD

That's a joke. You wouldn't know how to take care of
yourself. You oughta thank God I've been here to look
after you! And when are you gonna clean that bathroom,
like I asked, huh?

MATTHEW
(*sincere*)
But I did. I did it before I went to work . . .

DAD

You call that clean?

MATTHEW

Yeah . . .

DAD

Do it again!

Matthew turns and goes out.

You eat yet?

MATTHEW
(off)

I'm not hungry.

DAD
(shakes his head)

Fucking kid's gonna waste away.

INT. MATTHEW'S BATHROOM — DAY — A LITTLE LATER

Matthew dutifully scrubs the bathroom. The sink, the bathtub, the toilet bowl.

INT. MATTHEW'S OWN ROOM — DAY — LATER

Matthew's room has nothing in it except a mattress thrown on the floor, a chair by the window, and books. Hundreds of books are scattered all over the place. He's sitting on the edge of his bed reading a book entitled Information Theory.

The door slams open and he looks up to see . . .

Dad standing there, furious, but trying to keep calm.

DAD

How many times have I got to tell you to clean that god-damn bathroom?

MATTHEW

But . . . I . . .

                              DAD
   Do it! NOW!

INT. BATHROOM — DAY — MOMENTS LATER

Matthew scrubs his heart out. With his cigarette smoking and his sleeves rolled up, he's breaking into a sweat scrubbing the toilet bowl.

INT. CLOTHING STORE — DAY

Maria sorts through clothes with a salesgirl roughly her age. She is depressed and shops with a vengeance.

                              GIRL
   That would look great on you.

                             MARIA
   I like this one too.

                              GIRL
   Try on both.

                             MARIA
   Can I charge these on my parents' credit card?

                              GIRL
   Sure. The dressing room is right over there.

Maria walks over and enters the dressing room.

INT. DRESSING ROOM — DAY

Maria slips into one of the dresses. She looks at herself in the mirror and her eyes are eventually drawn to her . . .

Stomach, which is certainly not showing any signs of pregnancy. She places her hands on her belly and tries to imagine what she'd look like pregnant.

After a moment she relaxes and slumps down into the chair behind her.

She stares at herself in the mirror. She sits there, sadly contemplating herself.

EXT. MATTHEW'S YARD — DAY

Dad is watering the lawn. He sees . . .

Mrs Blech, who is not a bad looking mom in her late thirties, having trouble starting her car.

Dad stops what he's doing and approaches, easy-going, good-natured, and sincerely concerned.

                              DAD
What's the problem?

                          MRS BLECH
Oh, I wish I knew. This damn car. It's always something.

                              DAD
Sounds like the battery.

INT. MATTHEW'S BATHROOM — DAY — SAME TIME

The place is sparkling. Matthew looks around to see if he's forgotten anything. He sees that he's left the sponge on the floor. He places his cigarette on the edge of the sink and bends down to get it. He tosses it in his bucket and goes out.

BUT . . . his cigarette remains on the edge of the sink, its ash growing on and on.

INT. MATTHEW'S BROOM CLOSET — DAY

The door swings open and Matthew places the bucket on its shelf.

INT. MATTHEW'S BATHROOM — DAY — SAME TIME

The cigarette's ash trembles precariously and bits of it . . .

Fall down into the spotless sink.

EXT. MATTHEW'S YARD — DAY — SAME TIME

Joey Blech and his twelve-year-old sister, Grace, come up to the car while Dad is looking into it.

                              GRACE

Hi, Mr Slaughter!

                               DAD

Hi, Grace. Joey, how are you?

                              JOEY

Fine.

                               DAD

It's nothing serious, Mrs Blech. Just all this corrosion here
on your battery terminals.
                          (*to Joey*)
Joey, you wanna do me a favor, please? Go in the garage
there and get me a piece of sandpaper and a screwdriver,
OK?

                              JOEY

OK!

                               DAD

This won't take a minute, Mrs Blech.

INT. MATTHEW'S BEDROOM — DAY — SAME TIME

*The voices of Dad and the kids carry inside. Matthew is looking
thoughtfully at the floor. He reaches into the side pocket of his jacket
to get . . .*

*A hand grenade. He holds it to his chest and looks out toward the
window.*

EXT. CLINIC — DAY

*There is a group of protesters milling around before the entrance of a
women's health clinic, carrying placards that read: 'Save our children! Close it down!'*

*Across the street, Nurse Paine pulls up in her dented and rusting
little Pinto. She steps out of the car, tosses away her cigarette, and
regards the protesters with a wry, cynical shake of the head. She's
an attractive, hard-boiled, devoted social-worker type. She sighs,*

slams the car door, and moves forcefully toward the clinic.

The protesters see her approaching and descend upon her, wild and righteous.

PROTESTER 1

That's her! That's her!

PROTESTER 2

Murderer!

PROTESTER 3

Baby killer!

Nurse Paine continues on through the barrage of insults hurled at her.

INT. CLINIC (OFFICE) – DAY

Maria sits staring at the edge of the desk, childishly uncommunicative. Paine watches her patiently. After a while . . .

PAINE

What kind of questions do you have?

MARIA

I don't know.

PAINE

Do you want to have an abortion?

MARIA

I don't know.

PAINE

Do you have a boyfriend?

MARIA

No.

PAINE

Who is the father?

MARIA

There is no father.

Paine holds the girl's stubborn gaze a moment. Maria looks back down. Paine watches her, then takes off her nurse's cap. She reaches down into her desk drawer and takes out a fifth of bourbon and two shot glasses.

Maria looks on surprised, but not shocked.

                         PAINE
                      (*of bourbon*)
You?

                         MARIA
Sure.

Paine pours and they drink. They sit in silence, enjoying their bourbon. Then . . .

You know, I'm looking at this guy, right? And I looked at him a lot before. So now I know that I've got this little piece of him actually in me. Physically in me. And it makes me feel completely different. I don't know, sorta special or something. And so I'm talking to him. I'm talking to him and I realize . . . I'm talking to him and I realize that he doesn't even see me. And I wonder what it was he was seeing when we did this. I go over it in my head and I know now what he's seeing. It's really simple. He's seeing my legs. He's seeing my breasts. My mouth. My ass. He's seeing my cunt.
                   (*looks up at Paine . . .*)
How could I have been so stupid? That's really all there is to see, isn't it?

                         PAINE
That's not true.

                         MARIA
I don't know.

                         PAINE
It's not true and you know that.

> MARIA

I don't know anything.

INT. MATTHEW'S BEDROOM — DAY

Matthew is sitting with the grenade in his hand, smoking.

INT. MATTHEW'S KITCHEN — DAY — MOMENTS LATER

Dad comes in through the door, feeling pretty good about himself. He opens the fridge and drinks from a quart of milk. He stands there a moment, swallows, burps, and then remembers Matthew. He listens.

Nothing.

INT. MATTHEW'S BATHROOM — DAY

Dad pushes open the door, looks around, enters, and stops, horrified, when he sees . . .

The cigarette in the sink.

The quart of milk slips from Dad's hand and . . .

Hits the floor, splashing out on to the sparkling tiles.

INT. MATTHEW'S BEDROOM — DAY

Matthew, holding the grenade to his cheek like some precious pet, looks up from the floor and opens his eyes. He breathes deep, relaxed. A moment of silence, then . . .

BOOM! The door is thrown off its hinges and falls, hanging cock-eyed to the side.

Matthew slips the grenade under a book on the floor.

Dad is there at the door. Heaving with violence, he steps into the room.

Matthew stands up slowly.

Dad closes his eyes, clenches his fists, breathes deep, and looks up at his son.

Matthew waits.

DAD

Who the hell do you think you are?

MATTHEW

I don't think I'm anybody.

DAD

You think you're somebody special, don't you?

MATTHEW

Just tell me what I've done wrong.

DAD

You think you shit ice-cream cones, is that it?

MATTHEW

All I want to do is clean the bathroom.

Dad punches him in the stomach and Matthew falls to his knees, holding his gut. Dad goes down on his knees, face to face with Matthew.

DAD

I've seen your kind. I've seen 'em all my life. You just keep taking. Taking, like everything was owed to you. Like the rest of us owed you something! You're like a little child! Gimme this! Gimme that! Other people need things too, you know, Matthew! You ever think about that? You ever think about other people? You ever think about *me*!

MATTHEW

I think about you all the time.

DAD

What!

No answer. He grabs Matthew by the hair . . .

Did you say something?

MATTHEW

I don't know what you want!

DAD

I want . . . a little *cooperation*!

He releases Matthew's head. Matthew stays where he is, his face to the floor. Dad sits on the edge of a chair, hangs his head, and sighs.

I don't know. Maybe it's my fault.

                    MATTHEW

It's not your fault.

                    DAD

Well, then whose fault is it?

Matthew doesn't answer.

Huh!

Matthew looks down.

Whose fault is it, Matthew?

Matthew is silent.

If it isn't my fault, whose fault is it?

                    MATTHEW
                    (*softly*)

It's my fault.

                    DAD

What was that?

                    MATTHEW

It's *my* fault!

                    DAD

It's your fault.

                    MATTHEW

It's my *fault*!

                    DAD

That's real big of you, Matthew. You think that *changes* anything?

Matthew says nothing.

INT. MARIA'S REAR HALLWAY — THAT AFTERNOON

Maria comes in the back door and looks around for someone. She checks her face in the mirror and tries to seem cheerful.

> MARIA
>
> Mom? Anybody home?

She moves into the kitchen.

INT. MARIA'S KITCHEN — DAY — SAME TIME

> MARIA
> (*seeing people in the kitchen*)
> Aunt Fay? Uncle Leo? What's going on? We having a party?

She doesn't notice that they turn away and hang their heads. She moves over to Peg.

> Hey, Peg, we having a party? You gotta see this bitchin' top I got. Where's Mom? . . .

Peg moves away as Maria moves into the living room . . .

INT. LIVING ROOM — DAY

Jean is sitting on the couch, flanked by two other women. Tragedy flows from their faces, and even Maria stops in her tracks, stricken.

> MARIA
> (*pales*)
>
> Mom?

Jean stares, bitter beyond words. Maria collapses at her mother's feet.

> What happened? Where's Dad?

Jean looks up at Maria.

> JEAN
>
> He's dead.

MARIA

Dead?

JEAN

Dead.
                    (*slowly, cold*)
You killed him.

Maria drops her head. Jean grabs Maria's chin. Maria stares up at her mother, amazed and frightened. Jean is clear-eyed and terrifying.

Get outta my house.

EXT. STREETS — DAY

Maria staggers blindly through the streets.

EXT. PHONE BOOTH — DAY

Maria clings desperately to the receiver.

MARIA
                    (*into phone*)
Hi, Carol. It's me. How do I know? I . . . I didn't *mean* to! What? I don't know. Look, I don't have any place to go. What? Because you're my best friend.

Click. Carol hangs up. Maria looks at the receiver, stunned.

EXT. DELI — LATE AFTERNOON

There's a bench just outside the door of the deli. A neat and kindly forty-year-old woman, Rachel, sits at one end, watching the traffic go by.

Maria comes up and collapses on to the bench. She sits staring at her feet, dejected.

Rachel looks over at Maria. She grows concerned and leans over carefully.

RACHEL

Excuse me . . . Maybe it's none of my business, but . . .
Are you all right?

No response.

I only ask because you seem a little pale. Are you hungry?

Still no response.

Has something happened? Are you hurt?

*Suddenly, Maria breaks down and falls on Rachel's chest, sobbing
into the woman's coat. Rachel is surprised and a little scared at first,
but then puts her arm around the girl and holds her.*

Now, now. Everything will be all right. Everything will be
OK.

*Maria moves back to her side of the bench and stares at the ground
again.*

MARIA

That's such a *stupid* thing to say! Really stupid! How the
hell do you know?

RACHEL

I'm sorry. It just seemed like the thing to say.

MARIA

Why say anything?

RACHEL

I don't know.

MARIA

There's nothing to say!

RACHEL

Maybe.

MARIA

Gimme five dollars.

She looks up at the woman. Rachel hesitates, but then reaches into her bag and hands Maria a five-dollar bill. Maria takes it, then looks down, ashamed. She hands it back.

I'm sorry.

RACHEL
It's OK. Go ahead. Take it. I want you to have it.

Maria waits a moment, then sighs and stuffs the money in her pocket. Rachel watches her and smiles warmly.

MARIA
I killed my father this morning.

RACHEL
(*not listening*)
My daughter would have been just about your age.

MARIA
I didn't mean to, honest. It was an accident. We were just arguing.

RACHEL
I've spent some time in a psychiatric hospital.

MARIA
I didn't know he had a bad heart.

RACHEL
After that my husband just didn't want children.

MARIA
He always *seemed* healthy enough.

RACHEL
I wonder if deep down he blames me for her death.

MARIA
I just slapped him.

A scrawny, bleach-blonde biker mom wheels up a baby stroller, parks it near the bench, kisses the baby, then goes into the deli, smoking a joint.

                              RACHEL
I hate my husband.

                              MARIA
You just never know.

                              RACHEL
He's just like a child himself.

                              MARIA
How can a slap in the face kill a man?

                              RACHEL
He is so absurdly like a little boy. Every summer we've got
to go to this ridiculous resort called Cape Holiday.

                              MARIA
                          (*to Rachel*)
What?

                              RACHEL
I hate Cape Holiday.

                              MARIA
I'm sorry.

                              RACHEL
And our days are like clockwork. The same routine year in
and year out. Him off to the city every morning with his
briefcase and pipe. Then back again each evening on the
5.15 train.

*Maria listens and realizes that Rachel is somewhere far away in her
own head. But she listens politely . . .*

And me at home dusting a house that never gets dirty.
Never gets messed up. There's no one there to mess it up.
Sometimes I come home and I find myself hoping the
house is a wreck. Filthy. Complete disarray. Sometimes I
come home and find myself hoping the house has been
destroyed by fire.

Maria watches the woman oddly, waiting. Rachel just stares off into space, thinking, biting her lip. The biker mom's baby chortles and burps in its stroller.

Maria gets up slowly, and places her hand on Rachel's arm . . .

> MARIA
> Well, thanks for the five dollars.

Rachel doesn't respond. She concentrates on something unknown. Maria steps away awkwardly and enters the deli.

Rachel snaps out of it and looks over at . . .

The baby peering out at her from over the edge of the stroller. He's grasping a little plastic submachine-gun.

INT. DELI — LATE AFTERNOON

Maria comes in and passes the biker mom, who is on the pay phone.

> BIKER MOM
> I don't care about any of that! What am I supposed to pay the rent with? Are you still sleeping with that slut? Yeah, well you tell her I'm gonna rip her lungs out next time I see her . . .

Maria takes a six-pack out of the refrigerator and lays it on the counter. She sighs and throws down her five dollars. The deli man is a heavy-set, pasty-faced guy in his forties.

> DELI MAN
> Let me see some proof.

> MARIA
> What?

> DELI MAN
> Come on.

> MARIA
> I buy beer here all the time.

> DELI MAN
> Not from me you don't.

MARIA

Where's the other guy? Or that lady?

DELI MAN

Look, they're not working right now. I am. If you wanna
buy beer *now*, you gotta show *me* proof.

MARIA

Listen, mister. I've had a really *bad* day. Just take the
money. Please.

Maria pushes the money toward him. They stare each other down.
Maria is so worn down and wired she looks like a drug addict. The
deli man looks her up and down, thinks a moment, looks around the
store, then takes the money. He puts the beer in a bag and she
reaches for it, but . . .

He snatches it back. She looks at him. He stares at her a moment,
then motions to the back room.

DELI MAN

Come back here a minute.

Maria doesn't move. She stares at him, edgy.

Come on. You want the beer?

MARIA

Yeah, I want the beer. Why do I have to go back there?

DELI MAN

I don't want you to go out the front. People might see
you. They can close me down for selling you beer!

Maria waits, looks around, then cautiously moves past the counter.

INT. DELI BACK ROOM — LATE AFTERNOON

Maria enters, followed by the deli man. She looks around and sees . . .

MARIA

There's no back *door* here.

DELI MAN
(*leers at her*)
Come on, gimme a kiss.

MARIA
Oh, gross!

DELI MAN
Hey, you want the beer, you gotta gimme a kiss.

MARIA
Just gimme back the money.

DELI MAN
No way.

MARIA
Come on! That's not fair!

DELI MAN
(*comes close*)
You think it's fair you comin' in here jeopardizing my business?

MARIA
I ain't jeopardizing anything! I wanna *do* business!

DELI MAN
Right, so gimme a kiss.

MARIA
Let me outta here. You can *keep* the money.

She tries to get past him. He grabs her.

DELI MAN
I don't want the money. I want a kiss.

MARIA
You can't have both.

DELI MAN
(*gives back money*)
OK. Here's the five dollars. Now gimme a kiss. On the lips.

MARIA

Drop dead.

DELI MAN
(*cheated*)
You have to. I gave you back the five dollars!

MARIA

It was mine to begin with!

DELI MAN

Listen, you want the beer or not?

MARIA

If you don't let me go I'm gonna scream.

DELI MAN

Go ahead. My brother's the chief of police. I'll say you
were stealing. They'll believe me. Not you.

Maria looks at him in disbelief.

MARIA

Come on.

DELI MAN
(*approaches*)
Just a little kiss.

He moves in to kiss her. She jumps away and gets clear.

MARIA

Listen, I am *not* gonna kiss you. Face it.

DELI MAN

Look, I don't have to be nice about it. Now why don't you
make it easy on yourself.

*She's cornered and she knows it. She hangs her head, thinks a
moment, then . . .*

MARIA

Gimme a cigarette.

DELI MAN

If I give you a cigarette, you have to take off your shirt.

MARIA

You're really disgusting.

DELI MAN

It's just business, honey. Free trade.

MARIA

Shut up and gimme a cigarette.

He gives her a cigarette and lights it for her.

DELI MAN

Take off your shirt.

MARIA

Just wait a minute, will ya!

He keeps pressing closer and closer . . .

DELI MAN

Let me see you touch yourself.

MARIA

I bet this gets you really excited, huh?

DELI MAN
(*sweating*)

It sure does! How 'bout you?

Maria takes a good, long drag off her cigarette, lets him get closer, then . . .

Sticks the cigarette in his eye . . .

YEOWWWWW!

He falls back into a stack of boxes. Maria picks up the beer and runs out.

INT. DELI — LATE AFTERNOON

Maria runs through the store and out on to the sidewalk.

EXT. DELI SIDEWALK — LATE AFTERNOON

Maria slams out the door and stops dead in her tracks when she sees . . .

The biker mom standing, horror stricken, staring down into . . .

The empty baby stroller.

                              BIKER MOM
    They stole my baby!

Maria looks over at . . .

The bench. Rachel is gone.

The deli man stumbles out the door, howling in pain, and falls to the ground. Maria runs off in a panic.

                    (knocking over the baby stroller)
    Fuck!

EXT. STREET — LATE AFTERNOON

Maria wanders aimlessly through the streets, clutching her bag of beer.

EXT. ABANDONED HOUSE — NIGHT

Matthew approaches a derelict house.

INT. ABANDONED HOUSE — NIGHT

Matthew sits down, takes the hand grenade out of his pocket, and places it on the shelf next to him. As he lights a cigarette he hears a noise. Nothing. He turns away, but as he is about to take a drag on his cigarette he hears something move.

INT. ABANDONED HOUSE — NIGHT

Matthew wanders through the house toward where he heard the noise. He sees Maria huddled in a corner. They stare at each other, then Matthew starts to move away.

MARIA

What do you want?

MATTHEW

I don't want anything.

MARIA

Really.

MATTHEW

Yeah.

MARIA

Why?

MATTHEW

Because I don't think anything's going to help.

MARIA

What do you mean by that?

MATTHEW

You drink all that beer by yourself?

MARIA

Do you live around here?

MATTHEW

Not far.

MARIA

I don't have anywhere to go.

MATTHEW

So?

MARIA

Forget it.

Matthew stands there, staring.

So, what do you want?

MATTHEW

I said, I don't want anything.

MARIA

So then, get lost.

MATTHEW

What do *you* want?

MARIA

I don't want anything from you. That's for sure.

MATTHEW

Really?

MARIA

Yeah. Really.

Matthew nods his head thoughtfully, then moves over and crouches down next to Maria.

MATTHEW

Say it.

It takes a good long time, but finally she lets down her defenses and sighs wearily.

MARIA

I . . . I need some place to sleep.

INT. MATTHEW'S BEDROOM — MORNING

Books are strewn across the room. Maria is asleep in Matthew's bed. She wakes up and looks around her.

EXT. MATTHEW'S HOUSE — MORNING

Matthew has been shopping. He comes up to the door, gets rid of his cigarette, and enters the house.

INT. MATTHEW'S BEDROOM — MORNING

Maria is sitting on the bed, reading a passage from Matthew's copy of Man in the Universe. *It strikes her as strange, but intriguing. She puts the book down, but keeps looking at it, frowning.*

Matthew enters with a small bag of groceries. He places before

Maria a bag of potato chips, a Coke, and a bottle of stomach medicine.

> MARIA
> (*of the medicine*)

What are these?

> MATTHEW

They'll make your stomach feel better.

Maria takes a sip of Coke.

Where are you from?

> MARIA

Around.

> MATTHEW

Are you a runaway or something?

> MARIA

I'm a murderer.

> MATTHEW
> (*unfazed*)

Really? Who'd you kill?

> MARIA

Well, I'm not actually a murderer. But I've thought about killing myself.

> MATTHEW

I know what you mean.

> MARIA

You do?

Matthew shows Maria his grenade.

> MATTHEW

I carry this with me at all times.

> MARIA

A hand grenade?

MATTHEW

Yeah.

MARIA

Is it real?

MATTHEW

My dad brought it back from Korea.

MARIA

What for?

MATTHEW

Souvenir, I guess.

MARIA

No, I mean, why do you carry it around with you all the time?

MATTHEW

Just in case.

MARIA

Just in case what?

MATTHEW

Just in case.

MARIA

Are you emotionally disturbed?

MATTHEW

Look, I just showed it to you because of what you said.

MARIA

Forget what I said. Put that thing away.

MATTHEW

Do you really think it's a good idea to drink soda for breakfast?

MARIA

It keeps my skin clear.

MATTHEW

What?

MARIA

It's true.

MATTHEW

In ten years your bones are gonna snap like twigs. You oughta have a glass of milk.

MARIA

Milk gives me pimples.

MATTHEW

You probably get more pimples from all that make-up you're wearing.

MARIA

Make-up *hides* my pimples.

MATTHEW

Sorry.

MARIA

Do you live here alone?

MATTHEW

With my dad.

Maria looks around nervously.

MARIA

Where is he?

MATTHEW

Visiting his sister.
                    (*pause*)
Well, I've got to go see this jerk about a job.

MARIA

Can I take a shower?

MATTHEW

Sure.

                            MARIA
    Thanks.

Matthew looks at her.

                          MATTHEW
    It's OK.

*Matthew goes out. Maria sits there a moment and realizes that her
clothes stink.*

INT. TV REPAIR OUTLET — DAY — A LITTLE LATER

*There is a line of people holding broken TV sets that goes out the
door and around the corner. Matthew enters. There is a guy about
his age, Bruce, working the front counter. Anthony is at the counter.*

                          ANTHONY
    So, what's wrong with it?

                           BRUCE
    Listen, cookie-puss, your warranty's expired. So just shut
    up and blow.

Matthew shoves Anthony out of the way.

    What do you want?

                          MATTHEW
    I'm here to see Mr Santiago.

                           BRUCE
    He ain't in.

                          MATTHEW
    Get him.

                           BRUCE
    What do you want?

                          SANTIAGO
                            (*off*)
    Who is it, Bruce?

BRUCE

Nothing. Nothing much at all.

Santiago comes out.

SANTIAGO

So, Matthew.

Matthew keeps his eyes lowered.

Your father tells me you need a job.

MATTHEW

He tells me you need help.

SANTIAGO

Don't start in with me, Matthew! I'm only doing this for your father!

MATTHEW

I don't do TVs.

SANTIAGO

But TVs is what we fix.

MATTHEW

Television is the opium of the masses.

SANTIAGO

Matthew, be reasonable. I know you need a job. You know you need a job. It may not be what you're used to, but a paycheck's a paycheck.

MATTHEW

Radios. I'll fix radios. Phone answering machines. Calculators.

SANTIAGO

I don't need help with that stuff! Look, three hundred a week. I'll give you all the radios and appliances you want, *but* you've gotta work on TVs.

MATTHEW

Two hundred a week and I do only radios and appliances.

SANTIAGO

But I need *help* with the *TVs*!

MATTHEW

I'm sorry, I can't do it!

SANTIAGO

Jesus Christ! I'm just trying to do your old man a favor!

MATTHEW

I'm sure he appreciates it.

Matthew turns to leave, but first punches Bruce in the stomach.

EXT. TV REPAIR OUTLET — DAY — MOMENTS LATER

Customers fall back in fear as . . .

Matthew throws open the door and steps out on to the sidewalk.

He bumps into a black nurse and her TV falls to the sidewalk and is smashed. She and Matthew look down at it.

MATTHEW

It was busted anyway.

He stalks on.

INT. KITCHEN — DAY — MEANWHILE

There is a washing machine and dryer in the large kitchen. Maria, wrapped only in a big bath towel, throws her clothes in the machine, adds detergent, and turns it on. It rumbles into action. She lights a cigarette.

She spots a toaster, finds some bread, and drops in a few slices. Picking up a glass of milk and a container with some cold soup, she goes over to the sink. She drops her cigarette into an old coffee cup, picks up a pan, and pours the soup into it. Noticing a radio, she reaches for it and turns it on — loud rock and roll music comes on. As she reaches for her glass of milk she knocks the pan of soup on to the floor. She looks at the mess, then picking up the glass of milk, she goes across the room, leaving the milk on the top of the washing

*machine where it trembles precariously. Maria grabs hold of a
sponge mop that is leaning against the wall, but her attention is
diverted by* ...

The newspaper headline: INFANT KIDNAPPED AT BUS STOP.

*Maria picks the newspaper up. Preoccupied, she drops the paper,
smells her hair, and goes out of the kitchen leaving behind her: the
glass of milk trembling precariously on the edge of the washer, the
cigarette floating in the dregs of the coffee cup, the soup on the floor,
the bread burning in the toaster.*

INT. MATTHEW'S BATHROOM — DAY

Maria washes her hair in the shower.

EXT. MATTHEW'S FRONT YARD/DRIVEWAY — DAY — SAME TIME

Dad pulls up and steps out of his car.

INT. MATTHEW'S KITCHEN — DAY — SAME TIME

The radio is blaring ... *the toaster is on fire* ... *the glass of milk is
moving closer to the edge of the washing machine.*

EXT. MATTHEW'S DRIVEWAY — DAY — SAME TIME

Dad closes the garage door.

INT. MATTHEW'S KITCHEN — DAY — SAME TIME

*The glass of milk topples over the edge of the washer and crashes on
to the floor.*

INT. MATTHEW'S BATHROOM — DAY — SAME TIME

Pensive, Maria sits on the toilet seat smoking a cigarette.

EXT. MATTHEW'S HOUSE — DAY — SAME TIME

Dad puts his key in the lock and enters the house.

INT. MATTHEW'S BATHROOM — DAY — SAME TIME

Maria gets up and puts the cigarette butt in the toilet as she leaves.

INT. MATTHEW'S KITCHEN — DAY — SAME TIME

Dad surveys the damage. Maria enters still wrapped in the bath towel.

                         MARIA
   Hi.

                          DAD
   Who the hell are you?

                         MARIA
   I'm a friend of your son's.

                          DAD
   My son doesn't have any friends.

At this point Matthew enters, sizes up the situation, and goes rigid with fear. Maria and Dad look at him, waiting, but he just stares at the floor. Dad looks back at Maria, fuming, then approaches Matthew and slaps him across the face. Maria cringes.

   What the hell is going on around here?

Matthew is unable to speak. He opens his mouth, but can't form words. He is traumatized. Dad hits him again. Maria steps forward.

   Answer me!

                         MARIA
   Hey!

                          DAD
                      (*to Maria*)
   You keep outta this!
                     (*to Matthew*)
   Answer me! Matthew!

                         MARIA
   Why don't you just leave him alone!

DAD

Listen, missy, you better just put your clothes back on and get the hell outta my house!

MARIA

I'm going to put my clothes in that dryer and I'm going to wait until they are dry. And *then* I'll leave.

DAD

Is that right?

MARIA

Yeah, that's right.

DAD

Well, I've got news for you, you little harlot!

Dad rushes over, throws open the machine, and drags Maria's clothes out, tossing them on the floor amongst the spilled milk and soup.

MARIA
(*to Matthew*)

Are you all right?

Matthew runs out the back door.

DAD

Matthew! Where are you going? Matthew! Get back here!
(*to Maria*)
You better be gone when I get back.

Dad runs out after Matthew. Maria looks around at the devastated kitchen. She bends down and lifts her soiled clothes. She looks at them, sighs, and drops them to the floor.

INT. MASTER BEDROOM — DAY — MOMENTS LATER

Maria is poking around trying to find some clothes. She goes toward the closet, opens it, and sees, naturally, only men's clothes. But all the way in the back, she spots . . .

Some real old dresses. She reaches in and takes one out and then leaves the room.

INT. MATTHEW'S BEDROOM — DAY — MOMENTS LATER

With no make-up, her hair pulled back, and wearing the simple dress, Maria looks like a completely different person. She looks down on the bed and sees the book, Man and the Universe.

EXT. STREET — DAY

Matthew walking.

EXT. STREETS — DAY THROUGH EVENING

Maria spends the day walking around town, searching for Matthew. There's no sign of him anywhere. She forges ahead as evening falls . . .

INT. BAR — NIGHT

Matthew is stooping to pick up some cigarettes from a machine. He glares at Bruce as he enters the bar. Peg notices his entrance. Matthew looks particularly lethal this evening. The deli man is watching TV and laughing. He has a patch over his eye. Matthew spins him around, punches him in the stomach, and then pushes Anthony away from the bar.

The bartender, Phil, approaches and turns off the TV, worried.

> PHIL
> (*panicked*)
> Matthew, really, sorry. Look, I'm turning it off!

Matthew takes a cassette tape from his pocket and thrusts it at Phil.

> MATTHEW
> Play it and shut up. Bring me a bottle of scotch.
> (*to someone on his left*)
> What the hell are you looking at?

Everyone in the place looks away and pretends to be calm.

Phil nervously shoves the cassette tape in the tape deck and comes back with a bottle of scotch as Beethoven starts filtering in over the sound system.

PHIL

Here you go, Matthew. On the house.

MATTHEW

Shut up.

He grabs the bottle and steps further down the bar and pours himself a drink.

Peg sits herself down next to Matthew.

PEG
(*of bottle*)
How'd you know what I was drinking?

MATTHEW
(*growls*)
Get lost.

PEG

Your friend the bartender warned me about you.

MATTHEW

I don't have any friends.

PEG

He says women aren't very safe in here.

MATTHEW

Is that so?

PEG

I know some people who think you oughta be locked up.

MATTHEW

You gonna drink or you gonna talk?

Peg just looks at him, unintimidated. She's as tough as he is.

PEG

Oh, you really *are* fucked up.

MATTHEW

And you're not?

PEG

Well, at least I'm a grown-up.

MATTHEW

Listen, I don't wanna discuss your problems.

PEG

Then let's discuss yours.

MATTHEW

Why are you dressed in black?

PEG

Is that a *problem* for you?

MATTHEW

No, I just think a woman who comes into a bar like this, all dressed in black, may not be the kind of woman who likes to *talk* much.

PEG

Oh, but I love to talk.

MATTHEW
(*sighs*)

OK, what do you want to talk about?

PEG
(*coy*)

Oh, I don't know. Nothing in particular. The weather, maybe.

MATTHEW

The weather sucks.

PEG

I think it's kinda warm for this time of year, don't you think?

MATTHEW

It's the damage to the ozone.

PEG

What?

MATTHEW

Ozone.

PEG

What's that?

MATTHEW

It keeps the sun's ultraviolet rays from burning us up!
Where the hell you been the last ten years?

PEG

Married.

MATTHEW

I don't think this conversation's going anywhere.

PEG

Sure it is. I'm learning all this stuff about the ozone.

MATTHEW

Great.

PEG

So, do you have a girlfriend?

MATTHEW

What's *that* got to do with anything?

PEG

Maybe that's your problem.

MATTHEW

Do I have a problem?

PEG

Of course you do.

MATTHEW

Oh yeah, and what do *you* think my problem is?

PEG

I don't think you get laid enough.

MATTHEW

Is that so?

PEG

Well, what kind of relationship could a man as screwed up as you possibly have?

MATTHEW

I don't have relationships.

PEG

You love 'em and leave 'em, huh?

MATTHEW

I don't *love* anybody.

PEG

You mean, you just *have* a girl.

MATTHEW

I take what I can get. Now if you're through talking, do you want to go out back and fuck?

PEG
(*speechless*)

You're talking to the mother of two. You know that! You can't be talking to somebody's mother like that. Bastard!

Matthew gives her a glass.

MATTHEW

Here, have a drink.

PEG

Oh, fuck off.

MATTHEW

No, seriously. I mean it. Stay.

He pours her a drink.

PEG

Everything's been very screwed up since my divorce. He took the kids away from me like I'm unfit or something.

MATTHEW

Have you got a car?

*Maria enters and comes toward Matthew, exhausted. She doesn't
notice Peg.*

> MARIA
> (*to Matthew*)
> *There* you are! I've been looking all over for you!

> PEG

Maria!

> MARIA
> (*surprised*)

Peg!

> MATTHEW

Where'd you get that dress?

> PEG
> (*to Maria*)

Do you *know* him?

> MARIA
> (*to Matthew*)

Matthew, come home with us.

> PEG

What!

> MARIA
> (*to Peg*)

He has to, Peg.

> PEG

Maria, if you go home now, Mom's gonna stab you in the
heart with a steak knife, OK?

> MATTHEW
> (*realizing*)

You two are sisters?

> MARIA

Don't go back to your father's house.

MATTHEW

I have to go back.

MARIA

Why?

MATTHEW

I have to.

MARIA

Matthew, he's a monster.

PEG

What's going on here?

MARIA
(*to Peg*)
Matthew's coming home to live with us for a while.

PEG
(*outraged*)
Maria, do you *know* who this guy is?

MARIA

I don't care who he is.
(*then, to Matthew*)
Who are you?

PEG

Maybe he doesn't want to come home with us!

The girls look at Matthew. He looks away.

MATTHEW

Leave me alone.

PEG
(*relieved*)
There, OK? Come on, Maria. Let's get outta here.

*Peg gets up. Maria stays there and stares into Matthew's face as he
gazes at his hands on the bar before him. A few moments pass, then . . .*

MARIA

Are you sure?

MATTHEW
(*lies*)

Yeah.

PEG

Maria, come on!

Maria stares at him a moment longer.

MARIA
(*to Matthew*)
Please come back to the house with me.

MATTHEW
(*looks at her*)

Why?

MARIA
(*honestly*)
I'm afraid of my mother.

INT. MARIA'S KITCHEN — NIGHT

Jean is sitting alone at the kitchen table, dressed in black, drinking gin and staring at the floor. She notices a roast chicken by the sink and picks up the carving knife to cut it when the back door opens.

Maria, Peg, and Matthew clamber in the back door and crowd into a little frightened huddle when they see . . .

Jean with the knife in her hand.

Maria slowly pushes her way past the others and comes forward into the kitchen.

Jean stands still, not looking at the others.

Peg and Matthew watch from the doorway. Peg is nervous. Matthew is confused.

Maria moves toward Jean, who turns around pointing the knife at her.

> PEG
> (*leaving the room*)

Christ!

Maria and Jean stare each other down for a moment, then . . .

> JEAN
> (*ice*)

I'm never gonna forgive you.

> MARIA

I know.

> JEAN

As long as I live I'm gonna work your fingers to the bone.

> MARIA

OK.

> JEAN

Did you eat anything today?

> MARIA
> (*weak*)

No.

> JEAN
> (*turns away*)

Sit down. I'll fix you something.
> (*looks back at Matthew*)

Who's your friend?

INT. MARIA'S KITCHEN — NIGHT

*They're all sitting or standing around the kitchen. Jean brushes
Maria's hair.*

> MARIA

. . . so then he gives me *back* the five dollars and still wants
me to kiss him.

> PEG

Oh, gross!

JEAN

Disgusting . . .

MARIA

I was so scared. And he's like sweating and rubbing his
crotch and everything . . .

PEG

So, what'd you do?

MARIA

What'd you think I did?

MATTHEW

You burned him with the cigarette.

MARIA

Right in the eye.

PEG

Ouch!

JEAN

That man is going straight to hell.

MARIA

And he's threatening to call the cops on *me*.

MATTHEW

So, was this before or after the baby disappeared?

MARIA

Just before it.

PEG

You've gotta go to the police, Maria.

JEAN

Yes, that man should be punished!

PEG

No, about the baby.

MARIA

Well, I don't know. I can't be sure. I didn't *see* anything.

PEG

But at least they could talk to her.

MARIA

She seemed so sad. So mixed up.

PEG

We're all mixed up, Maria, but we don't go around stealing babies.

MARIA

You see, you're already convinced that she did it.

PEG
(*to Maria*)

So, what are you gonna do?

MARIA

About what?

PEG

About being pregnant.

JEAN
(*to Matthew*)

You ain't the father, are you?

MATTHEW

No, ma'am.

MARIA
(*embarrassed*)

Mom!

JEAN
(*to Maria*)

Eat your sandwich!

MARIA
(*to Peg*)

I went to the clinic yesterday and I spoke to this lady . . .

PEG

How much?

MARIA

I'd need about two hundred and fifty dollars.

She looks at Jean.

JEAN

What, for an abortion? Don't look at me. I spent everything we had on your father's casket.

Maria looks to Peg, who shrugs sadly.

PEG

The divorce lawyers took all my money.

Maria shrugs and accepts the burden.

MARIA

Then I'll get a job.

MATTHEW

I've got money.

MARIA

No, thank you.

MATTHEW

It's OK.

PEG

Why don't you get it from Anthony?

MARIA

I don't ever want to see that jerk again.

MATTHEW

Take the money from me.

MARIA

No. You don't have a job either.

MATTHEW

I'm going to take this job fixing TVs.

PEG

Maria, where'd you get that dress?

Maria looks at Matthew and bites her lip. Peg and Jean follow her gaze to . . .

Matthew as he calmly regards the dress . . .

> MATTHEW
> It belonged to my mother.

INT. MARIA'S UPSTAIRS HALLWAY — NIGHT

From the hall, we see Maria dismantling her room. It is a typically tasteless teenage girl's room. She's tearing posters off the walls. Then she lugs a mattress through the hall and into the next room. Peg comes up the stairs and goes into her own room.

INT. PEG'S BEDROOM — NIGHT

Matthew is fixing Peg's TV. He sets it upright, turns it on, and it works.

> PEG
> You fix it?

> MATTHEW
> Yeah.

> PEG
> Thanks.

> MATTHEW
> You're welcome.

> PEG
> You wanna watch some TV?

> MATTHEW
> I don't watch TV.

> PEG
> Why not?

> MATTHEW
> It gives you cancer.

PEG

It does not.

MATTHEW
(*shrugs*)

Well, see for yourself.

Maria appears in the hall beside Matthew with the book she took from his room.

MARIA

Do you know what the word 'empirical' means?

PEG

Don't ask him. He thinks TV gives you cancer.

MATTHEW

It means information based on experience.

Maria shakes her head in confusion.

You can't know something unless you experience it first.

Peg rolls her eyes in exasperation and closes her door.

PEG

Jesus!

Maria and Matthew are alone in the hall a moment. He sees the book she is holding.

MARIA

I borrowed it. Do you mind?

MATTHEW

No.

MARIA

I put a bed in here for you.

They look in at the bed.

MATTHEW

Where do you sleep?

MARIA
(*of her room*)

I sleep in there.

MATTHEW
(*looks in*)

There's no bed in here.

MARIA

I don't need one.

MATTHEW

Are you nearsighted?

MARIA

Yeah.

MATTHEW

Why don't you wear your glasses?

MARIA

They make me look stupid.

MATTHEW

How do you mean?

MARIA

You know, brainy, like a librarian.

MATTHEW

I like librarians.

Maria waits a moment, then puts on her glasses and lets him see.

Matthew is immobilized by desire. Maria sees this, blushing.

She waits expectantly, watching as he leans toward her – seemingly against his will.

Maria lifts her face to be kissed, breathless and still. Matthew's face comes toward hers. They both linger – unsure. A moment.

Then Matthew moves back.

Maria stands there, dizzy, looking at the floor.

Matthew stands back, also looking at the floor.

> MARIA
> *(weakly)*

Give me your hand grenade.

> MATTHEW
> *(looks up)*

What?

> MARIA

Give it to me.

She puts out her hand.

Matthew reaches into his pocket and takes it out. He hands it over.

Jean appears at the bottom of the stairs.

> JEAN

Maria!

Maria jumps into her room and closes the door. Matthew remains in the hallway looking down at Jean, who is still at the bottom of the stairs.

I don't want you getting any ideas.

> MATTHEW

Ideas about what?

> JEAN

You know what. Tomorrow you find somewhere else to sleep. Get it?

> MATTHEW

OK.

> JEAN

I don't know what your problem is, but I've got problems of my own!

Matthew nods as Jean moves away. He then goes toward his own room.

INT. MARIA'S ROOM — NIGHT

Maria looks at the grenade in her hand and then puts it in the top drawer of her desk. She then closes the drawer, picks up her pen, and starts writing in her notebook . . .

> MARIA
> (*writing*)
> I am ashamed. I am ashamed of being young. I am ashamed of being stupid.

Maria pauses, closes her notebook, and turns off the light. She curls up on the floor, pulling a blanket over her. She takes off her glasses and closes her eyes.

INT. MARIA'S KITCHEN — DAY

Maria is doing the laundry, while Peg sits at the table with her friend Lori, who is about Peg's age (twenty-eight).

From now on, Maria only wears the dress she took from Matthew's house. She usually wears her glasses and her hair is pulled back away from her face.

> LORI
> (*to Maria*)
> So, have you been over to the clinic?

> MARIA
> Yes.

> LORI
> Are you gonna have an abortion?

> MARIA
> I suppose.

> PEG
> I think that's the right move.

> MARIA
> (*to Peg*)
> Did you ever have one?

PEG

An abortion?

MARIA

Yeah.

PEG

Sure.

LORI

When?

PEG

A couple of years ago.

MARIA

After you'd already had children?

PEG

Exactly.

MARIA

Why?

PEG

Well, because I already had two kids I couldn't handle.
And I hated my husband.

LORI

My second baby saved my marriage.

PEG

My marriage was beyond saving.

MARIA
(*to Lori*)

Did you have the baby *because* your marriage needed help?

LORI

Definitely. But then, I really did want another baby. I like
being pregnant.

MARIA
(*to Peg*)
Did you want to get pregnant the first time?

PEG
I suppose. We didn't think about it. When we first got married we just spent all our time fucking. I mean, what the hell; we were married, right? Pretty soon I got pregnant and that was OK 'cause I was already kinda bored with my husband. I was seventeen.

MARIA
(*to Lori*)
How old were you when you got married?

LORI
Twenty.

MARIA
Did you want to have children right away?

LORI
Oh, yeah. I couldn't wait.

MARIA
Do you ever think about what your life might've been like if you never got married and had kids?

LORI
(*thinks, then . . .*)
No.

MARIA
Never?

LORI
Well, what's the use in thinking about *that* now?

MARIA
Did you think about it then?

LORI
Of course not. Did you, Peg?

PEG
(*shakes her head 'no'*)
Who thinks about that stuff when you're seventeen years old?

Peg and Lori turn silently and look at Maria.

INT. FACTORY — DAY

An older woman is showing Maria how to do assembly-line work. They are standing in front of a big drill press-type machine.

WOMAN
Now, you just stand here, like this, and take one of these slugs and you put it right in here where the groove is. Then, you press down on the pedal down here, see, with your foot. Like this. You pull down on this arm here till the drill goes right through to the mark, here. You got that?

MARIA
Right.

WOMAN
Then you let go of the arm and take your foot off the pedal. Let go of the arm *first*. Remember that.

MARIA
Let go of the arm first.

WOMAN
Right. You gotta let go of the arm first or you damage the whole machine.

MARIA
OK.

WOMAN
So, when you take your foot off the pedal, you just knock the slug off the plate and toss it into this barrel over here . . .

The woman proceeds to demonstrate the process.

INT. FACTORY — DAY — LATER

Maria, wearing goggles and a smock, works at the machine.

INT. TV REPAIR OUTLET — DAY

Matthew works on TVs.

EXT. TRAIN STATION — LATE AFTERNOON

Maria comes across the street and meets Matthew, who is sitting at the base of a column.

> MARIA
>
> Hi.

> MATTHEW
>
> How was work?

> MARIA
>
> Do you know how to type?

> MATTHEW
>
> I'm not good at it.

> MARIA
>
> I've got to learn how to type. Typing has to be better than drilling holes in little pieces of aluminum all day.
> (*pause*)
> What time is it?

> MATTHEW
>
> Five to five.

EXT. TRAIN PLATFORM — AFTERNOON — MOMENTS LATER

Maria and Matthew stand at the bottom of the stairs leading up to the train platform.

> MATTHEW
>
> Who are we waiting for?

> MARIA
>
> The husband of the lady I met on the bench.

MATTHEW

How do you know what he looks like?

MARIA

I remember her saying he carried a briefcase and smokes a
pipe.

MATTHEW

A lot of men fit that description.

MARIA

Yeah, but I think we'll know this guy when we see him.

MATTHEW

Why?

MARIA

He'll seem childish. Like a boy. Kinda nave.

*They watch the stairs. Then Matthew frowns to himself and looks at
Maria.*

MATTHEW

Kind of what?

MARIA

Nave.

MATTHEW

Nave?

*Maria looks at Matthew and becomes uncertain. She takes out a
small notebook she carries with her and flips the pages until . . .*

She points out a word.

'Naive.'

MARIA

Naive?

MATTHEW

Naive.

                          MARIA
     Oh.

Up above they hear . . .

The train pull into the station.

Matthew and Maria move closer to the stairs.

The train slowly screeches to a halt.

They wait anxiously, their eyes peeled on . . .

The top of the stairs.

*The train doors open and a mass of feet shuffle out toward the stairs
and . . .*

Come down the steps and stop, suddenly as one.

*Matthew and Maria stand there, blocking the bottom of the stairs,
staring curiously up at . . .*

*The dozens of men standing on the stairs, all dressed exactly alike,
holding briefcases and with pipes in their mouths. The men look
down just as curiously at . . .*

*Matthew and Maria. Maria looks at Matthew, shrugs her shoul-
ders, and walks away.*

INT. MARIA'S KITCHEN — EVENING

*Matthew is repairing an old electric typewriter at the kitchen table.
The girls are finishing their meal. Jean pours herself a gin and
glances at Matthew.*

                          JEAN
                     (*to Matthew*)
     Still here, huh?

                          MARIA
     Mom, he has nowhere to go.

                          JEAN
     Shut up, you, and finish those potatoes!

MARIA

Mom, if I eat anything else I'll explode.

JEAN

Eat 'em! And when you're through get started on those dishes!

MATTHEW

This is a well-built piece of machinery.

JEAN

They don't make things like they used to.

PEG

Mom, you never told us you were a secretary.

JEAN

I hated it. I hated working. I was so glad when your father proposed.

PEG

Don't you consider being a wife and mother work?

JEAN

With the likes of you two it was torture.

MARIA

Do you ever think of going back out to work?

JEAN

Never! *You're* going to support me! For the rest of my life you'll have to make sure there's food in my mouth and clothes on my back! Got it? Now, eat those potatoes!

MARIA

OK! OK!

JEAN

It's not gonna be easy!

MARIA

I know!

JEAN

You'll have to work every minute of your life!

PEG

Mom, ease up. Maybe you oughta lie down.

JEAN

Peg, don't play up to me.

Matthew flips a switch and the typewriter activates.

MATTHEW

OK. That's it.

He turns to Maria and pushes the typewriter over to her.

JEAN

I never wanted daughters in the first place.

Maria puts on her glasses and begins to operate the machine.

You'll have to type faster than that to keep us out of the poorhouse.

Maria looks off into space.

INT. MARIA'S KITCHEN — NIGHT — LATER

Maria has finished mopping the floor and is putting the mop and bucket away. She moves through the living room, passing Jean on the sofa.

MARIA

Goodnight, Mom.

Jean glances up at Maria, pensively.

INT. PEG'S BEDROOM — NIGHT

Peg is lying on the bed in her bathrobe, watching TV. Maria enters and lies on the bed next to her.

MARIA

Do you miss your kids?

                              PEG
Sure.

                             MARIA
Do you hate your husband?

                              PEG
Absolutely.

                             MARIA
Would you ever get married again?

                              PEG
Of course.

INT. MARIA'S KITCHEN — NIGHT — SAME TIME

Jean enters the dark kitchen and finds Matthew sitting at the table smoking and drinking scotch. She sits down opposite him.

                             JEAN
Why aren't you asleep?

                            MATTHEW
I don't sleep.

                             JEAN
Aren't you a little old to be running around with a seven-teen-year-old?

                            MATTHEW
You want me to go?

                             JEAN
                           (*shrugs*)
I don't know.

                            MATTHEW
I'm not here to cause trouble.

                             JEAN
There's no avoiding trouble.

> MATTHEW
> (*carefully*)

You ride Maria pretty hard.

> JEAN

How I raise my kids is none of your business.

> MATTHEW
> (*looks away*)

Sorry.

> JEAN

You like *her* more than Peg, don't you?

> MATTHEW

Who said anything about Peg?

> JEAN

I think Peg's prettier.

> MATTHEW

They're both pretty.

> JEAN

Peg's more level-headed too, but she's wild. Always been like that. Made a mess of her marriage.

> MATTHEW

Maria sleeps on the floor.

> JEAN

You really do like her more, huh?

> MATTHEW

I don't like to see her torture herself.

> JEAN

Have you two been screwing around?

The two of them stare at each other. They hold it for a moment. Then Matthew breaks it and reaches for his cigarette pack and offers Jean one.

MATTHEW

Want a cigarette?

JEAN

Don't change the subject.

MATTHEW

I haven't touched her.

JEAN
(*taking the cigarette*)
I don't think she knows much about how to make love to
a man.

MATTHEW

She must know something. She's pregnant.

JEAN

That's what I mean. A girl who knows how to make love
to a man would never let that happen.

MATTHEW

You think so?

JEAN

You stand a better chance with Peg, you know. And I bet
she's great in bed.

Jean leans forward so that Matthew can light her cigarette.

MATTHEW
(*pauses, then lights her cigarette*)
We don't have much in common.

JEAN

When was the last time you were with a woman?

MATTHEW

I don't remember.

JEAN
(*turns away from Matthew*)
I'm never going to let you take Maria away from me.

MATTHEW

I never said I wanted to.

JEAN

She's got to pay.

MATTHEW

Your husband died of a heart attack.

JEAN

No one dies of a heart attack. They die of disgust, disappointment.

MATTHEW

You're not the first woman in the world who's had a hard time.

JEAN

You're an outsider; you don't understand. A family's got to stick together, come hell or high water.

MATTHEW

A family's like a gun. You point it in the wrong direction, you're gonna kill somebody.

JEAN

Exactly.

Matthew looks at Jean.

INT. MATTHEW'S BEDROOM — NIGHT

Maria is sitting on Matthew's bed holding the hand grenade. Matthew enters.

MATTHEW

You've gotta leave this house.

MARIA

I have to take care of my mother.

MATTHEW

Your mother is a psychopath.

MARIA

She's just in pain.

MATTHEW
(*pause*)
What are you doing here?

MARIA

How does this work?

MATTHEW
What do you want to know that for? Give me that thing.

He goes toward the bed.

MARIA

No, how's it work?

MATTHEW

Why?

MARIA

I just want to know.

Matthew sits down close to Maria on the bed.

MATTHEW
(*points*)
You see this pin? You pull that, wait eight seconds, and
then . . .

MARIA

. . . boom.

MATTHEW
(*touching her*)
Sleep in here tonight.
(*moves his hand away*)
I don't mean with me. I just mean, sleep here. In a bed.

MARIA
Peg says you have a reputation.

MATTHEW

What kind of reputation?

MARIA

A dangerous reputation.

MATTHEW

Peg's got a reputation herself.

MARIA

I wanna become a nun.

MATTHEW

No you don't.

MARIA

Yes I do.

MATTHEW

No you *don't*. You're just having some kind of severe reaction.

MARIA

I don't want to feel anything.

MATTHEW

Well, I bet nuns feel things. You have to be dead not to feel things. You don't want to be dead, do you?

Maria turns toward Matthew. They look at each other and then kiss, tenderly. They stay with their foreheads touching, and then Maria turns her head toward the grenade in her hand and Matthew looks away.

MARIA

I'm gonna go to the clinic tomorrow to have the abortion. Will you come with me?

MATTHEW

If you want me to.

MARIA

Why do you do this?

MATTHEW

Do what?

MARIA

Why do you hang around here and look after me like this?

MATTHEW

Somebody has to.

MARIA

Why you?

INT. CLINIC — DAY

Maria and Matthew are sitting on chairs in the waiting room. Matthew puts a cigarette in his mouth. They both look anxious.

MATTHEW

How long do you think it'll take?

MARIA

I don't know. Not long, I guess.

MATTHEW

Are you OK?

MARIA

Yeah. You?

She takes the cigarette out of Matthew's mouth.

MATTHEW

I feel like smashing things up.

MARIA

Relax. There's nothing to worry about. Why don't you go for a walk?

MATTHEW

I don't want to take a walk. You sure you want to go through with this?

MARIA

What do you mean?

MATTHEW

Marry me.

MARIA

Don't be crazy.

MATTHEW

Marry me. Have the baby. We'll be a family.

MARIA

You're delirious.

MATTHEW

Sorry.

MARIA

It's OK.

Matthew breathes nervously.

MATTHEW

How long do you think it'll take?

MARIA

I don't know. Not long, I guess.

She takes the cigarette out of Matthew's mouth.

MATTHEW

Are you OK?

MARIA

Yeah. You?

MATTHEW

I feel like tearing somebody's head off.

VOICE
(*off*)

Maria Coughlin.

Maria and Matthew look at each other, then Maria resolutely gets up.

Matthew sighs, then looks at the other women in the room. He also glances at a guy, John, sitting among the women.

John comes and sits down next to Matthew.

> JOHN

How're you doin'?

> MATTHEW

I feel like smashing things up.

> JOHN

Yeah. Sometimes it gets like that. Your first time?

> MATTHEW

What?

> JOHN

Your first time here?

> MATTHEW

Of course.

> JOHN

I thought so.

> MATTHEW

Who the hell are you?

> JOHN

John. John Bill. How're you doin'?

He puts his hand out for Matthew to shake. Matthew ignores it.

> MATTHEW

I already told you. I feel like punchin' somebody's lights
out.

> JOHN

Yeah. The first time's kinda tough. But you know, it's an
amazing thing. You come in here the first time – your
whole life's a mess. All this tension and stuff. Then she
goes in there and when she comes out everything's fixed.

*Matthew looks at him, then he grabs John and throws him to the
floor. People scream as Matthew and John grapple with each other
on the floor.*

In the other room Maria is taking off her jacket. She stops when she hears the noise of fighting. She jumps off the table and goes out into the waiting room.

EXT. PARKING LOT NEAR TRAIN STATION — DAY — LATER

Maria and Matthew are sitting by the column.

> MARIA
>
> What time is it?

> MATTHEW
>
> Five-o-three.

> MARIA
>
> Did you mean it? Would you marry me?

> MATTHEW
>
> Yes.

> MARIA
>
> Why?

> MATTHEW
>
> Because I want to.

> MARIA
>
> Not because you love me or anything like that, huh?

> MATTHEW
>
> I respect and admire you.

> MARIA
>
> Isn't that love?

> MATTHEW
>
> No. That's respect and admiration. I think that's better than love.

> MARIA
>
> How?

> MATTHEW
>
> When people are in love they do all sorts of crazy things.

They get jealous, they lie, they cheat. They kill themselves.
They kill each other.

MARIA

It doesn't have to be that way.

MATTHEW

Maybe.

MARIA

You'd be the father of a child you know isn't yours.

MATTHEW

Kids are kids, what does it matter?

MARIA

Do you trust me?

MATTHEW

Do you trust me first?

MARIA

I trust you.

MATTHEW

You sure?

MARIA

Yes.

Matthew looks at Maria and then kneels down in front of her.

MATTHEW

Then marry me.

MARIA

I'll marry you if you admit that respect, admiration, and
trust equals love.

MATTHEW

OK. They equal love.

*Maria and Matthew kiss. Maria looks at Matthew, then removing
her glasses she climbs to the top of the base of the column and, turning around, falls backward off the base. Matthew runs and . . .*

catches her in his arms, shocked. She opens her eyes and smiles up at him. Matthew can't speak. He's gone white as a sheet.

> MARIA

Good. I trust you. Now it's your turn.

She rolls out of his arms and stands at the foot of the column base.

> MATTHEW

What?

> MARIA

Go on up.

> MATTHEW

Maria, that's pretty high.

> MARIA

Don't you trust me?

> MATTHEW

Of course I do.

> MARIA

Then go on up.

> MATTHEW

Maria, I'm twice your size. If I fall on you from that height I'll kill you.

> MARIA

Trust me.

Matthew hesitates. He looks at the column base and then back at her.

> MATTHEW

This is not a matter of trust.

> MARIA

Matthew, go up. I will break your fall. I promise.

Matthew holds her resolute gaze for a while, then sighs and heads up. He reaches the top and hesitates again.

MATTHEW

If I do this, will you leave your mother?

MARIA

What?

MATTHEW

You heard me.

MARIA

Maybe.

MATTHEW

Not good enough.

MARIA

You're being selfish.

MATTHEW

The woman's a sadist.

MARIA

She's just in shock. What's a sadist?

MATTHEW

Your mother or me.

MARIA

Wait a minute. Look!

Maria walks over to the parking lot. Matthew follows.

EXT. PARKING LOT — DAY

Maria is crouched in front of a car's bumper. There is a sticker on it advertising Cape Holiday.

MATTHEW

What is it?

MARIA

The woman said she and her husband go to Cape Holiday every summer.

MATTHEW
(*looking around the lot*)
There's another one.

Maria follows his gaze and sees . . .

A Cape Holiday sticker on another car.

MARIA
(*points*)
And over there too. There might be dozens.

MATTHEW
But how many belong to *men* who take the 5.15 *train*?

DISSOLVE TO:

EXT. STATION — DAY — MOMENTS LATER

The 5.15 pulls out of the station.

*Maria and Matthew come walking up between an aisle of cars,
scrutinizing the bumpers. Maria writes in her notebook . . .*

MARIA
(*calculating*)
Seven.

MATTHEW
And there were ten before the 5.15 came through.

MARIA
The white fancy one is gone.

MATTHEW
The yellow pick-up truck. The Japanese model. Three.

MARIA
Three.

MATTHEW
What are you going to do when you find this man?

MARIA
I don't know yet.

INT. MARIA'S LIVING ROOM — EVENING

Peg is sitting on the sofa watching TV. Jean comes in and sits beside her.

> JEAN
>
> Peg, don't you think Matthew's a handsome man?

> PEG
>
> He's OK.

> JEAN
>
> Why haven't you made a play for him?

> PEG
>
> Mom!

> JEAN
>
> What?

> PEG
>
> You're unbelievable.

> JEAN
>
> He's too old for Maria.

> PEG
>
> So, what do you want me to do about it?

> JEAN
>
> Throw yourself at him.

> PEG
>
> Mom, I do not *throw* myself at men, OK?

> JEAN
>
> You used to.

> PEG
>
> Shut up and watch TV.

> JEAN
>
> Don't snap at me like that.

                              PEG
He's not interested in me.

                              JEAN
That's what you think.

                              PEG
What do you mean?

                              JEAN
I've seen the way he looks at you.

                              PEG
Yeah, right. And *I've* seen the way he looks at Maria.

                              JEAN
Oh, you're just imagining it. He likes you. I can tell.

                              PEG
You can?

                              JEAN
She isn't giving him *any.*

                              PEG
You're kidding me.

                              JEAN
God's honest truth.

                              PEG
Really.

                              JEAN
Think about it.

INT. RUARK COMPUTER FACTORY — DAY

*Matthew is trying to get his job back. He is talking to the big boss,
an attractive and aggressive young woman.*

                              BOSS
What can I do for you, Matthew?

MATTHEW

I'd like my job back.

BOSS

That's impossible.

MATTHEW

I'm sorry about vicing Ed's head.

BOSS

That's not what I'm talking about.

MATTHEW

What?

BOSS

You lied to us.

MATTHEW

When?

BOSS

When you applied for this job you said you had attended
MIT.

MATTHEW

Did I say that?

BOSS

And you never told us about your police record and four
years of reform school.

MATTHEW

You never asked.

BOSS

We gave you a lot of responsibility.

MATTHEW

I did a good job.

BOSS

That's beside the point.

MATTHEW

What difference does it make?

BOSS

I can't do it.

MATTHEW

Why not?

BOSS

People are afraid of you.

MATTHEW

I'll be nice. Really, I promise.

BOSS

Are you working now?

MATTHEW

Yes.

BOSS

For a competitor?

MATTHEW

I fix televisions.

BOSS

Well, work is work . . .

MATTHEW

I need something stable. With benefits. Pension plan-type stuff, you know.

BOSS

Why the sudden interest in stability?

MATTHEW

I'm getting married.

BOSS

Really?

MATTHEW

Listen, I promise I won't lose my temper any more. I

won't make a fuss about bad manufacturing or faulty
designs. I won't *care* about *quality* at all. I just want a job
with normal benefits for me and my dependents.

The boss looks away and considers. Matthew waits.

> BOSS
> I can't give you your old job back.

> MATTHEW
> I'll take anything.

> BOSS
> Eligibility for benefits starts after six months.

> MATTHEW
> Fine.

> BOSS
> You'll have to take a few steps down.

INT. MATTHEW'S TV ROOM — DAY

*Dad is watching TV. He looks sad. He looks at the TV, then stands
up and, with a determined look on his face, pulls the plug out.*

The TV tube goes dead.

INT. TV REPAIR OUTLET — DAY

*Dad walks in carrying his TV. Bruce is standing by a set of TV
monitors. Dad sets his TV down in front of Bruce.*

> BRUCE
> Can I help you?

> DAD
> (*looking around*)
> My TV's busted.

> BRUCE
> Just leave it here. I'll have a look at it later on.

DAD

Where's Matthew?

BRUCE

He doesn't work here any more.

DAD

What?

BRUCE

He got fired.

DAD

You mean he quit.

BRUCE

No, I mean he got fired.

DAD

Bullshit. Nobody in their right mind would fire Matthew.
He can fix anything.

BRUCE

Look, I'm telling you. He got fired. He scared the customers.

DAD

Well, what the hell do the customers know? Matthew's a
genius.

BRUCE

Well, we don't need a genius. We need somebody who can
fix TVs.

DAD

Yeah. Well, that's your problem, pal.

He leaves the shop.

BRUCE

What do you want me to do with this TV?

DAD

Get the damn thing out of my sight!

EXT. TV REPAIR OUTLET — DAY

Dad thinks for a moment, then walks away.

INT. FACTORY — DAY

Maria is operating her machine.

> MARIA (V.O.)
> 'Vicissitude: 1a, the quality or state of being changeable;
> mutability; b, natural change or mutation visible in human
> nature or human affairs; 2a, a favorable or unfavorable
> event or situation that occurs by chance . . .'

She turns away from the machine and looks at the clock.

EXT. TRAIN STATION — DAY

> MARIA
> *(reading from her notebook)*
> 'Fluctuation of state or condition; alternating change. See
> change.'

She looks up, hearing . . .

The 5.15 pull into the station.

She jumps up and runs to a position where she can see . . .

The yellow Plymouth . . .

The station wagon . . .

And the Japanese model.

Commuters come stampeding down the stairs.

Maria looks over as . . .

Commuters fan out into the parking lot.

She looks back and forth between the cars.

*She sees a man with a pipe unlock one of the cars. As Maria comes
toward the car, he looks up and faints.*

Maria crouches over his prone body.

She shakes him.

Mister.

The man, Robert, does not respond. Maria turns toward the brief-case lying beside him and pulls out the tag with his name and address. Robert revives.

ROBERT

Who are you?

MARIA

My name's Maria.

ROBERT

What do you want?

MARIA

I think I know your wife.

Robert just looks at her, stone-faced, then away. He sighs wearily and gets up off the ground.

Reaching the driver's side door, he puts the key in the lock, and pauses. He thinks a moment.

Maria hovers behind him.

ROBERT

What do you intend to do?

MARIA
(*careful*)

I was in trouble and she gave me some money. I just want to return it.

Maria comes over to Robert with five dollars.

He just looks at it.

She holds it closer.

He takes it.

What's her name?

ROBERT

Who?

MARIA

Your wife's.

ROBERT

Rachel.

MARIA

Will you tell her I said thank you?

ROBERT
(*hesitates*)

Yes.

Another moment of awkward silence, then Maria walks away.
Robert hurries into his car, slamming the door behind him.

Maria stands back as he pulls out and speeds away.

INT. RUARK COMPUTER FACTORY — DAY — MEANWHILE

Ed is at his workbench. Matthew approaches him.

MATTHEW

Ed.

ED
(*defensively*)

What is it?

MATTHEW

Calm down, Ed.

ED

What do you want?

MATTHEW

I just happened to notice that these circuit boards we're
wiring into the new models are the A-67-9s.

ED

Brilliant. So what?

MATTHEW

We manufactured these boards last year and too high a
percentage of them proved faulty in these higher powered,
larger memory units so we stored them out back.

ED

I know that, Slaughter.

MATTHEW

Well, I just thought maybe there's been some kind of mistake or something.

ED

Why do you always have to be such a pain in the neck?

MATTHEW

I'm just doing my job.

ED

Your job is to put these things together the way we tell you
to.

*Matthew obviously wants to rip Ed's lungs out, but has to control
himself.*

MATTHEW

Right.

*Ed decides to be big about it and opens his specifications manual.
He flips through the pages as Matthew, smiling, looks on over his
shoulder.*

ED
(*points*)

There. You see, part A-67-9. See it?

MATTHEW
(*frowns*)

Yeah, I see it.

                    ED

Satisfied?

Matthew doesn't answer.

INT. MARIA'S LIVING ROOM — NIGHT

Matthew is watching TV, beer in his hand, eyes glazed over.

Maria comes in and sits down beside him.

                    MARIA
Since when do you watch TV?

                    MATTHEW
It was on when I came in.

                    MARIA
How was work today?

                    MATTHEW
I don't wanna talk about it.

                    MARIA
I've decided to go back to high school.

                    MATTHEW
Why?

                    MARIA
I don't want to work in a factory.

                    MATTHEW
When we get married you won't have to work at all.

                    MARIA
But I want to. Just not in a factory.

                    MATTHEW
How can you go to high school pregnant?

                    MARIA
Plenty of girls do it.

MATTHEW

I can teach you everything you can learn in high school.

MARIA

I don't want that.

MATTHEW

Why?

MARIA

Because I just don't want it.

Matthew watches TV. After a while . . .

I met the man today.

MATTHEW

What man?

MARIA

The husband of the lady on the bench.

MATTHEW

Oh, yeah. What was he like?

MARIA

Nervous.

MATTHEW

Did you ask him if his wife stole the baby?

MARIA

You don't care, do you?

MATTHEW

Care about what?

MARIA

Can you stop watching TV for a moment?

MATTHEW

No.

MARIA

Why?

MATTHEW

I had a *bad* day. I had to subvert my principles and kow-
tow to an idiot. Television makes these daily sacrifices possible. It deadens the inner core of my being.

Maria gets up and sits right in front of the TV.

MARIA

Let's move away, then.

MATTHEW

They have television everywhere. There's no escape. And
besides, you won't leave your mother.

MARIA

I will if you quit your job.

MATTHEW

What?

INT. MARIA'S KITCHEN — NIGHT

*Jean is at the sink, overhearing Maria and Matthew. She has a full
bottle of gin in her hand.*

INT. MARIA'S LIVING ROOM — NIGHT

MARIA

I don't like what's happening to you. If you don't like your
job, you shouldn't do it.

Matthew registers this change in her outlook. He thinks.

MATTHEW

You'd leave your mother?

MARIA

I'm not doing her any good staying.

MATTHEW

After the baby?

MARIA

No. Now.

> MATTHEW
Maria, having a baby costs money.

INT. MARIA'S KITCHEN — NIGHT

Jean stands to the side of the entrance to the living room, eavesdropping.

> MATTHEW (V.O.)
In six months I'll have complete medical coverage down at the plant.

INT. MARIA'S LIVING ROOM — NIGHT

> MATTHEW
> (*continued*)
I'm just trying to be practical. Level-headed.

> MARIA
What's so practical about being level-headed?

> MATTHEW
Move away from the TV. The news is on and I want to hear about the earthquake victims.

> MARIA
Why? What are you going to do for them?

> MATTHEW
Commiserate.

> MARIA
What's 'commiserate'?

> MATTHEW
To express sympathy. Now move aside.

> MARIA
Is that like compassion?

> MATTHEW
No. Compassion means to suffer *with*. Which is different than just feeling pity. You need a thesaurus.

MARIA

A what?

MATTHEW

A thesaurus. It's like a dictionary of synonyms.
                    (*drains the last of his beer*)
Would you get me another beer?

MARIA

You're already drunk.

MATTHEW

No, I'm not drunk. I don't get drunk.

MARIA

Your job is making you boring and mean.

MATTHEW

My job is making me a respectable member of society.

Maria gets up and puts on her jacket.

Where are you going?

Maria doesn't answer. She just walks out of the room.

INT. MARIA'S KITCHEN — NIGHT— SAME TIME

Maria comes in from the living room. Jean is standing by the entrance sewing something.

JEAN

Where are you going?

MARIA

To the supermarket. We need stuff.

JEAN

Come here. Your hair needs brushing.

Maria hangs her head, sighs, then comes over and sits at the kitchen table. Jean picks up her brush and starts . . .

Did you clean the bathroom?

MARIA

Yes.

JEAN

I want you to do this kitchen floor.

MARIA

I'll do it tonight when everyone's asleep.

JEAN

Did you vacuum upstairs?

MARIA

Yes.

JEAN

Change all the sheets tomorrow before you go to work
and hang out the clothes that are in the washing machine.

MARIA

OK.

JEAN

When's he going to fix my sewing machine?

MARIA

You never use it.

JEAN

I don't use it because it's broken.

Maria reaches back and stops the brushing.

MARIA

He'll get around to it.

She heads for the door.

JEAN

Don't forget milk. We need milk!

INT. MARIA'S LIVING ROOM — NIGHT — A LITTLE LATER

*Matthew is still watching the TV program. Jean comes in and sits
down next to him.*

JEAN

I want you out of my house.

MATTHEW

Fine. But if I leave, Maria leaves with me.

JEAN

No chance.

MATTHEW

We can go on like this for ever, Mom.

JEAN

Don't call me Mom!

MATTHEW

Like it or not: I'm here to stay.

JEAN

Freeloader.

MATTHEW

My paycheck kicks in to run this household too, you know.

JEAN

Who asked *you* for help, anyway?

MATTHEW

Maria did.

JEAN

Maria's a child.

MATTHEW

Soon to be my wife.

JEAN
(*stunned*)

Over my dead body!

MATTHEW

It's all set. We go to Town Hall on Monday.

Jean stares at Matthew, amazed.

You want a beer?

INT. MARIA'S KITCHEN — NIGHT — SAME TIME

Matthew opens the fridge.

> JEAN (V.O.)
> What the hell's wrong with Peg?

> MATTHEW
> There's nothing wrong with Peg. I just don't want to
> marry her.

> JEAN (V.O.)
> Peg could take a punk like you and make a real man out
> of ya!

> MATTHEW
> I don't think I could stand being a real man, to tell you
> the truth.

> JEAN
> *(enters)*
> You might be able to convince Maria to marry you, but
> you'll never be able to take her away from me. I know how
> to deal with Maria.

Matthew looks at her. He knows she's right.

> MATTHEW
> You're a selfish bitch.

> JEAN
> I brought her into this world. Don't you forget that.

> MATTHEW
> You don't deserve her.

> JEAN
> Neither do you.

MATTHEW
You wanna arm wrestle about it?

Jean steps back, sizes him up a moment, then turns away and goes to the sink where she picks up a bottle of scotch and a bottle of gin.

JEAN
We'll drink for it.

MATTHEW
What?

JEAN
We'll drink for it. Whoever's left standing, wins.

MATTHEW
Jean, I can drink you under the table.

JEAN
That's what you think. Scotch is your poison, isn't it? Mine's gin.

MATTHEW
Jean, this is going to be way too easy.

JEAN
I'll get you out of my house one way or another.

MATTHEW
You won't do it *this* way.

JEAN
You're full of hot air, pal.

MATTHEW
You'll regret this whole thing in the morning, Mom.

JEAN
Shot for shot. There are two more bottles under the sink. And don't you *ever* call me Mom.

MATTHEW
(*lifts the bottle of scotch and takes a drink*)
To motherhood.

                          JEAN
                    (*lifts her bottle*)
Bastard.

INT. DINER — NIGHT

Maria is sitting at the counter, reading Man and the Universe.
*When she comes across a word she needs to look up, she writes it
down in her notebook.*

She looks up as . . .

*Nurse Paine comes into the diner. She approaches the counter and
sits down next to Maria.*

The cook behind the counter is nervous.

                          PAINE
Coffee.

                          COOK
Look, we don't want any trouble!

                          PAINE
Coffee!

                          COOK
We're closing up.

                          PAINE
                    (*ignores him*)
Milk, no sugar.

                          MARIA
Hi.

                          PAINE
Hi.

                          MARIA
You work late?

                          PAINE
They smashed my car up again. Tipped it over into the street.

MARIA

Bastards.

PAINE

I'm doing what I believe in. And if you're going to *do* that, you've got to be ready to take a certain amount of shit.

MARIA

I'm going to have an abortion.

PAINE

Are you sure it's what you want?

MARIA

Yes.

PAINE

You have to be sure. You have to be sure or nothing ever changes. People spend their entire lives making the same mistakes again and again.

MARIA

I'm sure.

PAINE

Are you alone?

MARIA

I met a man.

PAINE

He knows you're pregnant.

MARIA

He wants to marry me.

PAINE

Do you want that?

MARIA

Sometimes I'm sure I do. Other times I'm not so certain. He's a good man. But he's out of control. It seems like meeting me has made him capable and ready to give himself. I mean, completely, you know?

PAINE

Isn't that a good thing?

MARIA

I like him the way he is.

PAINE

How is he?

MARIA

Dangerous. But sincere.

PAINE

Sincerely dangerous.

MARIA

No, dangerous *because* he's sincere.

PAINE

I see. And now he's becoming insincere?

MARIA

Not exactly. He's just sort of numb.

PAINE

Because you've changed him.

MARIA

I didn't mean to, honest.

PAINE

No, you didn't mean to, but still it happens. People change each other. People start becoming what others want them to be.

MARIA

I just want him to be himself.

PAINE

Impossible.

MARIA

Really?

PAINE

How can you expect him to stay the same when you've come into his life?

MARIA

You think I should leave him?

PAINE

Look, hasn't he changed you?

MARIA

I guess so.

PAINE

There you go.

MARIA

I don't understand.

PAINE

There's nothing to understand.
                (*looks around the diner*)
Here's my husband.

She turns and stubs out her cigarette.

MARIA

I'll be there tomorrow.

PAINE
                (*pauses*)
As long as you know what you're doing.

MARIA

I know what I'm doing.

INT. MARIA'S KITCHEN — NIGHT

There are two empty bottles.

Two more are half empty.

Matthew and Jean are sitting on the kitchen floor.

MATTHEW
Here, let me pour you another one, Jean.

JEAN
(*frowns*)
Thanks.

Matthew pours and hands Jean the drink. She takes it, sighs, then knocks it back. Matthew screws up his face, disappointed, and pours himself another.

MATTHEW
(*disturbed*)
Shit.

JEAN
I've been meaning to ask you something.

MATTHEW
What's that?

JEAN
What was your mother like?

Matthew polishes off another with some difficulty. He shakes his head clear and places the glass back on the floor.

MATTHEW
I don't remember her.

JEAN
You were that young when she died?

MATTHEW
She died giving birth to me.

JEAN
No.

MATTHEW
It's the truth.

JEAN
That's terrible.

MATTHEW

I agree.

JEAN

So unfair.

MATTHEW

Of course.

JEAN

I feel sorry for your father.

MATTHEW

I had a feeling you two would hit it off.

JEAN

You can't blame him for hating you.

MATTHEW

I never said he hated me.

JEAN

But you don't get along.

MATTHEW

No. We don't get along. But then neither do you and Maria.

JEAN

Me and Maria will get along just fine once you're out of the picture.

MATTHEW

She'll waste away here with you.

JEAN

And what the hell kinda life are you gonna be able to give her?

MATTHEW

Any kinda life she wants.

JEAN

She wants to stay with me.

MATTHEW

Says who?

JEAN

Look, let me tell you something. 'Cause, you know, it's
not like I hated you right off the bat or anything.

MATTHEW

I appreciate that.

JEAN

It's just that I don't want to see Maria make the same mistake I made. And that Peg made.

MATTHEW
(groggy)

What mistake is that?

JEAN

Men!

MATTHEW

Oh.

JEAN

Children are OK. But marriage is always a last resort. A
woman can have anything she wants. Anything. But we
always make the mistake of thinking we need a man to do
it.

MATTHEW

Well, I mean, correct me if I'm wrong, but . . . isn't it
sort've impossible to have a baby without a man around
the house?

JEAN

Wake up, Matthew, this is the twentieth century! You can
be artificially inseminated! They've got sperm banks and
everything! The possibilities are endless!

MATTHEW

You're out of your mind!

JEAN

I'm fed up! That's all! You know, when my husband died,
sure, I was in shock. But what I really felt was relief!

MATTHEW

What!

JEAN

Relief. Yeah. That man poisoned the past twenty years of
my life. Some nights I'd lay awake just hoping he'd sort've
just – well disappear or something. And then WHACK!
Maria, with one slap, knocks him right out of my life!
Incredible! I was amazed. The girl's a genius!

Matthew stares at her, stunned.

Do you love him?

MATTHEW

Who?

JEAN

Your father.

MATTHEW

I don't love anybody.

JEAN

Yeah, right. I keep forgetting. Drink up.

Matthew pours himself another and tries to concentrate.

MATTHEW

You know, with me and my dad, it was as if our relationship
was a record album. You know, and the phonograph that the
record was playing on had a very old and worn out needle.
Know what I'm saying? There were these *skips*. Bad *skips*.
These painful *gouges*. But in your *head*, you know, you com-
pensate for it. You keep the *beat* because you know the *song*.

Jean just watches him.

Most people buy laser discs now. CDs. They don't wear
out. You can't damage the surface of CDs. They're digital.

Not analog. Would you like for me to explain to you, Jean, the difference between analog and digital recording?

> JEAN

No.

> MATTHEW

It's really fascinating stuff.

> JEAN

I'm sure it is.

> MATTHEW
> (drinks)

Jean.

> JEAN

Huh.

> MATTHEW

I think . . . I think I'm . . . I think I'm actually drunk.

> JEAN

I think so too.

She gives him a little nudge with her finger and . . .

CRASH! Down he goes. It looks like he's passed out. Jean shakes him. Matthew opens his eyes.

> MATTHEW

What?

INT. STAIRWAY — NIGHT

Jean struggles up the stairs with Matthew hung over her shoulder.

INT. PEG'S BEDROOM — NIGHT

Jean slams in through the door with Matthew in tow. She heaves him across the room and tumbles him down on to . . . Peg's bed.

Jean steps back and catches her breath, then stoops over Matthew and listens closely to make sure he's . . .

Sleeping. She smiles victoriously, waits a moment, then starts undressing him. She undoes his trousers and pulls them off, takes off his shirt, strips him completely.

INT. UPSTAIRS HALLWAY — NIGHT — MOMENTS LATER

Jean closes the door. She starts up the hall, but then stops, remembering something. She takes the hair clip out of her hair and goes back into the room.

INT. PEG'S BEDROOM — NIGHT — SAME TIME

Jean turns on the TV and places the hair clip on top of it. She pauses a moment and gazes at Matthew lying naked under the sheets. She shakes her head and sighs.

Matthew sleeps.

INT. MARIA'S KITCHEN — NIGHT — MOMENTS LATER

Jean enters the kitchen and stops short when she sees . . .

Peg, just back from work. She's holding the half-empty bottle of gin.

                          PEG
            (*gesturing toward the bottle of scotch*)
    What's going on here, Mom?

                          JEAN
    None of your business.
                    (*picks up the bottle of scotch*)
    You should've been home half an hour ago.

                          PEG
    The other girl got sick.
                (*drinks out of the gin bottle in her hand*)
    What is this?

                          JEAN
    What?

                          PEG
    This isn't gin.

                              JEAN
Oh, that.

                              PEG
This is water.

                              JEAN
Gimme that.

                              PEG
Why are you watering down the gin, Mom?

                              JEAN
I'm not watering down the gin. I was using that to water
the plants.

                              PEG
What plants?

                              JEAN
Will you stop asking stupid questions and just go on up to
bed!

Peg pours a scotch instead. Checks it, and . . .

                              PEG
Well, at least the scotch is real.

*Peg takes her drink and leaves the kitchen. Jean stares off into
space.*

INT. STAIRWAY — NIGHT — SAME TIME

Peg starts up the stairs.

INT. PEG'S BEDROOM — NIGHT — SAME TIME

*Peg enters the room, but stops short when she sees Matthew sleeping
in her bed. She quickly closes the door.*

INT. MARIA'S KITCHEN — NIGHT — SAME TIME

Jean is sewing. She hears the sound of Peg's door closing.

EXT. SUPERMARKET — NIGHT

Maria comes out of the supermarket carrying her groceries.

Anthony is standing by his car.

                    ANTHONY
Maria.

                    MARIA
What do *you* want?

                    ANTHONY
I wanna apologize.

                    MARIA
Oh, great. What happened with your football scholarship?

                    ANTHONY
I didn't get it. I failed my college entrance exam.

                    MARIA
I'm sorry to hear that.

                    ANTHONY
Maria, I want you to forgive me.

                    MARIA
              (*sighs benevolently*)
Sure. Here, give me a lift.

                    ANTHONY
Let me take those.

                    MARIA
       (*giving Anthony the grocery bags*)
Thanks.

                    ANTHONY
What did you do to your hair?

                    MARIA
Nothing.

                              ANTHONY
     I didn't know you wore glasses.

INT. PEG'S BEDROOM — NIGHT — SAME TIME

*Peg is in her slip, propped up on an elbow beside Matthew. She has
her drink in her hand. She lightly slaps Matthew's face. He just
moans and continues sleeping.*

                               PEG
     Matthew.

*She waits, but there's no response. She takes out her gum and kisses
Matthew on the mouth. He smacks his lips, but remains asleep. Peg
puts her gum back in her mouth and sighs.*

EXT. MARIA'S HOUSE — NIGHT

Anthony is trying to kiss Maria.

                              MARIA
     Get your *hands* off of me, Anthony!

                             ANTHONY
     Don't come on so high and mighty with me, Maria!

                              MARIA
     I'm not being high and mighty. I just don't want your
     hands anywhere near me. Now, get me my groceries out
     of the trunk.

                             ANTHONY
     It's true about you and that psycho-case, isn't it?

                              MARIA
     What psycho-case?

                             ANTHONY
     Matthew Slaughter.

                              MARIA
     As a matter of fact, yes. It is. We're getting married on
     Monday. Now get my groceries out of the trunk.

> ANTHONY
> (*stunned*)

What!

> MARIA

Give me the keys. I'll get them myself.

> ANTHONY

You can't do that!

> MARIA

Why not?

> ANTHONY

What about us?

Maria looks at Anthony.

INT. MARIA'S KITCHEN — NIGHT

Maria comes in the back door with the groceries, seething.

Jean doesn't look up as Maria drops the packages on the table.

> JEAN

It's about time. I wanted a cup of tea, but there's no milk.

Maria glares sideways at Jean, then slams down the quart of milk on the table.

Jean starts. She watches from the corner of her eye as Maria throws her jacket off and begins putting things away.

Maria, I left my hair clip up in Peg's room. Can you go get it for me?

Maria stands for a moment and calms herself, then looks over at her mother. Jean looks back at her.

Did you hear me?

> MARIA

Why can't you get it yourself?

JEAN
(*stunned*)

What?

MARIA

Mom, you're a normal, healthy person. There's no reason
for me to do every little thing for you.

JEAN

What's gotten into *you*?

MARIA

Nothing's gotten into me. I'm just telling you how it is.

Jean is getting desperate.

JEAN

Go get my hair clip!

Maria sighs and then comes over and sits at the table with Jean.

MARIA

Listen, Mom. I'm sorry about Dad.

Jean just stares at her. Maria waits.

JEAN

Are you going to marry Matthew?

MARIA

Maybe.

JEAN
(*ice cold*)

It's your life. Do what you want with it.

MARIA

That's right. It's my life. And I'll do what I want with it.

*Maria watches her mother closely. Finally, Jean looks up, pauses,
and . . .*

JEAN

Go get my hair clip.

They stare each other down a moment longer, then Maria gets up and leaves the room. Jean stares a hole in the table, deeply shaken despite her ice-cold routine.

INT. STAIRWAY — NIGHT

Maria moves up the stairs toward Peg's room.

INT. MARIA'S KITCHEN — NIGHT — SAME TIME

Jean doesn't blink. She waits motionlessly, her sewing frozen in her hands. She is terribly frightened.

On the stove, the kettle starts to whistle.

Jean doesn't react. She breathes in deep, waiting.

The kettle whistles . . .

INT. STAIRWAY — NIGHT— SAME TIME

The empty stairway. From the kitchen we hear the kettle's shrill, relentless whistle.

INT. MARIA'S KITCHEN — NIGHT — SAME TIME

Jean at the table, not moving; stiff as a board, waiting. The kettle is deafening.

Jean's hands, with the sewing, slowly drop to the table.

She hangs her head there a moment, then . . .

The whistling stops.

Jean looks up, startled.

Maria is standing there, her hand still on the stove's burner knob.

She pours a cup of tea and brings it, with the hair clip, over to the table, setting it before Jean.

MARIA
Here you go. I'm going to bed. Good night.

*Jean sits there, uncomprehending, as Maria kisses her on the head
and leaves the kitchen. Maria seemed completely undisturbed. Jean
stares at her hair clip and at the tea, puzzled.*

INT. STAIRWAY — NIGHT — MOMENTS LATER

*Jean comes quietly, but determinedly, up the stairs and moves
toward Peg's room.*

INT. PEG'S BEDROOM — NIGHT — SAME TIME

Jean opens the door slowly.

The hallway light falls over . . .

Matthew and Peg, asleep together on the bed.

Jean just stares at them, dumbfounded.

INT. MARIA'S BATHROOM — NIGHT — SAME TIME

*In the shower, Maria is pressing her forehead into the corner of the
tiled wall with her eyes shut tight and her fists clenched and held up
just beneath her chin.*

The water pours down over her head.

The bathroom fills with steam.

   FADE TO BLACK.

INT. CLINIC — DAY

*Maria is being questioned by a nurse. She is wearing a hospital
gown. The nurse holds a clipboard.*

                         NURSE
Emphysema?

                         MARIA
No.

                         NURSE
Heart disease?

MARIA

No.

NURSE

Venereal disease?

MARIA

No.

NURSE

Are you allergic to penicillin?

MARIA

No.

NURSE

Other allergies?

MARIA

No.

NURSE

Have you been hospitalized for any illness within the past
six months?

MARIA

No.

NURSE

Have you had an abortion before?

MARIA

No.

NURSE

Social Security number?

MARIA

Is Nurse Paine here?

NURSE

Why?

MARIA

No reason.

NURSE

She's off today. Social Security number?

MARIA

081-50-9199.

NURSE

OK. Drink this.

MARIA

What is it?

NURSE

Just drink it and lean back.

MARIA
(*drinks, then lies back on the table*)
Will this hurt?

NURSE

Don't worry. It's a simple procedure.

INT. RUARK COMPUTER FACTORY — DAY — MEANWHILE

The rows of workers are busy at their benches. We move along until we come to . . .

Matthew at his bench. He has an enormous hangover and has his chin propped up in his hand. His eyes are closed. He opens them gradually, rubs his forehead, takes a drag on his cigarette, and tries to start working. He lifts . . .

The circuit board A-67-9.

He regards it for a long time.

INT. RUARK BOSS'S OFFICE — DAY — A LITTLE LATER

The boss is handing some documents to Ed as Matthew enters. They both regard Matthew apprehensively. Ed makes a quick exit.

BOSS

Yes, Matthew?

MATTHEW

Have you got a minute?

BOSS

Sure. What is it?

MATTHEW

I just have a question. I was a little confused. The specification manual for the new model we're assembling calls for a particular piece. A circuit board. A-67-9.

BOSS

I know the piece.

MATTHEW

Well, it's just that I remember we manufactured that piece last year and an unusually high number of them checked out faulty.

BOSS

Yes, I'm aware of that.

MATTHEW

There was a defect in the pressing of the . . .

BOSS

Matthew, I *understand*.

MATTHEW

Oh.

BOSS

Matthew, listen. I appreciate your diligence. But there are people in this company, highly qualified people, people in important positions making decisions about these things. And they know what they're doing.

Matthew just stares at her, pale and ill.

MATTHEW

Uh huh.

BOSS

Now, if these people saw fit to include part A-67-9 in the

new model, well then we have to trust that they have a
reason for doing so. Agreed?

                          MATTHEW
                          (*slowly*)
Yes.

                          BOSS
                          (*sincere*)
So, Matthew, once again, thank you for your diligence and
dedication, but please just go back down there and do
your job.

*Matthew waits a few moments before moving, staring at the floor,
then . . .*

                          MATTHEW
        Yes, sir.

                          BOSS
Excuse me?

                          MATTHEW
        I'm sorry.

                          BOSS
Good.

                          MATTHEW
        I quit.

The boss stares at Matthew as he leaves.

INT. CLINIC (RECOVERY ROOM) — DAY

*Maria sits, dressed, in an otherwise empty recovery room. She's calm
and remote. A small plastic cup of orange juice is beside her. She
looks up as . . .*

*Jean comes in. She sits beside Maria. They are silent for a while,
then . . .*

                          JEAN
        Do you want to go home now?

MARIA

No. I have some things to do.

Jean sits there, feeling sort of useless and intensely guilty.

Maria senses this and takes her hand.

I'll be home later.

Finally, Jean gets up and goes.

Maria takes something out of her pocket and looks down at . . .

The address label from Robert's briefcase.

EXT. ROBERT AND RACHEL'S HOUSE — DAY

Maria comes up to the door and knocks. She waits. No one answers. She knocks again. Waits. She knocks a third time . . .

The door opens a crack. She looks up and sees . . .

Robert looking out at her.

She says nothing.

He says nothing. After a moment, the door slowly opens wider.

Robert steps aside and Maria hesitates, then enters.

Robert reaches out and takes in the mail, looking around the neighborhood as he does so.

INT. ROBERT AND RACHEL'S HOUSE — DAY — MOMENTS LATER

There is a hall leading from the front door to the living room. Maria moves carefully and slowly down the hall toward the living room, as Robert brings in the newspaper and closes the door, lingering just inside it a moment.

Maria comes into the living room and finds . . .

Rachel sitting alone in a chair by the window. Her hands folded tightly before her, she stares off at nothing until, finally, she sees . . .

Maria across the room, politely keeping her distance. Robert appears behind her; nervous, helpless, a tired wreck. Rachel looks away and Maria approaches. She attempts to place her hand on Rachel's shoulder, but then draws back. There's a thud against the table and Maria looks over at . . .

The newspaper Robert has tossed. Its headline reads: STOLEN INFANT FOUND IN PHONE BOOTH.

Maria, amazed, looks up at Robert.

> ROBERT
> They found him this morning. The police got an unidentified phone call, apparently. They say he's OK. Just fine.

Robert turns and walks out of the room.

Maria watches him go, then looks back down at . . .

Rachel, who is locked in her own world.

INT. MARIA'S HOUSE — AFTERNOON

Matthew storms in the back door, happy. He's got a bunch of flowers in one hand and a brand new book in the other. He slams it down by the sink.

It's a thesaurus.

He takes off his coat and throws it, with a flourish, to the floor.

There's someone knocking at the door.

He goes toward the back door and when he sees who it is, with resignation, he opens the door.

Dad comes in, looking up at Matthew and scratching his chin uncertainly.

INT. MARIA'S KITCHEN — AFTERNOON — MOMENTS LATER

Dad and Matthew are standing side by side against the kitchen cabinets.

> DAD
> What are you doing here?

MATTHEW

I live here.

DAD

Come on home, Matthew.

MATTHEW

No.

DAD

Matthew, I spent all my life looking out for you, now you desert me.

MATTHEW

The two of us are better off on our own.

DAD

You're selfish.

MATTHEW

I'm just trying to be responsible.

DAD

You're a fool, Matthew. I've heard about all this. Everybody knows that girl's child isn't yours.

MATTHEW

Big deal.

DAD

Big deal. She's just taking advantage of you.

MATTHEW

We better not talk about this, Dad.

DAD

You'll always be a fool, Matthew. You need someone to look after you.

MATTHEW

Why don't you just say it?

DAD

Say what?

MATTHEW

That you want me to come home because you're lonely.

DAD

Bullshit.

MATTHEW

Why don't you just say you're sorry for the way things never seem to work out between the two of us?

DAD

You're saying it's my fault?

MATTHEW

It's nobody's fault.

DAD

It's that little slut's fault! That's whose fault it is.

MATTHEW

Watch it, Dad.

DAD

Fucking low-life bitch!

MATTHEW

You better get out of here, Dad.

DAD

What are you gonna do about it?

MATTHEW

I'm warning you, Dad.

DAD

Come on. What are you gonna do about it?

MATTHEW

I swear to God, I'm going to knock you out.

DAD

Try it! I'll knock your ass through your face! Come on, try it!

Matthew sighs.

What's the matter? You afraid?

WHAM! Matthew punches Dad in the stomach and the older man stumbles back, amazed and a little winded. Matthew looks on, worried.

Dad looks up at him, takes off his cap, and dives at his son. They go crashing down, through the kitchen table, knocking chairs over and shaking the whole house. They roll around on the floor, punching and kicking each other with all their might.

EXT. MARIA'S HOUSE — DAY — SAME TIME

Jean comes walking into the yard and stops when she hears the brutal sounds of fighting from inside the house: dishes smashing, furniture breaking . . .

INT. MARIA'S KITCHEN — DAY — MOMENTS LATER

Matthew takes Dad's arm, opens a drawer beneath the sink, and jams Dad's hand in.

KACHOONK! Matthew slams it closed on Dad's fingers. They go crashing across the kitchen as Jean enters. She stops dead in her tracks, looking at the fight, and then runs out of the kitchen as Dad gets Matthew in a headlock, opens the refrigerator door, and . . .

SLAM! He closes it against Matthew's head. Dad staggers back and waits.

EXT. MARIA'S HOUSE — DAY — SAME TIME

Maria comes walking up to the house and stops when she sees . . .

Jean standing, petrified, in the front yard. She turns and looks at Maria.

Maria hears the commotion and goes up to the house.

INT. MARIA'S KITCHEN — DAY — MOMENTS LATER

Maria steps carefully into the kitchen and sees . . .

Dad leaning over the sink, wetting a dish cloth and touching it to a cut on his face.

He looks over at Maria, slowly.

Maria holds Dad's gaze a moment, then turns and walks away.

INT. BATHROOM — DAY — MOMENTS LATER

Maria comes up the stairs and finds . . .

Matthew in the bathroom, leaning over the sink, also wetting a towel and cleaning up cuts on his face. He looks up at her and smiles.

Maria comes to him.

> MARIA
>
> Are you OK?

> MATTHEW
>
> I quit.

> MARIA
>
> What?

> MATTHEW
>
> I quit my job.

> MARIA
>
> Why?

Matthew sits on the edge of the tub.

> MATTHEW
>
> You're right. We've got to get out of here. This is no place to raise a child.

Maria sits on the edge of the toilet opposite Matthew.

> Maria, I woke up in Peg's bed this morning. I don't know how . . .

> MARIA
>
> Stop.

Matthew stops and looks helpless.

I've had an abortion.

*Matthew stares at her a moment, then looks down again, crushed.
She reaches out and caresses him. He hangs his head, disturbed and
confused.*

I don't want to get married.

*Maria holds Matthew's gaze. He looks back down and heaves a
sigh. Finally, he lifts the thesaurus off the floor and hands it to her.*

MATTHEW
I bought you this.

*Maria takes it, looks at it, then watches as Matthew gets up and
walks out of the bathroom.*

INT. MARIA'S KITCHEN — DAY — SAME TIME

Jean stands behind Dad, who's sitting at the kitchen table.

JEAN
(*frowning*)
And who do you think you are?

DAD
Leave me alone.

JEAN
Look what you've done to my cabinets.

DAD
Get me a hammer and I'll fix it.

JEAN
Do you want something to eat?

INT. MARIA'S BEDROOM — DAY

Maria's top drawer is open. Maria rushes to it and looks in to see . . .

The grenade is gone.

EXT. STREET — DAY — MOMENTS LATER

Maria walks quickly up the street. A police squad car passes her with its siren blaring.

EXT. RUARK COMPUTER FACTORY — DAY

Maria comes rushing up to a crowd of workers and others, who are all standing around at a safe distance from the factory.

A few more people run out of the factory, including Ed and the boss, who is demanding that Ed go back into the factory and get Matthew out.

Maria passes right by them and enters the factory.

INT. RUARK COMPUTER FACTORY — DAY — MOMENTS LATER

Maria rushes through the factory, finally slowing when she sees . . .

Matthew sitting on an overturned word processor, holding the grenade before him.

Maria comes forward.

Matthew looks up and sees her.

Maria strides bravely on and comes up to him. She stops and looks down at . . .

The grenade in his hand, then over at . . .

The grenade's pin in his other hand.

She looks up at . . .

Matthew, who looks from her to the pieces in his hand with a startled expression on his face.

MARIA
What happened?

MATTHEW
I don't know. It must not be any good.

MARIA

Are you sure?

MATTHEW

No.

MARIA

You mean, it might still go off?

MATTHEW

I guess so.

Maria thinks. They both look up at each other.

Matthew remains there, trapped. Maria moves slowly toward him. Silence.

EXT. RUARK COMPUTER FACTORY — DAY — SAME TIME

Jean, Peg, and Dad come running up and stand waiting with the others.

INT. RUARK COMPUTER FACTORY — DAY — SAME TIME

Maria slowly reaches over and gently lifts the grenade out of Matthew's hand.

Matthew holds his breath as he watches it rise up and . . .

Maria carries it away, held out in front of her.

Matthew stands and comes in behind her as . . .

Maria tosses the grenade. They turn away and shield themselves.

We see the grenade fall to the floor and roll away. No explosion.

They stand with their backs turned, tensed, but nothing happens and they look over their shoulders at . . .

The grenade lying on the floor across the factory.

Maria and Matthew wait.

EXT. RUARK COMPUTER FACTORY — DAY — SAME TIME

Outside – the crowd waits.

INT. RUARK COMPUTER FACTORY — DAY — SAME TIME

Close-up on grenade.

Maria and Matthew sigh with relief and take a few steps away . . .

KABOOM! The grenade goes off and pieces of everything go flying by over their heads as they dive to the floor.

EXT. RUARK COMPUTER FACTORY — DAY — SAME TIME

Peg and Jean faint in unison.

INT. RUARK COMPUTER FACTORY — DAY — SAME TIME

As the dust clears, Matthew and Maria are lying, head to head, on the floor.

> MATTHEW
> I'm sorry. I lost my head.

> MARIA
> It's OK.

> MATTHEW
> What do we do now?

> MARIA
> We could run?

> MATTHEW
> We'd never make it.

> MARIA
> I'll tell them it was my fault.

> MATTHEW
> They'll never believe you.

> MARIA
> I don't care if they believe me or not.

MATTHEW

Why have you done this?

MARIA

Done what?

MATTHEW

Why do you put up with me like this?

MARIA

Somebody had to.

MATTHEW

But why you?

MARIA

I just happened to be here.

Matthew is pulled to his feet by two policemen.

He stares at Maria as he is being dragged away.

Maria returns his look.

EXT. RUARK COMPUTER COMPANY — DAY — A LITTLE LATER

Matthew, handcuffed, is led to a squad car. The door is opened for him and they start to thrust him in, but he looks back at . . .

Maria as she steps forward, away from Jean, Peg, Dad, and the others.

Matthew holds her gaze a moment until, finally, they manage to shove him into the back seat of the squad car. But he twists himself around and looks out the back window at . . .

Maria gazing bravely back at him.

They slam the squad car door and peel out as they start away. Maria walks slowly forward after the car as it . . .

Speeds away down the road. Matthew is still peering out at her through the back window and . . .

Maria steps out into the street and walks on after the car, straining to see him as . . .

He moves farther and farther off down the road.

Maria walks on a little farther, straining her eyes, finally stopping to put on . . .

Close-up: her glasses.

The squad car moves even farther off into the distance, but . . .

Extreme close-up: Maria remains focused on . . .

The spot where the car and Matthew finally disappear over the horizon.

Hold on Maria in the middle of the road, looking off after him.

Simple Men

CAST AND CREW

MAIN CAST

BILL MCCABE	Robert Burke
DENNIS MCCABE	Bill Sage
KATE	Karen Sillas
ELINA	Elina Lowensohn
MARTIN	Martin Donovan
MIKE	M. C. Bailey
VIC	Christopher Cooke
NED RIFLE	Jeffrey Howard
KIM	Holly Marie Combs
JACK	Joe Stevens
SHERIFF	Damian Young
MOM	Marietta Marich
DAD	John MacKay
MARY	Bethany Wright
SECURITY GUARD	Richard Reyes
FRANK	James Hansen Prince
VERA	Mary McKenzie

MAIN CREW

Written and Directed by	Hal Hartley
Cinematographer	Michael Spiller
Production Designer	Dan Ouellette
Editor	Steve Hamilton
Music	Ned Rifle
Executive Producers	Jerome Brownstein
	Bruce Weiss
Producers	Ted Hope
	Hal Hartley

EXT. LOADING DOCK — EARLY MORNING

Vera is a sexy twenty-three-year-old with a gun aimed at the security guard's head. The security guard dare not move. He is blindfolded.

Behind them we see Frank and Bill loading a truck with boxes of high-tech computer equipment.

> VERA
> (*ferocious*)
>
> Don't move!

> GUARD
>
> OK.

> VERA
>
> Did you just move?

> GUARD
>
> My foot's asleep.

> VERA
>
> I said don't move!

Then Bill McCabe walks over. Of the three, he seems to be the boss criminal. He grabs Vera's gun, takes her by the chin, and kisses her passionately on the mouth. She melts. The guard doesn't move.

Then . . .

> BILL
>
> All right, good-lookin', get in the truck.

> VERA
>
> But, Bill . . .

> BILL
>
> Come on. I'm right behind you. Come on, Frank, what are you waiting for?

Vera starts to go, but stops and looks back at him. She runs back into his arms and they kiss again. Then . . .

What's wrong?

                              VERA
Do you love me?

                              BILL
Yes.

                              VERA
Am I beautiful?

                              BILL
Yes, you're beautiful.

She moves off and approaches the truck.

Bill is confident, smooth, and handsome. He thrusts the gun in his pocket and glances over at the guard as he lights a cigarette and oversees the last of the loading. To guard:

Don't move.

                              GUARD
OK.

Bill seems satisfied with this crime. He takes a hit off a flask of scotch he has with him and offers some to the guard.

                              BILL
You want a drink?

                              GUARD
No thanks.

                              BILL
You sure?

                              GUARD
I'm not allowed to drink on the job.

Bill sees the guard is wearing a little Catholic medallion bearing the image of the Virgin Mary. It strikes his fancy. He moves closer and lifts it.

> BILL

Hey, that's nice.

> GUARD

It's the Virgin Mary.

> BILL

She's good lookin', huh?

> GUARD

She brings me good luck.

> BILL

Can I have it?

> GUARD

But she keeps me out of danger.

> BILL

You're not in danger.

> GUARD

Is that true?

> BILL

Sure, it's true. My gun doesn't even work.

Convinced, the guard nods and lets Bill remove the medallion from around his neck. Bill puts it around his own neck.

Thanks.

> GUARD

Be good to her and she'll be good to you.

And with that Bill jumps off the loading dock and heads for the truck.

Frank is standing before the truck with Vera close beside him. He trains his gun on Bill.

                          FRANK
   Sorry, Bill. It's all over.

Bill stops, looks around, then takes a cautious step or two closer to
Frank and Vera.

                          BILL
                       (*confused*)
   What is this?

                          FRANK
   Vera's with me. I got ideas of my own about how to run
   things.

Bill goes white. He looks at Vera, but she turns away.

                          BILL
   Vera?

                          VERA
                      (*desperately*)
   I gotta do what I feel! I gotta be happy!

Bill pushes Frank's gun out of the way and approaches Vera.

                          BILL
   Since when are you unhappy?

                          VERA
   You deserve better than me, Bill!

Frank comes between her and Bill.

Bill just looks at her, dumbfounded, then at Frank. Then he looks
back at Vera.

She runs off to the truck.

And Frank hands him an envelope.

                          BILL
   What's this?

                          FRANK
   It's three grand.

BILL
(*appalled*)

Three grand! I put this whole thing together! I stand to make ten times this much once we deliver this stuff!

Frank backs away to the truck.

Bill is devastated. Not knowing what to do, he turns and looks back at the blindfolded security guard. The guard speaks into the wind . . .

GUARD

Be good to her and she'll be good to you!

Bill looks weakly back at the truck just as . . .

It pulls away and speeds up the deserted street.

Bill is left standing there in the street, clutching the envelope. He throws it to the ground. He takes out his gun, aims at the truck, and . . .

Click. Click. Click. It doesn't work. He drops his arm and stares dejectedly at the ground before him. Then he looks up. He hears a siren. He snatches the envelope up off the ground and runs.

INT. POLICE STATION — MORNING

Bill's younger brother, Dennis, comes striding into the police station.

COP

And what can I do for you, young man?

DENNIS

I believe my father is being held here.

COP

Who's your father?

DENNIS

William McCabe.

The cop looks up, impressed.

COP

No shit.

>   DENNIS
>   (*nods bashfully*)

Yes, sir.

The cop leans close . . .

>   COP

Listen, kid, I saw your father play with the Dodgers back
in '56. No matter what else people say about him, good or
bad, your old man was the greatest shortstop that ever
lived.

>   DENNIS

Can I see him?

>   COP
>   (*leans back*)

No.

>   DENNIS

Why not?

>   COP

He had a stroke in the holding cell. They took him to the
hospital.

INT. COFFEE SHOP — MEANWHILE

Bill enters and looks around, demoralized. He sees a young woman,
Mary, seated at the counter. He goes over and sits down beside her.
They acknowledge one another coldly.

>   BILL
>   (*to waitress*)

Coffee.

>   MARY

What's wrong with you?

>   BILL

Leave me alone.

MARY

They caught your father finally after twenty-three years.

Bill looks at her, nonplussed, then . . .

BILL

What?

MARY

Look, it's in all the papers.

He looks at the front-page story, then hands back the paper and turns to the counter.

BILL
(*weary*)

Big deal.

MARY

It is a big deal. It says right here he's responsible for that bombing.

WAITRESS
(*off*)

What bombing?

MARY

His dad. Twenty-three years ago he lobbed a bomb in the front door of the Pentagon.

BILL

That hasn't been proven yet.

WAITRESS
(*off*)

That's your father – William McCabe – the radical short-stop?

BILL
(*irritated*)

What about my coffee?

WAITRESS
(off)

The man's a hero.

BILL

My father's a crazy old man.

MARY

It says here seven people were killed and he's responsible.

BILL

And I suppose you believe everything you read, right?

MARY

Drop dead.

Bill reaches into his pocket and brings out the three grand. He gives her half of it. She picks it up off the counter and looks at it, impressed.

BILL

Here, this oughta hold you for a good long while.

She slips it into her bag and sips her coffee. Finally . . .

MARY

I got married.

BILL
(unimpressed)

Oh yeah, to who?

MARY

Him.

She motions across the room and Bill follows her gaze. He sees a young guy with a lot of tattoos playing pinball. Bill turns back around without comment and sips his coffee.

BILL

How's the kid?

                           MARY
                        (*getting up*)
OK.

                           BILL
                        (*stops her*)
That money's for him.

                           MARY
                         (*icy*)
Don't take your bad conscience out on me, Bill.

*This stings him. She moves away and exits with her husband. As
they are exiting we see Dennis passing by. He sees Mary and stops.
She gestures inside and Dennis sees Bill. He comes in.*

                          DENNIS
Hey, what are you doing in town?

                           BILL
Working.

                          DENNIS
You hear about Dad?

                           BILL
Yeah.

                          DENNIS
He's in the hospital.

Bill looks up, surprised.

INT. HOSPITAL — TWENTY MINUTES LATER

*Bill and Dennis come striding in through the doors to the emergency
desk. Once in, Bill grabs Dennis by the arm and freezes, going
white.*

Six policemen are running up the hall toward them.

Dennis is confused; Bill is mortified.

But the policemen troop right on past them and out into the street.

Bill relaxes and Dennis leads the way to the desk.

INT. HOSPITAL — MORNING

At the desk: the nurses are all confused and excited.

> NURSE OTTO
> (*breathless*)
>
> Can I help you?

> DENNIS
>
> Yeah. We're here to see about a patient. William McCabe.

All the bustling nurses stop. They look at Bill and Dennis. There's a moment of awkward silence, then . . .

> NURSE LOUISE
> (*steps forward*)
>
> Are you his family?

> BILL
> (*impatient*)
>
> He's our father.

> DENNIS
>
> Is he OK?

> NURSE LOUISE
>
> I think your father's a wonderful man! I don't care what the newspapers say about him!

> NURSE OTTO
>
> Go back to your station, Louise!

> NURSE LOUISE
> (*being pulled away*)
>
> He wouldn't have blown up that building if he knew people were in there! He's a great man! Falsely accused!

> NURSE OTTO
>
> Louise!

> BILL
>
> Look, lady, can we see him or what?

> NURSE OTTO
> (*turns back*)

No, you can't.

> BILL

Why not?

> NURSE OTTO

Because he's gone.

> BILL

Gone where?

> NURSE OTTO

He's escaped.

INT. MOM'S APARTMENT — A LITTLE LATER

Meg McCabe is sitting at the kitchen table when she hears the boys enter.

> DENNIS

Mom, what's going on?

> MEG

I'm leaving, Dennis. I'm going to Florida. I'm afraid your father might show up and I just don't wanna ever see him again.
> (*to Bill*)
What are you doing in town, Bill?!

> BILL

Got anything to eat?

> MEG

Have you seen Mary?

> BILL
> (*opens fridge*)
I'm taking this bottle of scotch.

> MEG

She lets that child run wild in the streets, you know.

Dennis is at the table, preoccupied.

> DENNIS
>
> Mom, you know where he might go?

> MEG
>
> Who?

> DENNIS
>
> Dad.

INT. LIVING ROOM

Mom packs to leave as Bill sits on the couch.

> MEG
>
> Keep an eye on Dennis. Don't let him do anything stupid.

> BILL
>
> Look, take this.

He takes the wad of cash out of his coat and hands it to her.

> MEG
>
> Where'd you get that?

> BILL
>
> Never mind where I got it. Will you just take it? You'll
> need it.

She takes it, hesitating, then . . .

> MEG
>
> Is this dirty money?

> BILL
>
> All money is dirty money, Mom. Now will you shut up
> and take it before I don't wanna give it to you any more!

He stands and slams shut her suitcase.

INT. MOM'S KITCHEN — DAY

In the kitchen: Dennis is still at the table concentrating.

MEG

When I saw him last he made me memorize this telephone
number. He said in case of an emergency I should ask for
Tara.

She hands him the number. He looks at it, then . . .

DENNIS

You don't want to call?

MEG

It's over with us, Dennis. It has been for years.
    (*after a moment, she gets up and puts on her coat*)
You should be back in school.

DENNIS

I still have time.

MEG

Did you get the money?

DENNIS
        (*nods evasively*)

Yeah.

MEG

Good. Keep an eye on Bill. Keep him outta trouble.

DENNIS

Right.

She kisses him and leaves.

*He listens to her leave the apartment. When the front door slams, he
looks down at the number in his hand. He turns it over and sees it is
a photo of Meg as a pretty young woman on the beach at Coney
Island.*

He moves to the phone and dials. He waits, then . . .

OPERATOR
        (*off*)

The number you have dialed has been disconnected.

EXT. MOM'S APARTMENT — DAY

Bill and Dennis are sitting on the front stoop. Bill is looking at the phone number on the back of the photo.

> BILL
>
> What area code is this?

> DENNIS
>
> Long Island, I think.

> BILL
> *(hands back photo)*
>
> What's it mean?

> DENNIS
>
> I don't know. It might be where Dad is.

> BILL
>
> Did you try calling it?

> DENNIS
>
> It's disconnected.

> BILL
>
> You oughta walk away from this thing, Dennis. Dad's in deep shit. You oughta just go back to school.

> DENNIS
>
> I'm not going back to school.

> BILL
>
> Don't be stupid.

> DENNIS
> *(adamant)*
>
> I'm not going back.

> BILL
>
> What are you gonna do then?

> DENNIS
>
> I'm gonna find Dad.

BILL

Dennis, don't do that!

DENNIS

I'm not asking you to come!

BILL

Well, good! Because I'm not! I'm just telling you it's a stupid thing to do!

(*pause, then . . .*)

Look, lend me a hundred bucks, will ya? I gotta get outta town.

DENNIS

I don't have any money.

BILL

Well, go to the cash machine.

DENNIS

I don't have any money in the bank.

BILL

What about your scholarship money?

DENNIS

I gave it to Mom.

BILL

(*furious*)

You gave it to Mom?!

DENNIS

Yeah. I was gonna ask you for money.

BILL

I don't have any money.

DENNIS

I've got twenty dollars, if you want that?

BILL

(*wild*)

Twenty dollars! What am I gonna do with twenty dollars!

                          DENNIS
    Are you in trouble?

*Bill glares at him resentfully. Then he turns away and smokes. He
sits on the stoop.*

                          BILL
    I don't know.

                          DENNIS
    What happened?

                          BILL
    I robbed some computers.

                          DENNIS
    But you didn't get caught, right?

                          BILL
    I got double-crossed.

They sit in silence. Dennis waits for further explanation.

                          DENNIS
    So what's that mean?

                          BILL
    I don't know what it means. I just gotta get outta town!

They sit there in silence again for a while, then . . .

                          DENNIS
    Come with me.

                          BILL
    Where?

                          DENNIS
    To find Dad.

                          BILL
    How?

                          DENNIS
    I don't know exactly. I guess I'll try to track down this Tara.

BILL
(*skeptical*)

With twenty dollars?

DENNIS

Well, that oughta get us to Long Island, don't you think?

BILL

How should I know?

DENNIS

I've never been to Long Island.

BILL

Yes, you have.

DENNIS

I have?

BILL

Yeah, you've been to Queens. Queens is Long Island.

DENNIS

Queens is part of New York City. I don't think it's really considered Long Island.

BILL

It's part of New York City, but it's *on* Long Island.

DENNIS

Queens is a borough.

BILL

A borough *on* Long Island.

DENNIS

A borough of New York City.

BILL

Right.

DENNIS

Long Island's a terminal moraine.

                              BILL

What?

                             DENNIS

Terminal moraine. It's the earth deposited by a receding
glacier.

                              BILL
                      (*stubs out cigarette*)
Well, shit! What the hell are we waiting for? Come on!

He stands and walks off. Dennis follows.

INT. PENN STATION — LATER

Bill and Dennis are at the ticket window.

                              BILL

Yeah, um. How far out on Long Island can two people go
for, say, fifteen dollars?

The teller browses over a chart, figures, then ...

                             TELLER

Not far.

                             DENNIS

Will it get us to a 516 area code?

                             TELLER

Yes.

EXT. SUBURBAN TRAIN STATION — AFTERNOON

*The train leaves the station and Bill and Dennis are revealed on the
lonely platform looking out over the town. Bill surveys the wide, flat,
nondescript suburb. Then ...*

                              BILL

Don't do anything suspicious, all right?

                             DENNIS

Like what?

BILL

You know what I mean.

And he moves off. Dennis hesitates, then follows.

EXT. STREET — MOMENTS LATER

They come walking across the street from the station toward a closed-up bar called the Station Café. The sign still hangs, weather-beaten and off-kilter, above the door.

They walk around the side and Dennis starts peeking in through the dusty windows. They go around back to where they hear some sort of commotion.

EXT. BACK OF CAFÉ — SAME TIME

Ned Rifle is a guy about thirty years old with the words 'missed opportunity' written all over his face. He is kicking the shit out of an old and broken-down motorcycle.

Bill and Dennis watch in amazement. Ned keeps lifting up the motorcycle and throwing it down again in the dirt. He jumps on it, spits at it, kicks it, and finally jumps down and wrestles it into sub-mission. He punches its headlight out and stops when he sees Bill and Dennis.

They stare, dumbfounded, then also notice . . .

Kim, a dangerously sexy thirteen-year-old in a convent-school uni-form and a black leather jacket. She's got a nose ring. She looks up over the newspaper she's reading and stares at the two brothers, unsettling them. They look back at Ned.

Heaving with exhaustion, he comes a few steps closer.

NED

Where'd you come from?

BILL
(*uneasy*)

New York City.

                              NED
Big deal.

                              BILL
                           (*of bike*)
What the hell are you doing to that machine?

*Ned doesn't answer at first. He tries to think and then just passes his
hand over his face. He attempts to form words, to give shape to the
vast and complicated situation that seems to be tormenting him. But
he fails. His wrath dissolves into sadness.*

*Bill can hardly believe what he's witnessing. He looks at Dennis, but
Dennis just looks away, embarrassed.*

*Ned throws himself on the ground. Kim gets up and, folding her
paper, walks away. Dennis follows her.*

Bill hesitates, then moves cautiously forward and kneels over Ned.

Listen, pal, take it easy.

                              NED
It's the fucking clutch assembly! It won't stay in gear!

EXT. FRONT OF CAFÉ — SAME TIME

*Dennis comes around the front of the building and finds Kim lean-
ing against the windows. He passes her and looks in.*

                              KIM
It's open.

                            DENNIS
What?

She enters. Dennis waits, but then follows her in.

EXT. BACK OF CAFÉ — SAME TIME

*Bill has lifted the bike up and is inspecting it while Ned leans
against the café, scowling.*

                         BILL
Hey. What's your name?

                         NED
                 (*slowly, reluctantly*)
Ned.

                         BILL
                 (*approaches*)
Listen, Ned. How much will you pay me to fix this motorcycle?

                         NED
It can't be fixed.

                         BILL
Yes, it can.

                         NED
It will never run again.

                         BILL
Yes, it will, I promise.

Ned gets up and sits by the curb.

                         NED
There's nothing like a machine to make a man feel
insignificant.

*Ned looks across the street and sees a nun having a smoke – she
moves off.*

INT. CAFÉ – SAME TIME

Dennis wanders through the place looking for a phone book.

                         KIM
Ned's parents used to own this café.

                         DENNIS
                      (*busy*)
Oh yeah?

                              KIM

They're dead now.

                            DENNIS

I'm sorry to hear that.

                              KIM

They had a suicide pact.

                            DENNIS
                          (*looks up*)

What?

                              KIM

It was awful. Blood all over the place.

Dennis looks around at the place with a new sense of dread, then he shows her the phone number.

                            DENNIS

You have any idea what area this exchange might belong to?

She drops her books and approaches.

                              KIM
                           (*looks*)

Eight eight four. I don't know. Let's call the operator. Gotta quarter?

He gives her one and she moves to the phone booth. He follows her and stands aside as . . .

She speaks into the phone.

Hello, operator. I need to know what region of Long Island has the exchange 884.
                     (*listens, then . . .*)
Yeah, I realize it's an uncommon request, but my boyfriend is bleeding to death.
                     (*waits, then . . .*)
Thank you.

(*to Dennis*)
She's looking it up.

She then lets the photo of Dennis's mom drop to the floor of the booth. Dennis, who can see it plainly, reaches in for it, balancing himself by placing his hand on Kim's knee. Meanwhile she's responding to the operator . . .

Sagaponeck?

The nun enters and almost lights herself a cigarette. Then she looks over and sees . . .

Dennis, with his hand on Kim's leg above her knee and his face just beneath the level of her skirt, and Kim, seated before him with her legs open. Dennis suddenly realizes his hand is touching the girl and whips it away. He stands and steps back.

The nun takes a step into the room.

Kim stands and takes a few steps away from the phone booth toward the nun, looking around the room with a bored expression.

NUN
What's going on in here?

KIM
(*coy*)
Oh, nothing.

Dennis doesn't move. The nun walks in toward him. Passing Kim, she hits her in the back of the head . . .

NUN
Get back over and get on the bus!

Kim runs out. The nun comes right up to Dennis and stares him down.

And who are you?

DENNIS
I'm a friend of Ned's.

                         NUN
You don't look familiar.

                         DENNIS
I'm not from around here.

                         NUN
I see.

EXT. BEHIND CAFÉ — MOMENTS LATER

Bill hides his gun as . . .

*Kim is ushered back toward the convent school by the scowling nun.
Bill looks up from his work as they pass.*

                         KIM
                    (*sotto to Bill*)
Sagaponeck.

                         BILL
                    (*confused*)
Don't mention it.

*The nun shows Kim into the bus and scowls at Bill before moving
off.*

INT. CAFÉ — LATER THAT NIGHT

*Across the café, by the front windows, Bill and Dennis each take a
hit off the bottle of scotch and resume their conversation. They're
drunk.*

                         BILL
What difference does it make?

                         DENNIS
It would mean he's innocent.

                         BILL
The man's a fanatic. A dangerous fanatic; whether he's
innocent or not.

DENNIS

He was a radical. That doesn't make him a fanatic. A lot
of people were radical back then.

BILL

But you do agree he's a criminal?

DENNIS

Well, so are you!

BILL

That's different.

DENNIS

How's that different?

BILL

Dennis, the difference between Dad and me is that I've
just fucked with the law and he's fucked with the government.

DENNIS

The law and the government are the same thing.

BILL

No, it's not. The government doesn't have to obey the law.

DENNIS

Well, maybe that's not the way things should be.

BILL

Who wants a government that's gotta obey the law?

DENNIS

A lot of people do!

BILL

Yeah, well, that's why a lot of people aren't running the
country.

Dennis moves off to go to sleep in the phone booth. Bill follows him.

DENNIS

You're drunk!

BILL

Listen, Dennis, let me tell you something about the law.
The law is just a contract. A contract between the rich
people who own everything and the poor people who want
to take it away from them. The contract says: if you break
the law and you get away with it, fine. But if you break the
law and get caught you gotta play by the rules and pay the
price. It's no big moral thing. You don't have to have an
ideology to knock over a liquor store!

DENNIS

Leave me alone.

BILL
(*all fired up*)

And another thing. If we do catch up with the old man,
I'm gonna give him a piece of my mind!

DENNIS

Yeah, right.

BILL

What's that supposed to mean?

DENNIS

You wouldn't last ten seconds with the old man.

BILL

Oh, you don't think so, huh?

DENNIS

He'd kick your ass.

BILL

The old man's a fool. He was a great shortstop but he
blew it.

DENNIS

He was dedicated to a cause.

BILL

He neglected his wife and children.

DENNIS

Well, nobody's perfect.

Bill moves back to his seat.

BILL

The old man's finished. Out of date. He's a relic.

DENNIS

Please be quiet and go to sleep!

Bill is too wired to even sit still. He paces, then sits again . . .

BILL

I can't sleep.

DENNIS

Why not?

BILL

I'm in pain.

DENNIS
(*leans out of the phone booth*)

What?

BILL

I've got a broken heart, man.

DENNIS
(*incredulous*)

Bullshit.

BILL
(*defensive*)

I do.

Dennis comes over and sits with him.

DENNIS

What happened?

Bill drinks and takes a significant pause, then . . .

                              BILL
I was set up. Double-crossed. Betrayed by the woman I
love.

                              DENNIS
Who, Mom?

                              BILL
No, Vera.

                              DENNIS
Who's Vera?

                              BILL
I don't want to talk about it.

                              DENNIS
Suit yourself.

                              BILL
                        (*takes out his wallet*)
You wanna see a picture of her?

He shows Dennis the picture.

                              DENNIS
Wow. She's pretty.

                              BILL
I would've done anything for her.

                              DENNIS
Sorry.

                              BILL
I just can't understand it.

                              DENNIS
You'll get over it.

*Bill begins putting the picture away in his wallet. He insists with a
deadly seriousness . . .*

                              BILL
No. Dennis, I will not get over it.

DENNIS

Yes, you will.

Bill stops and looks right at Dennis.

BILL

Dennis, I love this woman.

DENNIS

You've loved other women.

Bill puts his wallet away.

BILL

Not like Vera. Vera was special.

DENNIS

Believe me, you'll get over it.

Bill takes another hit off the scotch and thinks. Then . . .

BILL

Yeah, you're right.
                    (*considers, then . . .*)
Tomorrow. I'll get over it tomorrow.

DENNIS

Now go to sleep.

BILL

But I'm not gonna fall in love any more.

DENNIS

Fine.

BILL

Women don't want you to love them!

Dennis lies down to sleep on a diner-booth bench.

Tomorrow. The first good-looking woman I see . . . I'm
not gonna fall in love with her. That'll show her!
                    (*paces*)
Yeah. The first good-looking . . . *blonde* woman I see. I'm
gonna make her fall in love with *me*. I'll do everything

right. Be a little aloof at first. Mysterious. Seem sort of . . .
thoughtful and deep. But possibly a bit dangerous too.
Flatter her in little ways. But be modest myself. They all
fall for that shit. Make her fall hopelessly in love with me.
    (stops, thinks, and takes a hit off the scotch, then . . .)
Yup. Mysterious. Thoughtful. Deep but modest. And then
I'm gonna fuck her.

*Dennis opens his eyes and slowly looks up and watches Bill as he
moves to his seat once again.*

But I'm not gonna care about her. To me she's gonna be
another piece of ass. Somebody else's little girl who I'm
gonna treat like dirt and make her beg for it too.
    (almost drinks again, but . . .)
I'm just gonna use her up. Have my way with her. Like a
little toy, a plaything.
    (drinks . . .)
And when I'm done I'm just gonna throw her away.

He trails off and remains staring out into the night.

DENNIS
(embarrassed)

Are you through?

*Bill only slowly recognizes his brother's voice and looks back in at
him.*

BILL

I haven't even begun yet.

DENNIS

Go to sleep.

*And Dennis curls back up in his coat and lies down. Bill stares at
nothing for a while. Then . . .*

BILL

I can't sleep.
    (pauses, then softly . . .)
I'm in pain.

INT. CAFÉ — NEXT MORNING

Dennis is still sleeping.

Kim appears at the front door and looks in at him. Bill is nowhere to be seen. She enters.

She has a newspaper with her. She comes down beside Dennis and pokes him in the arm. He wakes up, befuddled, then gets his bearings. He sees her there beside him and clears his eyes.

> DENNIS

What's up?

> KIM

Look.

She hands him the newspaper.

EXT. BACK OF CAFÉ — NEXT MORNING

Click. Click. Ned toys with the gun Bill used during the heist.

Bill is preparing to leave on the bike. He is preoccupied with . . .

A police car parked outside the convent seventy yards away.

> NED

You know, I've never held a gun before.

> BILL
> (*preoccupied*)

Yeah, well, don't hold it too long. Listen, you just take that to a gun shop and don't take anything less than a hundred and fifty bucks for it. OK?

> NED

OK.

> BILL

I'm gonna take these tools.

> NED
> (*sees medallion*)

What is that thing?

BILL

That's the Blessed Virgin, Ned.

NED

She's pretty, huh?

BILL

Not only is she pretty, but she's got a nice personality. *And*
she's the mother of God.

NED

Can I keep it?

BILL

Be good to her and she'll be good to you.

NED

Thanks, Bill.

BILL

Don't mention it.

NED

I wish I could be more like you.

BILL

You don't wanna be like me.

NED

I mean, you just get up and go. You take charge of things.
You're your own man.

BILL
(*seriously*)

Ned, I don't even know where I'm going.

NED

But that's what life's all about! The adventure! The not
knowing!

BILL

No it isn't.

NED

I want adventure. I want romance.

Bill looks at him for a moment and then sighs. He places his hand on Ned's shoulder and tries to explain.

BILL

Ned, there is no such thing as adventure. There's no such thing as romance. There's only trouble and desire.

NED

Trouble and desire.

BILL

That's right. And the funny thing is, when you desire something you immediately get in trouble. And when you're in trouble you don't desire anything at all.

NED

I see.

BILL

It's impossible.

NED

It's ironic.

BILL

It's a fucking tragedy is what it is, Ned.

Bill sees the nun and a young, boyish cop come out of the convent. The nun is talking. She points to the café.

Listen, I gotta go.

NED

So soon?

BILL
(*pushing bike*)

Yeah.

NED

Will you be coming back?

Bill pushes the bike around front, always watching . . .

The cop and nun. The cop looks over, then starts following the angry nun as she marches toward the café.

Bill curses under his breath and wheels the bike as fast as he can.

> BILL
>
> That's hard to say.

> NED
>
> Let me come with you?

EXT. FRONT OF CAFÉ — SAME TIME

Bill muscles the bike on to the front sidewalk just as Dennis comes stepping out of the café with Kim.

> BILL
>
> Come on, Dennis! Hurry up!

> DENNIS
> (*of newspaper*)
>
> Look, there's a story about the robbery!

But Bill is having a hard time starting the bike. Dennis and Kim see . . .

The nun and the cop stop dead in their tracks, alarmed when they see . . .

Kim with Dennis. Nobody moves. Suddenly, Dennis turns and moves awkwardly away, stumbling as he makes for the bike.

This is enough evidence for the nun and cop to start running.

Bill is frantic, but finally gets the bike to roll over. Dennis jumps on. Ned runs along beside them, calling over the roar of the engine . . .

> NED
>
> I'll never forget you guys!

And Kim runs over and grabs Ned by the arm and drags him toward the café.

The cop comes tearing around the corner just as . . . Bill and Dennis peel out and screech into the street.

The cop starts to run back for his car, but the nun reaches him and screams to . . .

Kim, as the girl lets go of Ned.

> NUN
> (*frantic*)
> Kim, look out!

Ned spins to see them and stops when he sees the cop's gun drawn.

> NED
> It's not loaded! Look . . .

BOOM! He fires a shot into the air.

Bill and Dennis speed away up the street.

The cop, with the help of the nun, finally wrestles the gun away from Ned.

The nun grabs Ned by the hair.

> NUN
> Where did you get that weapon?

> NED
> There's nothing but trouble and desire.

The cop grabs the medallion . . .

> COP
> What's this?

> NUN
> It's the holy Blessed Virgin, you idiot!

Ned tries to grab it back, but can't . . .

> NED
> Bill gave it to me!

                              NUN
                            (*to cop*)
Give it back!

                              COP
I can't! It's evidence!

                              NUN
Evidence of what?

                              COP
I don't know!

The nun punches him in the stomach and wrestles the cop to the ground.

Ned falls back and begins mumbling . . .

                              NED
There's nothing but trouble and desire.
There's nothing but trouble and desire.
There's nothing but . . .

Bill and Dennis careen through traffic and make for the outskirts of town . . .

The cop and nun slug it out in the street . . .

Kim leans her head against the glass of the phone booth and closes her eyes . . .

Ned continues . . .

. . . trouble and desire.
There's nothing but trouble and desire.
There's nothing but trouble and desire.
There's nothing but trouble and desire.
There's nothing but trouble and desire . . .

CUT TO BLACK.

A few moments of silence, then . . .

                                KATE
                                (off)
He wanted me to lie for him. But I don't lie for anybody.

EXT. A FIELD — DAY

Kate is in a field of tall swaying grass on the east end of Long Island. She is searching through the grass for something small. Kate is beautiful and blonde. She is in her early thirties and is a straightforward no-nonsense woman. She has her back to her friend, Elina, as she speaks.

                                KATE
We were standing over there by the fence. I followed him
out here because he was so drunk. I was afraid he might
hurt himself. It was so dark.

As she talks we move out across the field to where Elina is also searching. Elina is a younger woman, quiet and mysterious.

He started shooting into the air and shouting. He said he
was going to kill me. Somebody must've heard the shots.
The police came racing down the road here. I remember,
when he heard the sirens, he threw the gun out this way.
                       (pauses and thinks, then . . .)
But it might have been the other field. I can't remember.

She notices Elina is nowhere to be seen. She stops and looks around.

Kate runs forward and finds . . .

Elina lying there, tossed around by violent spasms. Kate falls to her knees but doesn't know what to do.

EXT. A NEARBY ROAD — SAME TIME

Meanwhile, Bill and Dennis are at the side of a back road tending to the worn-out motorcycle. Bill sweats as he works on the engine. Dennis sits a little way off, reading the newspaper.

                              DENNIS
Six hundred and fifty thousand dollars' worth of computer equipment?

                              BILL
Hand me that wrench, will ya?

                              DENNIS
                         (*hands it to him*)
That's a lotta money.

                              BILL
It was a beautiful crime.

                              DENNIS
How did you do it?

                              BILL
I sent Vera up here to get a job at that corporation. This is
like three months ago. Back in Maryland, I even sent her to
computer-training school. Then Frank . . . you don't know
Frank . . . Frank came up and started driving for this particular trucking outfit . . . I set myself up as an independent
contractor selling computer software designs . . .

                              DENNIS
Sounds like a tough way to make a living, Bill.

Bill is having a hard time with the engine.

                              BILL
Fuck!

                              DENNIS
I mean, who are these people? Frank? Vera? How could
you be in love with a woman and not know she's the type
of person that'll turn on you like that?

Bill looks up over the gas tank and thinks, then . . .

                              BILL
She was beautiful.

DENNIS
She was *that* beautiful?

BILL
Yes. Here, hold this.

Dennis comes over and holds a wrench in place while Bill takes a vice grip to whatever it is he's doing.

I was in love, I guess.

DENNIS
You weren't in love. You were thinking with your prick.

Bill looks at him over the engine, then goes back to work.

BILL
What's the difference?

DENNIS
Hey, look.

Bill follows Dennis's gaze and sees . . .

Kate standing in the road, frazzled and out of breath.

EXT. FIELD — MOMENTS LATER

Kate comes running across the field, followed by Bill and Dennis. She reaches Elina and stops, looking on anxiously as Dennis kneels over the unconscious figure in the grass. He listens for breath, checks the pulse, and so on.

Bill stands off to the side a little, feeling useless.

DENNIS
Seems OK. Just unconscious.

BILL
(*to Kate*)
Do you live around here?

KATE
(*cautiously*)
Up the road a little.

EXT. FIELD — DAY

Moments later: Dennis carries Elina in his arms as he follows Kate and Bill back across the field.

INT. BAR & GRILL — LATER

Dennis sits reading at the empty bar. He gets up and goes outside.

EXT. BAR & GRILL — SAME TIME

Dennis comes down off the front porch and hears some activity around back.

EXT. GARAGE — SAME TIME

Dennis finds a fisherman, Martin, filleting fish. Dennis approaches, interested in the fish guts.

> MARTIN
> (*off*)

Is that girl epileptic?

> DENNIS
> (*looks up*)

Excuse me?

> MARTIN

Seems like epilepsy to me.

> DENNIS
> (*realizes*)

Oh. Yeah. I think so too.

> MARTIN

I had a cousin like that. Be fine for months and then bang. Not a lot you can do about it, is there?

> DENNIS
> (*of guts*)

What do you do with these fish guts?

                        MARTIN
Fertilizer.

He gestures toward Kate, who is coming down the steps from her apartment above the bar.

    She wants to plant trees.

INT. BAR — SAME TIME

The place is empty and Bill has his hand in the register. He hears Kate come in the back way and quickly moves away. She comes in. She sees Bill and stops.

                        BILL
Everything OK?

                        KATE
Yes.

                        BILL
                    (*sits at bar*)
So you run this place yourself, huh?

                        KATE
Yes.

                        BILL
                    (*hesitates . . .*)
How about a beer?

As she gets his beer, she is looking out into the street; always on the lookout. Bill looks her up and down while her back is turned. He raises his eyebrows, impressed, then looks away as she returns with the beer.

    Thanks.

Kate watches him, then . . .

                        KATE
Where are you guys from?

Bill lowers his beer and watches her carefully, then . . .

> BILL

Why?

> KATE

I'm expecting someone and I don't know if they're coming alone or not.

> BILL

We're from New York.

> KATE
> (*conversationally*)

On vacation?

> BILL

We're looking for a place called Sagaponeck.

> KATE

What's in Sagaponeck?

He thinks of some appropriate lie.

> BILL
> (*drinks*)

A house my father once lived in.

Kate watches him and nods as he looks away and drinks. She leans back off the bar and stretches her neck to look out into the road.

> KATE

If you guys need a place to stay for a few days, there's the bungalow out back.

Bill lifts his beer, then . . .

> BILL
> (*cool*)

I wouldn't wanna be . . . in the way or anything.

> KATE
> (*opens door*)

You wouldn't be. I'd like you to stay.

She holds his gaze a moment longer, then goes out. Bill sits there, watching her go.

EXT. BAR — SAME TIME

Dennis is busy preparing to leave on the motorcycle. Bill comes out of the bar and looks off at Kate as she walks by. Dennis follows his gaze.

> BILL
> (*of Kate*)
>
> She's pretty, huh?

Dennis looks back out at . . .

Kate as she enters the field. She lifts a bucket of fish guts and a shovel.

> DENNIS
>
> Are you going to fuck her?

Bill shoots him a look, then lights a cigarette and replies . . .

> BILL
>
> Maybe.

Dennis sighs and looks around, impatient.

> DENNIS
>
> I think we should push on.

> BILL
>
> Now?

> DENNIS
>
> Yeah.

Bill looks out at Kate.

> BILL
>
> I'm tired. I think I'm going to rest a while.

Dennis is disappointed and annoyed with Bill. He watches Bill watching Kate. Then . . .

DENNIS
(*of motorcycle*)

Is this thing broken?

BILL

Yeah. It's shot.

Dennis just looks away, then . . .

DENNIS

There's a gas station up the road a few miles down.
Maybe we can get some money for it.

BILL

Good idea.

And Bill walks away toward the field to join Kate.

INT. BAR — LATER

*Martin comes in and finds Dennis at a table with a thin telephone
book. He is searching for the number. Martin watches a while,
then . . .*

MARTIN

What are you doing?

DENNIS

Looking for an address.

MARTIN

You know, they organize that book in alphabetical order.

DENNIS

Oh, I know. All I have is the phone number. I don't know
who I'm looking for.

Martin looks at the number, pauses, then looks back at Dennis.

MARTIN

You gonna go through the whole goddamn book?

DENNIS

There aren't many numbers in it.

MARTIN

Let me help you.

And he takes the book away from Dennis. He stands at the bar and flips through it without looking away from Dennis.

DENNIS

You work here?

MARTIN

No. I gotta charter boat down at the pier.

DENNIS

Have you known Kate long?

MARTIN

I've known her a while. Her ex-husband, Jack, he used to own this place. But then he got into trouble with the law. When she divorced him the judge gave the place to her.

DENNIS

Where is this guy now?

MARTIN

Jack?

DENNIS

Yeah.

MARTIN

In jail. He came back here about two years ago threatening to kill her or something.

DENNIS
(*looks up*)

Really?

MARTIN

Jack's nasty. I mean, he's my best friend and all, but shit, enough's enough.

DENNIS

What happened?

MARTIN

Somebody called the cops and they came and dragged him outta here. Then they found he was wanted for something in Pennsylvania.

DENNIS

Wow.

MARTIN

That's your brother out there?

DENNIS

Yeah.

MARTIN

Your older brother?

DENNIS

Yeah.

MARTIN

You do whatever he says, huh?

DENNIS
(*defensive*)

Well, no. Not always.

MARTIN

He looks bossy.

DENNIS

He's OK.

MARTIN

He likes Kate.

DENNIS

You think so?

MARTIN

Most men like Kate.

DENNIS

Do you?

MARTIN

Yes, I do. You gotta see her in a bathing suit. But she won't have nothing to do with me.

DENNIS

She seems kind of . . . jumpy.

MARTIN

Jumpy women are great.

Dennis just looks across the table at Martin, then goes back to work.

DENNIS

Yeah, well, I wouldn't know about that.

MARTIN

No, I guess you wouldn't.

He finds the number and places the book back on the table before Dennis.

Here you go. See you later.

He goes out, leaving Dennis alone.

INT. PAVILLION — LATER

Out back of the bar there is a roofed party area with a pool table. Dennis stands leaning on his pool cue, studying the table. Bill enters and stands there beside him, watching.

Dennis glances over at him, then returns his attention to the table.

Bill looks on, waiting for something to happen.

But Dennis just continues studying the table. After a while he shifts his weight, frowns, and chalks his pool cue.

Bill stands back and folds his arms, curious as to the shot Dennis plans to make.

But Dennis just stands and studies the table some more.

BILL

They don't move by themselves, you know.

DENNIS
(*ignores him, then . . .*)
There's geometry involved.

But finally, he leans down and shoots. He sinks a few balls.

BILL
Listen. I've been thinking. You're right. Maybe we should ditch the bike somewhere. Kate says we can stay here a couple of extra days.

Dennis looks up from the table, thinks a moment, then hands Bill the photo. Bill sees the address and name added and is surprised.

T. Mulligan? Where'd you find this?

DENNIS
The telephone book.

Bill, impressed, hands back the photo.

BILL
Maybe we can get her to take us out there.

DENNIS
Who?

BILL
Kate.

DENNIS
(*disappointed*)
Oh.

BILL
What?

DENNIS
Nothing.

He looks at the table again, almost shoots, but then . . .

Look, you stay here. I'll go and try to find it myself.

BILL

Don't be an idiot. It could be miles away and you don't
know where you're going. Six ball – corner pocket.

DENNIS

That's a stupid shot. It's easy to make, but it won't leave
me anywhere. Look, Bill, you can have sex with every
woman between here and New York City, but it's not
gonna make you feel any better about Vera.

BILL

How do you know?

DENNIS

We're supposed to be out here trying to find the old man
and you're running around trying to get laid!

BILL

We're supposed to be *what*? No, *you're* the one who's out
here trying to find the old man. I couldn't give a shit!

DENNIS

Then why the hell have you come all this way then?

BILL

Because you asked me to!

DENNIS

Because you had nowhere else to go.

BILL

Look, I'm out here because Mom told me to keep an eye
on you.

DENNIS

Bullshit!

BILL

It's true.

Dennis puts down his pool cue and makes for the door in a huff.

DENNIS

Look, I'm moving on!

But Bill reaches out, grabs him by the collar, and swings him back into the room. Dennis falls against the pool table, and before he can get up again Bill pins him by his throat.

> BILL
>
> Gimme that address!

Dennis gives it to him. Bill lets him go. Dennis waits, still afraid, keeping his eye on Bill.

Bill finds his jacket on a chair. He moves to the door, but stops. He feels bad, but doesn't want to apologize.

> Look, go take care of the motorcycle. Will ya?

> DENNIS
>
> Fuck you, I wanna play pool.

> BILL
> (*furious*)
> You don't play pool! You shoot pool!!

KATE'S CAR — A LITTLE LATER

Kate and Bill are driving past farmland.

> KATE
>
> What's Dennis study at school?

> BILL
>
> Philosophy.
> (*of farms*)
> What do they grow out here anyway?

> KATE
>
> Those are potatoes.

> BILL
>
> Really?

> KATE
>
> It used to be all potato and duck farms out this way years ago. It used to be famous for that.

                          BILL
For ducks?

                          KATE
                        (*smiles*)
Yeah, ducks.

                          BILL
Ducks are funny animals.

                          KATE
I think the hockey team is called the Ducks.

                          BILL
They have a hockey team?

                          KATE
Yeah. I think so. The Long Island Ducks. I don't know,
maybe it's soccer. I'm from Pittsburgh myself.

                          BILL
Long Island's a terminal moraine.

                          KATE
It's a what?

                          BILL
It's the dirt dumped by a glacier when it melts.

She watches him skeptically.

EXT. ROAD — KATE'S CAR

*On the road: Kate and Bill drive by, passing a car parked by the
side of the road.*

*It is a red car. As they pass by, it moves off toward where they've
come from.*

EXT. GAS STATION — DAY

*Dennis comes in off the road, pushing the motorcycle. He is sweat-
ing.*

There is a young guy, Mike, standing at the gas pumps playing 'Greensleeves' on the electric guitar.

Dennis waits for him to finish, then . . .

                              MIKE
        Bonjour, monsieur.

                              DENNIS
    What?

                              MIKE
    It's French.

                              DENNIS
    Oh.

                              MIKE
                            (*of bike*)
    Outta gas?

                              DENNIS
    No. It's busted.

                              MIKE
        Qu'est-ce qui ne va pas?

Dennis thinks for a second, then . . .

                              DENNIS
    You mean, what's wrong with it?

                              MIKE
    You *parlez-vous francais?*

                              DENNIS
    Un peu.

                              MIKE
    Excuse me?

                              DENNIS
    Just a little.

                        MIKE
Far out, man.

And he shakes Dennis's hand. Dennis resumes ...

                        DENNIS
As far as I can tell, the clutch assembly is shot.

                        MIKE
You'd have to leave it for a couple of days.

                        DENNIS
I was thinking you might want to buy it. Cheap. For parts.

                        MIKE
We'd have to talk to the boss about that.

                        DENNIS
Is he here now?

                        MIKE
No. He's getting divorced. He won't be back till later.

Dennis looks back out at the road, then returns to Mike ...

                        DENNIS
Can I leave it here and come back when he returns?

                        MIKE
C'est entendu.

And he underlines this with a wailing little lick on the guitar.

EXT. ROAD IN SAGAPONECK — AFTERNOON

Kate pulls the car to the side of the road and cuts the engine. She and Bill look out at what used to be the address. Bill eventually gets out and looks over the car at ...

The rubble of a burnt down house. Only the foundation remains. He comes around the car and Kate joins him as he approaches the ruins. He casts a glance at the charred mailbox and checks the address. (This is it.) He moves on.

Kate watches as he moves comfortably amidst the blackened rubble and starts poking around like some sort of inspector.

                         KATE
I hate fire.

                         BILL
Don't worry about this.

                         KATE
When I look at something like this, I can't help but wonder if there were people sleeping when it happened.

                         BILL
No. I'm sure no one was hurt.

                         KATE
Really? How do you know?

                         BILL
This was a professional job.

                         KATE
What do you mean?

                         BILL
It looks to me like an insurance scam.

                         KATE
Really? You think so?

                         BILL
Yeah, you can tell by looking at the type of damage what
sort've fire it was.
                    (*looks at the rubble . . .*)
Yeah, this . . . this was an easy nobody-gets-hurt profes-
sional insurance scam.

                         KATE
Seems you know a lot about all this.

                         BILL
I used to do it for a living.

                              KATE
You were in the insurance business?

He looks at her askance.

                              BILL
Well, yeah, sort of.

EXT. BAR — A LITTLE LATER

Dennis comes walking back up the road and sees . . .

Elina standing on the porch watching him.

                            DENNIS
Hi.

                            ELINA
                       (*foreign accent*)
Hello.

                            DENNIS
Wanna cigarette?

                            ELINA
Where is everyone?

                            DENNIS
Bill left with Kate. They'll be back soon, though.

                            ELINA
Bill who?

                            DENNIS
My brother.

                            ELINA
And who are you?

                            DENNIS
I'm Dennis.

He offers his hand but she just looks away. Then . . .

ELINA

My name is Elina.

DENNIS

How are you feeling?

ELINA

I'm feeling fine.

DENNIS

We met up the road. You had a . . .

ELINA

Yes.

DENNIS

I carried you back here.

ELINA

Thank you.

DENNIS

It's OK.

ELINA

It's epilepsy.

DENNIS

I thought so.

ELINA

Come inside.

And they go inside.

EXT. BURNT DOWN HOUSE — DAY

KATE

I think you should know about my husband.

Bill freezes, then . . .

BILL

Husband?

                                  KATE
Ex-husband. He was released from prison a few days ago.

                                  BILL
Prison, huh?

                                  KATE
I just thought I should say something. I mean, to be perfectly honest, I'm a little nervous about being alone at the
place right now. That's why I invited you to stay.

He considers all this, then . . .

                                  BILL
Does he live around here?

                                  KATE
No. He called yesterday from someplace in Pennsylvania.

                                  BILL
What do I need to know?

                                  KATE
Just that I appreciate your company.

                                  BILL
And you and him, you don't get along very well, huh?

                                  KATE
No, we don't.

                                  BILL
What's he like?

                                  KATE
He's psychotic.

INT. BAR — MOMENTS LATER

Elina stands silently watching Dennis, who is sitting.

Finally . . .

                                  DENNIS
Do you live here?

                              ELINA
No.

                              DENNIS
Just visiting?

                              ELINA
Not really.

                              DENNIS
I see.

She joins him at the table.

                              ELINA
What about you?

                              DENNIS
What about me?

                              ELINA
What are you doing here?

                              DENNIS
I'm just passing through.

                              ELINA
That's pretty vague.

                              DENNIS
What kind of accent is that?

                              ELINA
Why?

                              DENNIS
No reason.

                              ELINA
Romanian.

She hears a car approaching and stands to look. She sees something in the road and jumps down to the floor.

Get down! Get down!

He gets down. They press themselves against the wall beside the bar as . . .

Outside: through the screen door we see . . .

The red car slowly pulls into the dirt parking lot. The driver gets out, but we don't see him. He comes up to the front door and stops. All we see is his hand on the window. He turns and leaves.

Elina and Dennis gradually begin breathing again. She gets up.

Dennis, uninformed and confused, raises himself up slowly and approaches the bar.

DENNIS
(*finally*)

What the hell's going on around here?

And she slaps him. His beer goes flying. Elina steps away, seething.

ELINA

Go away from here! You're going to ruin everything! Why have you come?

Dennis is stunned. He holds his face and looks at her, speechless. She suddenly feels confused and guilty and runs out of the room.

Dennis just stands there, holding his face, amazed.

EXT. BURNT DOWN HOUSE — DAY

KATE

So tell me about yourself.

He looks at her and smiles. He tries to think of what to say, but then . . .

BILL

Oh, there's nothing to tell.

KATE

That sounds mysterious.

This bothers Bill, reminding him of his speech the night before. He stops and looks at her.

BILL
(*honestly*)
I don't mean to sound that way.

KATE
You seem like a man with a lot of experience.

BILL
Do I?

KATE
Yes.

BILL
How?

KATE
Somehow very thoughtful, deep.

BILL
Do you have a cigarette?

KATE
No, I don't smoke.

BILL
I'm not deep and it's not that I'm so very thoughtful
either, it's just, you know, I'm tired.

KATE
You're being modest.

Bill almost shouts. But he contains himself.

BILL
I think we should be heading back.

KATE
Are you through here?

BILL
Yeah, I'm all finished.

And he starts to lead her away, but . . .

She spots something at the edge of the property.

He follows her over to ...

A small tree.

> KATE
>
> I want to dig up this tree.

> BILL
>
> Why?

> KATE
>
> I want to transplant it.

INT. GAS STATION/BODY SHOP — THAT AFTERNOON

Mike is sitting there in the cluttered office, practicing French.

> MIKE
> *(reading)*
> 'Est-ce que les nanas sont intéressantes? Are the broads inter-
> esting? Oui, ce sont les nanas intéressantes. Yes, the broads
> are interesting.'

Then Mike's boss, Vic, comes in. He's always in a bad mood.

> VIC
>
> Do I pay you to sit around and talk French all day?

> MIKE
>
> Is it a black chair? Oui, c'est une chaise noire.

> VIC
>
> Move over!

Mike makes room for Vic to pass.

> MIKE
>
> How'd it go?

> VIC
>
> I'm a free man, but I'm broke. What the hell are you
> learning French for anyway?

                                MIKE
It's a beautiful language.

                                 VIC
Yeah, well, so's Navaho!

                                MIKE
I've gotta date with that French check-out girl at the Deli-
Mart.

                                 VIC
She ain't French!

                                MIKE
Sure she is.

                                 VIC
She is not. She's Italian.

                                MIKE
No way!

                                 VIC
She is.

                                MIKE
                        (*throws down the book*)
Fuck!

                                 VIC
What's that motorcycle doing out there?

                                MIKE
Some guy brought it in here earlier. He wants to sell it to
us.

                                 VIC
Does it run?

                                MIKE
It needs a new clutch assembly.

                                 VIC
Who was this guy anyway?

MIKE

I'd never seen him before.

VIC

Did he have the registration for it?

MIKE

I didn't ask.

Vic is immediately suspicious. He walks out and looks the bike over, then comes back in.

VIC

He didn't leave a phone number or anything?

MIKE

Non, monsieur.

VIC

You idiot, that motorcycle could be stolen for all we know!

MIKE

I don't think this guy was a thief.

VIC

Why not?

MIKE

He didn't look like a thief.

VIC

What was he like?

MIKE

Well, he spoke French.

Vic rolls his eyes back and holds his head. Then . . .

VIC

Call in the license plate number and make sure it hasn't been reported as stolen.

MIKE

Oui, monsieur.

                              VIC
And stop that!

                              MIKE
Relax.

EXT. BURNT DOWN HOUSE — A LITTLE LATER

Kate is carefully digging up the tree. Bill stands by, waiting for something to do.

                              BILL
Can I do anything?

                              KATE
                          (*digging*)
No.

                              BILL
You know a lot about trees, huh?

                              KATE
No more than anybody else, I suppose. It's really just a
hobby.

                              BILL
You know, I was reading something somewhere, something
about how — something about, you know, how, uh, trees
are important.

                              KATE
Yeah, I guess they are.

                              BILL
They help the atmosphere.

                              KATE
They help replenish the ozone layer.

                              BILL
That's it! The 'ozone layer.'

KATE

Can you spread that piece of burlap on the ground over here, please.

Bill takes a three-foot square piece of burlap and spreads it out on the ground near the tree. Kate puts down the shovel and steps down into the little ditch she's made around the tree. She carefully but forcefully lifts the tree. Small roots snap as she pulls it out of the ground and places it, finally, on to the burlap.

BILL

I guess it's not good to cut down too many trees, huh?

KATE

No, I guess not. I'm no scientist or anything. It just relaxes me to work with them.

She stands.

BILL

That's what I need, a hobby.

KATE

It keeps me busy and I like that.

Bill grabs her and kisses her on the mouth. It's a long, smooth, well-handled kiss.

He leans back.

Kate is stunned.

Bill holds her gaze, himself breathless and amazed.

CRACK! She slaps him and stomps angrily back to the car.

Bill picks himself up, holding his face, shocked and confused.

Kate closes the trunk, gets in the car, and slams the door. She points out at Bill, furious.

I didn't do one thing to make you think you could do that!

Bill stands there, amazed.

Kate starts the car, heaves a sigh, then looks back out at him.

Are you coming or what?

He hesitates, but then lowers his hand from his face and cautiously approaches the car.

EXT. ROAD/GAS STATION — MOMENTS LATER

Kate goes whizzing by at top angry speed.

EXT. GAS STATION — DAY

Mike is taking money from a young woman customer in a car with a friend.

>   MIKE
> Merci, madame.

The young women giggle appreciatively as they drive away, and Mike grins mischievously as he pockets the money and walks over to . . .

Vic and the sheriff. The sheriff is another tortured and confused man with a drinking problem and a disastrous love life. He is continually preoccupied.

>   SHERIFF
> Yeah. That's it. That's the motorcycle we're looking for.

>   VIC
>   (to Mike)
> See! What did I tell ya!

The sheriff wanders back to his car . . .

>   SHERIFF
> If the guy comes back here, try to detain him.

>   VIC
> Detain him?

>   SHERIFF
> Yeah.

>   VIC
> How?

SHERIFF

I don't know! Offer him a cup of coffee or something.

VIC

And then what?

The sheriff stops and turns, irritated.

SHERIFF

Then, you know, call me! I'll come and arrest him, I guess!

VIC

And in the meantime this French sociopath stabs me and Mike to death!

MIKE

Fuck that, man!

The sheriff flies off the handle.

SHERIFF

Oh, you want my job?

VIC

No, we don't want your job! We just want a little protection!

The sheriff falls back in disbelief, lighting himself a cigarette.

SHERIFF

Protection!

VIC

Yeah!

The sheriff throws his hat to the ground.

SHERIFF

Protection! Certainty! Assurance! Security!

VIC
(*lost*)

Well, yeah. That too, I guess.

> SHERIFF
> (*in a fit*)
>
> You want confidence! A pledge! Safety! Guarantee!
> Promises! Expectation! Consideration! Sincerity! Selfless-
> ness! Intimacy. Attraction. Gentleness. Understanding. An
> understanding without words. Dependence without
> resentment.
>
> (*begins trailing off*)
>
> Affection . . . To belong . . . Possession . . . Loss.

He stops finally and collapses. He sits on the cement base of the gas pumps and hangs his head. Vic looks on in horror.

Mike approaches and lays a hand on the man's shoulder.

> MIKE
>
> Hey, sheriff, everything OK at home?

> SHERIFF
> (*weakly*)
>
> Why do women exist?

Mike pats him on the back, comfortingly.

EXT. BAR — SAME TIME

Dennis is sitting on the porch steps, deep in troubled thought. Kate drives up and skids to a stop in the parking lot. She and Bill get out, slam doors, glare at each other, go their separate ways, etc. . . .

Kate goes inside and lets the screen door slam shut as Bill comes up on to the porch.

Dennis waits, then . . .

> DENNIS
>
> Well?

> BILL
>
> Give me my cigarettes. There's nothing there.

> DENNIS
>
> What do you mean?

BILL
(*hands back photo*)
Whatever was there was burnt right down to the ground.
Recently. Nothing left but ashes.

*Dennis is disappointed. He looks at the address sadly, then up at
Bill.*

Bill is edgy, he comes over and sits beside Dennis.

You know what's going on here, don't you?

DENNIS
(*not sure*)
I guess.

BILL
We're being set up.

DENNIS
What?

BILL
These two . . . Kate and the other one . . . they're . . .
(*leans close*)
. . . lesbian lovers.

Dennis is nonplussed.

Yeah, that's it. Don't you see? I can't believe I didn't see it
sooner. And her *husband*, who's a psychopath, is on his
way back here right now and he's probably plenty pissed
off!
(*and then adds . . .*)
And I don't blame 'im.
(*smokes, then . . .*)
That's why she wants us to hang around, you see. To give
the impression, you know, that there's nothing . . . unnatu-
ral going on around here!

Dennis is still staring at Bill, confused. Bill becomes irritated . . .

Well, say something!

                    DENNIS
                 (*thinks, then . . .*)
What do you want me to say?

                    BILL
Tell me I'm right!

                    DENNIS
I don't know if you're right.

Kate leans out the screen door, no longer angry . . .

                    KATE
Would you like to eat with us?

*Bill doesn't respond. He just stares off at the road. Dennis looks back
at her and nods politely . . .*

                    DENNIS
Yes, thank you. Can we give you a hand with anything?

                    KATE
                 (*re-enters*)
No, thank you.

Dennis watches her go, then looks back at Bill.

EXT. PAVILLION — LATER

                    DENNIS
I don't know if she prefers women or not, but Elina's definitely involved.

                    BILL
Who's Elina?

                    DENNIS
The girl. The other one.

                    BILL
What the hell kind of name is Elina?

DENNIS
(*significantly*)

Romanian.

BILL

Romanian?

DENNIS

Weird, huh?

BILL

Why's it weird?

DENNIS

Well, have you ever met a Romanian?

BILL

No.

DENNIS

I think she's involved.

BILL

With what?

DENNIS

With Dad.

BILL

Dennis, pull yourself together.

DENNIS

She slapped me.

BILL

Who slapped you?

DENNIS

Elina.

BILL

Elina slapped you?

DENNIS

Yeah.

                              BILL
What did you do to her?

                            DENNIS
I didn't do anything to her!

                              BILL
You didn't try to kiss her?

                            DENNIS
                          (*confused*)
No! Why would I do that?

                              BILL
I don't know, she's kinda cute.

Dennis looks back at the house, remembering.

                            DENNIS
Look, that's not the point. She slapped me because she
knows who we are. And she's afraid we're gonna lead the
cops to Dad.

                              BILL
She told you this?

                            DENNIS
No. But it seems pretty clear to me.

                              BILL
Dennis, just because a girl slaps you for making a pass at her
doesn't mean she's a member of some terrorist organization.

                            DENNIS
I didn't make a pass at her!

                              BILL
Dennis, the only clue you have to Dad is a burnt down
house. Give it up. He's gone. Either that or he went up in
smoke with the house.

                            DENNIS
There's more, though. Somebody drove up in a car and
looked around the place.

                          BILL

Was it the police?

                          DENNIS

I couldn't see who it was.

                          BILL

Did they see you?

                          DENNIS

No. We were hiding.

                          BILL

You and Elina were hiding?

                          DENNIS

Yeah.

                          BILL

What was she hiding for?

                          DENNIS
                       (*exasperated*)

That's what I'm trying to tell you! She was hiding for
some reason, and I think it's because she's involved somehow with Dad!

Bill paces a little, thinking. He looks back at Dennis, very serious.

                          BILL

Look, if it was the cops, they're probably looking for me,
not Dad.

                          DENNIS

I didn't think of that.

They stand there in silence for a while, then . . .

                          BILL

Come on, let's go eat.

INT. BAR — EVENING

The place is empty. No business. Kate and Elina sit at separate

tables while Bill and Dennis sit at another. Everyone eats in silence.
Finally . . .

> DENNIS
>
> Not much business here, is there?

> KATE
> (*amiably*)
>
> It's the end of the season.

> DENNIS
> (*nods*)
>
> I see.
> (*looks to Elina, considering, then back to Kate . . .*)
> This is good food.

> BILL
> (*impatient*)
>
> Will you shut up and eat!

Dennis swings back around and continues eating. Kate looks on,
annoyed with Bill.

> KATE
>
> Elina, you can sleep on the couch upstairs tonight if you
> want. Bill and Dennis are going to spend the night in the
> bungalow.

> ELINA
>
> Thank you. That will be fine.

Dennis keeps eating, but Bill happens to look up and comes eye to
eye with Kate as she gets up and leaves the room.

Elina gets up and goes outside. She reappears behind Bill and Den-
nis, listening at the window.

> BILL
>
> What do you say, wanna go?

> DENNIS
> (*surprised*)
>
> No.

BILL
(*urgently*)
I think we should split. Right away.

DENNIS
I want to talk to Elina. Find out what she knows.

Bill pushes his plate away and leans on the table, deep in troubled thought.

BILL
I'm afraid of what went down back there with Ned.

DENNIS
Well, then it's better that you stay here, isn't it?

BILL
This isn't a good place for me to stay.

DENNIS
Why not?

Bill glances over toward the kitchen where Kate can be seen through the door.

BILL
Because if I don't leave right now, I might not leave.

Dennis looks back over his shoulder at the kitchen, then returns to Bill.

DENNIS
I thought you said she was a lesbian?

BILL
(*shrugs*)
I was pissed off. I lost my head.

Dennis pauses, watching Bill. Then . . .

DENNIS
I think she likes you.

BILL
You do?

                          DENNIS
    Definitely.

*Bill just sighs and looks at his hands. Dennis waits a moment, then
goes outside after Elina.*

EXT. BAR — SAME TIME

*Dennis comes out and Elina ducks into a tool shed. He passes by her
and walks out to the garage.*

*Elina comes out and checks to see if he's gone. She climbs the stairs
to Kate's living quarters. Dennis comes back around from the garage
and hears Elina enter the apartment.*

He hurries up after her.

INT. KATE'S APARTMENT — SAME TIME

*Dennis searches the place, and Elina eludes him by hiding in the
various rooms.*

Finally, he spots her and chases her into the bathroom.

She closes the door and locks herself in.

INT. BAR — SAME TIME

*Bill lingers by the bar as Kate cleans up. She walks by him and he
stops her. She stands there holding the dishes for a moment, then . . .*

                          BILL
    Look, I'm sorry.

                          KATE
    I didn't slap you because you kissed me. I slapped you
    because you thought I couldn't refuse.

                          BILL
    I kissed you because I couldn't help myself.

*They stand there in silence, both looking around the room awk-
wardly. Finally, she looks back at him.*

KATE

If you kiss me now, I promise I won't hit you.

They look into one another's eyes and wait. Then . . .

She drops all the dishes to the floor. They rush together and kiss passionately.

INT. KATE'S APARTMENT — SAME TIME

Dennis stands outside the bathroom.

ELINA

Leave me alone!

DENNIS

Look, I don't mean any harm. I just want to talk.

ELINA

Go talk to someone else!

He sighs and rubs his head. He walks halfway up the hall, thinking, then comes back to the door.

DENNIS

Do you know who I am?

Silence . . .

Come on! Answer me! Do you know who me and my brother are?

No answer at first. Then, quietly . . .

ELINA

Yes.

Dennis sighs, relieved, but far from satisfied.

DENNIS

You know my father?

ELINA

Yes.

>   DENNIS
> Do you know where he is?

>   ELINA
> No.

>   DENNIS
> Why are you afraid of me?

>   ELINA
> I'm not afraid of you.

>   DENNIS
> You know what I mean.

>   ELINA
> I'm afraid you'll ruin everything.

>   DENNIS
> Ruin what? His escape?

No answer.

> You can't stay in there for ever.

>   ELINA
>   (*quietly*)
> Go away.

Exhausted and hurt, Dennis gives up for now. He sighs and walks slowly up the hall and out of the house.

EXT. BAR — MOMENTS LATER

Dennis comes around the building and walks up on to the front porch. But he stops when he happens to glance into the bar and sees . . .

Bill helping Kate clean up.

EXT. BAR/PORCH — MOMENTS LATER

Dennis quietly steps back down and sits on the stoop. He sits there silently for a time, when he suddenly realizes . . .

Elina is standing at the far end of the porch.

He watches her as she stands there looking at him. Finally she comes over and sits on the stoop too.

ELINA

I think something must have happened.

DENNIS

You mean, you think something went wrong?

ELINA

I don't know. I'm only supposed to wait here.

DENNIS

For him?

ELINA

Either for him or someone else who will take me to him.
(*looks away, sadly*)
But he should have been here by now.
(*then, to Dennis*)
He's done it again. He's left me behind.

She hangs her head, infinitely disappointed. Dennis waits, respectfully, but then . . .

DENNIS

Excuse me for asking, but . . . are you and my father, you know, close?

ELINA

Yes.

DENNIS

How close?

ELINA

Very close.

DENNIS

You mean, you're his girlfriend?

She gets really defensive.

ELINA

Have you got something to say about that?

DENNIS

Just that the man's nearly seventy years old.

ELINA

You and your brother both put together will never be the
man your father is!

DENNIS

Well, maybe not.
                    (*gets up and paces, then . . .*)
Listen, you've got to help me to see him.

ELINA

Please don't ask me to do that.

DENNIS

I won't ruin anything. I just want to talk to him.

ELINA

It's too late for that.
                    (*looks down, hopelessly . . .*)
And besides, he's probably gone.

DENNIS
                    (*comes closer*)
What was supposed to happen?

ELINA

When?

DENNIS

When he got here.

ELINA

We were going to leave the country.

DENNIS

How?

ELINA

I don't know. At first I thought you must be the person
who would take me to Bill.

DENNIS

You call my father Bill?

ELINA

Well, what am I supposed to call him?

DENNIS

Even my mother calls him William.

Elina jumps up, runs into the parking lot, and throws herself on the ground with a sob.

Dennis gets up, terribly ashamed of himself, and rushes over to her.

Listen, I didn't mean anything by that. I'm sorry. Really.

ELINA
(*distraught*)

He's not coming! I know it! He's left me behind! I know he has!

DENNIS

Oh, hey, come on! He wouldn't do that! He'll be here. He will.

She looks up at him.

ELINA

How do you know! You don't even know the man!

DENNIS

I know he's a man of his word. I know he believes in things!

She watches him a moment, then sits up and collects herself, staring at the ground.

ELINA

He's a womanizer.

DENNIS
(*reluctantly*)

Yeah, well, he wouldn't leave a woman as attractive as yourself behind.

She looks at him, gives him the once over, then looks away.

                    ELINA
   You are a womanizer too, then.

                    DENNIS
   I'm just trying to make you feel good.

She looks back at him, then stands up.

                    ELINA
   Thank you.

Martin comes roaring up the road in his pick-up. He skids to a stop in the parking lot, hops out of the truck, falls to his knees in the dirt, and screams . . .

                    MARTIN
   I CAN'T STAND THE QUIET!

INT. PAVILLION — NIGHT

Roaring rhythmic rock and roll fills the pavillion.

Tables have been upended.

Empty beer cans and bottles of booze line the bar.

Kate, Bill, Elina, Dennis, and Martin dance.

It's hot.

Steamy.

Sloppy.

Fun.

INT. PAVILLION — LATER

A drunken debate about Madonna and economics.

Angle: close on Kate . . .

                    KATE
   Madonna exploits her sexuality on her own terms.

ELINA

What does it mean to exploit your sexuality on your own terms?

BILL

It means you name the price.

KATE

Madonna is a successful business person.

MARTIN

I like old-fashioned, straight ahead rock and roll.

DENNIS

She sings OK.

Angle: close on Elina . . .

ELINA

The representation of female sexuality that she offers is of strength and self-determination.

MARTIN

I don't listen to much new popular music myself.

KATE

Love songs are usually about weakness.

BILL

You can learn a lot about love from popular music.

ELINA

Is there a difference between exploiting your own body for profit and having someone else exploit it for you?

Angle: close on Dennis . . .

DENNIS

Everyone is involved with exploitation: the person whose body it is, the salesperson, and the audience that is entertained.

BILL

The significant distinction is: who earns more money, the exploited body or the salesperson?

KATE
And what about the audience?

DENNIS
What about them?

Angle: close on Bill . . .

The nature of exploitation never improves, it only
changes.

BILL
Where did you read that?

ELINA
Is it a feminist achievement for a woman to maintain such
control over her own career?

MARTIN
I thought we were talking about music?

BILL
Exploitation of sexuality has achieved a new respectability
because some of the women whose bodies are exploited
have gained control over that exploitation.

DENNIS
They earn more money.

BILL
(*concurring*)
They call the shots.

KATE
They're not thought of as victims.

BILL
If they earn the most money, no, they probably don't
think of themselves as victims either.

DENNIS
But what about the audience?

BILL

What about them?

Angle: close on Martin . . .

MARTIN

Hendrix. Clapton. Allman Brothers. Zeppelin. Tull. BTO.
Stones. Grand Funk Railroad. James Gang. T. Rex. MC5.
Skynyrd. Lesley West. Blackmore. The Who. The old
Who. Ten Years After. Santana. Thin Lizzy. Aerosmith.
Hot fucking Tuna.

INT. PAVILLION — LATER

*It's quiet now. Kate and Bill are dancing close and slow to some old
tune on the jukebox. Martin is talking to himself at the bar. Kate
lays her head on Bill's shoulder as they dance across the room.*

KATE
(sleepy)

After a while, I'm going to plant many different kinds of
trees. Eucalyptus, olive trees, Japanese maples, mimosa
. . . all different kinds of trees.

EXT. YARD — SAME TIME

Elina brings Dennis a glass of water.

ELINA

You shouldn't drink so much.

DENNIS

I guess not.

ELINA

Here, drink this.

DENNIS

What is it?

ELINA

Water.

He drinks a little. They sit in silence a moment, looking at one another, then Dennis leans forward and kisses her. He leans back.

You shouldn't do that.

                           DENNIS
Why not?

                           ELINA
Because I'm your father's girlfriend.

                           DENNIS
My father's a womanizer. He's a married man. And he stood you up.

                           ELINA
You have no respect for your father.

                           DENNIS
I don't know him. But I respect his taste in women.

                           ELINA
So then go make love to your mother.

INT. PAVILLION — SAME TIME

Kate is lying on the pool table, asleep.

Bill sits at the table with Martin, watching her sleep.

                           BILL
Pretty woman.

                           MARTIN
She's got principles!

                           BILL
A principled pretty woman.

                           MARTIN
Kate ain't told a lie in her whole life.

                           BILL
Have you known her long?

MARTIN

For a while. I used to work with her ex-husband.

BILL

You mean the angry and dangerous psychotic ex-husband?

MARTIN

Now just hold on. Jack may be dangerous, and maybe even psychotic, but I don't think he's angry.

BILL

How long have they been divorced?

MARTIN

Why? Are you looking for a wife?

BILL

I was just wondering.

MARTIN

Two and a half years, maybe.

BILL

She been alone all that time?

MARTIN

I proposed to her.

BILL
(*amused*)

Really?

MARTIN

As soon as I knew Jack was safely behind bars, yeah. I jumped at it.

BILL

You snake.

MARTIN

She won't have nothing to do with me, though.

BILL

No, huh?

MARTIN

Sometimes I think she just don't like men.

BILL
(*indignant*)

Bullshit! She likes me.

MARTIN
(*laughs*)

Yeah, I bet all the girls like you!

BILL
(*defensive*)

What's that supposed to mean?

Martin stands to go.

MARTIN

I gotta go.

BILL

No!

MARTIN

I get too emotional when I drink.

BILL

Have another beer!

MARTIN

I gotta get up early!

BILL

No, you don't. Sit down.

MARTIN
(*sits back down*)

I get too emotional when I drink.

BILL

Will you have another beer?

MARTIN
(*stands up again*)

I gotta go!

BILL

Why?

MARTIN

I gotta get up early in the morning.

BILL

Martin, you're drunk!

MARTIN

And emotional.

BILL

You gotta go.

MARTIN

Why?

BILL

You gotta get up early in the morning.

MARTIN

Yeah. You're right. Here, have another drink.

BILL

No. I gotta get up early in the morning too.

MARTIN

No, you don't. Sit down.

They drink.

BILL

Go on. Get outta here.

Martin slaps Bill on the shoulder and leaves.

Bill watches him go, then looks over and sees . . .

Kate sleeping on the pool table.

She wakes up and sits on the edge of the pool table.

KATE

What time is it?

BILL

It's almost morning.

KATE

I'm glad you stayed.

BILL

Is it true you've never told a lie?

KATE

No, I've told plenty of lies.

BILL

Why?

KATE

Because I thought they would make things easier.

BILL

And they didn't?

KATE

No. They made things worse.

BILL

You should probably go back to the house and get some sleep.

KATE

I want to sleep alone tonight.

BILL
(*easily*)

OK.

KATE
(*concerned*)

I don't want to lead you on.

BILL

You're not.

KATE

How long will you stay?

BILL

I'm going to spend the rest of my life here.

KATE

Really?

BILL

With you.

KATE

You seem pretty confident about that.

BILL

I am.

KATE

I hardly know you.

BILL

Oh, you'll get to know me in time. I'm gonna dig up that field and plant every tree you can name. I'll work all day and bartend at night.

She watches him closely.

KATE

You're not just trying to impress me, are you?

BILL

I know what I want when I see it.

KATE

Do you always get what you want?

BILL

Usually.

KATE

Really, everything?

BILL

Well, not always.

KATE

Life gets easier when you realize you can't have everything.

BILL

You can't?

KATE

No.

BILL

What can you have?

KATE

I think you can have what you want, or what you need. But you can't have both. Usually. Unless you're very lucky.

BILL

Or very smart.

KATE

I guess I'm not very lucky or smart.

BILL

Everything is different now.

KATE

Other men have loved me, you know.

BILL

I figured as much.

KATE

And I've loved them too.

BILL

That's only natural.

KATE

And all of those men have gone out of my life. Why do you think that is?

                                    BILL

Because they weren't me.

                                    KATE

And who are you?

                                    BILL

I'm the man who is going to make you happy.

                                    KATE

That's very romantic.

                                    BILL

Be good to her and she'll be good to you.

                                    KATE

Are you sure you're not just trying to seduce me?

                                    BILL

It's you who has seduced me.

*They lock gazes for a moment, then move together as one and kiss.
Finally, she steps back and smiles.*

                                    KATE

We'll see.

EXT. YARD — SAME TIME

Bill comes out and finds Dennis still sitting there.

                                    BILL

You OK?

                                    DENNIS

Yeah.

                                    BILL

Where's Elina?

                                    DENNIS

She went to bed.

                                    BILL

She tell you anything?

                    DENNIS
Plenty.

                    BILL
Yeah, like what?

                    DENNIS
She's Dad's girlfriend.

                    BILL
                 (*incredulous*)
Bullshit!

                    DENNIS
It's true. She loves him even though he stood her up and
left her behind.

                    BILL
                 (*comes closer*)
Was he supposed to meet her?

                    DENNIS
Yeah.

                    BILL
Here?

                    DENNIS
Yeah.

                    BILL
That bastard!

Dennis hears something and looks out into the dark field.

                    DENNIS
What was that?

                    BILL
What?

                    DENNIS
Listen.

They listen.

Nothing.

Dennis looks back at Bill.

> BILL
>
> Listen, Dennis. I'm gonna stay here with Kate.

> DENNIS
>
> You mean, for good?

> BILL
>
> Yeah.

Dennis considers this and looks out at the night.

> DENNIS
>
> What will you do?

> BILL
>
> I'll run this tree farm over here she wants to start.

> DENNIS
>
> A nursery.

> BILL
>
> Yeah, a nursery.
> > (*sips his beer, then . . .*)
> I'd be good at that.

> DENNIS
>
> You'll give up crime?

Bill gives him a sharp look, as if Dennis were trying to pick a fight with him. But he can see his brother is just honestly inquisitive. Bill relaxes and looks away.

> BILL
>
> Crime isn't a way of life for me. It's a . . . knowledge. It's an intelligence about things that I've been able to . . . capitalize on. But yeah, I'll give it up.

Again, Dennis hears something. Bill has heard it too. They stand still and listen. Then . . .

> That's just the breeze.

DENNIS
I thought I heard footsteps.

They listen again.

Nothing.

Finally . . .

It's nothing, I guess.

SLAP! Now they have definitely heard the rear kitchen door slap shut. They freeze and stare at one another.

INT./EXT. BAR — MOMENTS LATER

Bill leads the way as he and Dennis creep furtively into the bar through the back door, listening carefully.

Bill grabs a knife off the counter.

Dennis grabs a cleaver.

Bill bumps into a chair and motions for Dennis to be quiet.

They continue through the bar and come out on to the front porch.

They stop and listen.

Then, Bill sees Dennis's cleaver and takes it from him.

BILL
Gimme that.

EXT. BACK OF BAR/YARD — MOMENTS LATER

Bill and Dennis come around back with their weapons at the ready.

Bill kicks open the gate to the yard and knocks over a bucket of fish guts.

BILL
Fuck! What is that?

DENNIS
It's fertilizer.

Bill puts down his cleaver and takes the shovel. They begin cleaning up the mess of fish innards he has spilled.

Then Kate opens the door and looks out at them. They stop and look up at her.

> KATE
>
> What happened?

> BILL
>
> We thought we heard something.

> KATE
>
> Yeah, me too.

She looks around into the darkness, worried, and goes back inside.

Bill and Dennis drop what they're doing and follow.

INT. KITCHEN — MOMENTS LATER

Kate comes in and sits.

> KATE
>
> It's him. I know it's him.

> BILL
>
> Don't panic. Me and Dennis will stay up till daylight.

> DENNIS
>
> Where's Elina?

> KATE
>
> She's asleep on the couch.

> DENNIS
>
> No, she's not.

They see that the couch is empty and the window wide open.

INT. HALLWAY — MOMENTS LATER

Dennis steps into the hall.

                         DENNIS
  It's him!

                          BILL
  It's who?

                          KATE
  It's Jack!

                         DENNIS
  No, it's Dad!

                          KATE
  Whose dad?

                          BILL
  Our dad.

                          KATE
  What?

Dennis approaches Kate.

                         DENNIS
  Kate, what does Tara mean?

                          KATE
  Tara?

                         DENNIS
  T-A-R-A.

She looks at the two of them, at a loss, then . . .

                          KATE
  That's the name of Martin's boat.

Dennis nearly falls over. He looks at Bill.

EXT. KATE'S HOUSE — MOMENTS LATER

*The sky is getting light. Dennis gets into Kate's car; Bill tries to stop
him.*

> BILL

Dennis, just let 'em go!

> DENNIS

No way! Not after I've gotten this close!

> BILL

He must have known you're here and he didn't want to see you!

> DENNIS

This isn't about what he wants! This is about what I want!

Dennis takes off.

Bill watches him drive away, then looks back at Kate.

EXT. KATE'S HOUSE — MOMENTS LATER

Bill comes up the stairs to where Kate stands in the doorway.

They say nothing, but she goes inside and leaves the door ajar.

After a few moments, Bill follows her in.

EXT. GAS STATION — MOMENTS LATER

Dennis goes roaring by and passes . . .

Vic, who is hosing down the pavement around the gas pumps. He stops and watches Dennis disappear down the road, then drops the hose and walks into the office.

INT. OFFICE — SAME TIME

Vic enters and picks up the phone. He dials.

EXT. DOCK — MOMENTS LATER

It's dawn and the sky is getting bright. Dennis swerves off the road, drives over a small embankment, and charges right out on to the dock.

Elina and . . .

William McCabe (Dad) are climbing into Martin's big old boat, the
Tara. They stop, look up, and watch as . . .

Dennis jumps out of the car and comes striding purposefully along
the dock toward them.

Elina looks at Dad. He looks at her and she looks down. Dad looks
back out at Dennis.

He steps back up on to the dock and walks a few paces forward,
then stops and waits for Dennis to reach him.

Dennis is almost there, walking straight for the powerful and hand-
some old man, staring him dead in the eyes the whole time.

Dad glares out at him and lets him approach.

Dennis stops about three feet away from him. He says nothing.

Dad holds his son's stare with a challenging smirk.

Elina steps up on to the dock and waits anxiously.

Finally . . .

DAD
Who do you think you are?

DENNIS
I'm your son.

Dad is as still and immovable as rock. Dennis is not intimidated,
but he looks down at his feet a second, then straight back at the old
man.

Dad puts out his hand.

Dennis looks at it, then reaches out to take it. They shake hands
firmly. Then . . .

POW! Dad smacks Dennis in the head. Dennis falls back.

DAD
(*pointing at him*)
How old are you, Dennis?

DENNIS

Twenty-three.

DAD

Keep your hands off my woman! You got that!

Dennis still has to shake his head clear before he can make sense of this. Finally, and genuinely . . .

DENNIS
(*groggy*)

OK.

Dad steps back.

DAD

OK. We're even. Want some coffee?

DENNIS

Sure.

When they reach her at the end of the dock, Elina hauls off and slaps Dad in the face.

DAD

What!

Then she changes her mind and falls against his chest, exhausted. He puts his arm around her and looks at Dennis.

Dennis looks from his father to . . .

Martin, who steps out of the cabin of the boat. He shoves Martin and Martin shoves him back.

INT. KATE'S APARTMENT — SAME TIME

Bill and Kate are lying together in her bed. He's asleep, but she's still on the alert. She gets out of the bed, careful not to wake Bill.

EXT. KATE'S HOUSE — MOMENTS LATER

She comes down the stairs from the apartment and sets right the bucket Bill knocked over the night before. She then sees the red car parked in front of the bar.

INT. BAR — MOMENTS LATER

Kate approaches the back door, but stops when she sees . . .

Through the bar, a man sitting on the front porch. She is frightened and backs away quietly.

INT. KATE'S APARTMENT — MOMENTS LATER

Kate comes in and sits on the edge of the bed. She gently wakes Bill.

> KATE
>
> He's here.

> BILL
>
> Who is?

> KATE
>
> Jack.

EXT. HOUSE — MOMENTS LATER

Bill, still half asleep, staggers down the stairs and kicks over the fish guts again.

INT. BAR — MOMENTS LATER

Kate and Bill creep up to the back door and look through at . . .

Jack, sitting on the front porch.

He smokes with his back to them and stares out at the road. Bill collects himself, silently reassures Kate, then comes into the bar and approaches the front door.

EXT. FRONT PORCH — SAME TIME

Bill reaches the front door, pauses, then steps out on to the porch. He tries to seem imposing as he looks over at Jack, but he stops.

He is a little surprised.

Jack is a small man: weary, strangely intense, and with a scar across his face, but not the maniac Bill expected.

Jack doesn't acknowledge Bill; he just stares out at the road and smokes.

Bill relaxes a little. He glances back at Kate, then steps over and sits at a safe distance from Jack. Jack still doesn't react. Bill watches him from out the corner of his eye, trying nevertheless to be a forceful presence.

Jack very slowly leans over to Bill, still with his eyes straight ahead. This alarms Bill, but then he leans cautiously closer to Jack, thinking Jack wants to say something. But Jack just sits back, having changed his mind.

Bill looks at him oddly, then sits back himself, becoming impatient. But then Jack throws down his cigarette and sighs . . .

JACK

I just came back for my leather jacket.
(looks at Bill)
I'm cold.

EXT. ON THE DECK OF THE *TARA* — DAY

Elina, Dennis, and Martin repeat after Dad as he reads aloud from a book entitled Anarchy.

DAD

'We do not know when the revolution will triumph.
– But we know that the revolution is with us.
– And there is no doubt that if the revolution is crushed,
– it will be crushed because, on this occasion, we have been defeated;
– and never because we believed it useful to compromise.'

DENNIS

Listen, Dad, ah . . . can we talk?

DAD

Sit still, Dennis.
'We will have on events
the kind of influence
which will reflect our numerical strength

our energy
our intelligence
and our intransigence.
Even if we are defeated,
we will have performed a worthy task.
For human progress is measured
by the persistence and regeneration
of selflessness
and a willingness
to see beyond the limits of our own time.
And if today we fall without compromising,
we can be sure of victory tomorrow!'

He closes the book.

EXT. A DIFFERENT PART OF THE BOAT — MOMENTS LATER

Dad sits and looks out at the water. Dennis approaches.

> DENNIS
> Dad, did you bomb the Pentagon?

Dad looks back over his shoulder at him.

> DAD
> What?

> DENNIS
> You heard me. Are you responsible for that bombing in
> '68?

Dad thinks before answering, eyeing Dennis carefully.

> DAD
> Why do you wanna know that?

> DENNIS
> I need to know if my father is a premeditated murderer.

> DAD
> Is that why you've come looking for me?

> DENNIS

Yes.

> DAD
> (*chuckles*)

Dennis, you impress me more and more by the minute.

> DENNIS

You haven't answered my question.

> DAD

No.

> DENNIS

No what?

> DAD

No, I didn't.

> DENNIS

No, you didn't plant the bomb?

> DAD

That's right.

> DENNIS

Do you know who did?

> DAD

No. But even if I did, I wouldn't have told.

> DENNIS

So you've been in hiding all this time for nothing?

Dad just shrugs and looks out at the water. He pauses, then looks back . . .

> DAD

I'm good at it.

He walks off.

EXT. ANOTHER PART OF THE BOAT — MOMENTS LATER

Elina is tense, pacing back and forth and watching Dennis.

Dad waits. She stops and looks at him.

> DAD

Relax.

She storms off in a huff.

EXT. GAS STATION — TEN MINUTES LATER

Dennis comes driving up the road and pulls up before the pumps. He gets out and . . .

Mike comes out from the garage to meet him.

> DENNIS

Good morning.

> MIKE

Bonjour.

> DENNIS

So is your boss interested in buying the motorcycle?

> MIKE

Not really.

> DENNIS

How much will he give me?

> MIKE

Not much.

> DENNIS

How much?

> MIKE

Fifty bucks, maybe.

> DENNIS
> (*impressed*)

Fifty bucks! That's plenty!

> MIKE
> (*desperate*)

You can get a lot more somewhere else!

Dennis is moving toward the office.

> DENNIS

Is he inside?

> MIKE

Can you come back tomorrow?

> DENNIS

I've got to leave today.

> MIKE

Look, he's in a real bad mood.

> DENNIS

Besides, I'll take half that much.

He enters the office.

INT. OFFICE — SAME TIME

Dennis comes in, followed by Mike.

Vic appears from behind the desk with a gun trained on Dennis.

Dennis freezes.

> VIC

Hold it right there, pal!

> DENNIS
> (*to Mike*)

What is this?

> MIKE

Vic, you never told me you were packing a rod!

> VIC
> (*to Dennis*)

What have you done to Kate?

> DENNIS

I haven't done anything to Kate!

VIC

That's her car out there, isn't it?

DENNIS

I just borrowed it!

VIC

Yeah, right, the way you borrowed that motorcycle!

DENNIS

The motorcycle was given to us!

VIC

To *us*?

DENNIS
(*corrects himself*)

To me.

VIC

You said us.

DENNIS

I don't have to talk to you.

VIC

Shut up and sit down!

Dennis sits. Vic puts the gun to his neck.

DENNIS

Go ahead and call her!

MIKE

Call who?

DENNIS

Call Kate. She'll tell you. She lent me the car.

INT. BAR — SAME TIME

Kate and Jack are sitting in the bar. Jack is eating breakfast. Kate hears the phone ring and goes to answer it.

INT. KATE'S APARTMENT — SAME TIME

Bill, in the bedroom, hears a car pull away and looks out the window.

EXT. BAR — MOMENTS LATER

Kate and Jack drive away in the red car.

INT. KATE'S APARTMENT — SAME TIME

Bill leans back away from the window, wondering.

INT. GAS STATION — MOMENTS LATER

Dennis watches as Jack and Kate pull up and get out of the car.

Mike and Vic are suddenly terrified.

> MIKE
>
> Hey, is that . . . Jack?

> VIC
>
> I hope not.

> MIKE
>
> I think it is.

Jack stands by the car as Kate walks up to the office and enters.

Once in, she stops and looks at Mike and Vic.

Is that Jack?

Kate takes Vic's gun and throws it aside.

> KATE
>
> Go outside!

Mike and Vic look out at Jack fearfully.

> VIC
>
> But, Kate . . .

> KATE
>
> Go on!

They scurry out, scared.

Kate moves over to Dennis.

> Dennis, what's going on?

> DENNIS
> I'm not sure.

Vic and Mike burst back in.

> VIC
> We can't let him go, Kate. The sheriff's on his way over.

> KATE
> But what has he done!

> VIC
> He stole that motorcycle and he was involved in some big
> robbery the day before yesterday! It's right here in the
> paper.

He shows her the paper.

> KATE
> Get out of here!

They run back out. Kate turns to Dennis.

> Is that true?

> DENNIS
> No.

Kate is at a loss.

> KATE
> I'm going to go get Bill.

Dennis looks up, urgently.

> DENNIS
> No! Don't let Bill come down here.

This cuts straight through her. A suspicion seeps into her.

Dennis sees this.

KATE

Why?

DENNIS

Just don't.

Kate looks away, hurt.

Dennis stands and puts his hand on her shoulder.

Listen. I'm sorry about this.

She looks up weakly.

KATE

Can I do anything?

DENNIS

Yes.

KATE

What?

Dennis hesitates, then . . .

DENNIS

Help Bill get away to Martin's boat.

KATE

I can't do that.

DENNIS

Please just do it, our father's there waiting for him.

She hangs her head, hopelessly, and sighs. Then . . .

KATE

Is your father a criminal too?

DENNIS

No. He's a baseball player.

EXT. GAS STATION — MOMENTS LATER

Kate and Jack leave in their respective cars just as the sheriff drives up.

The sheriff staggers from his squad car and bursts into the office.

MIKE

Morning, sheriff.

SHERIFF

Yeah, right! Get me some coffee!

INT. GAS STATION

The sheriff staggers in and collapses into a chair.

SHERIFF

Are you the suspect?

DENNIS

Yes.

SHERIFF

What's your name?

DENNIS

Dennis.

The sheriff lights up a cigarette and takes a deep, consoling drag. He looks out the window and shakes his head in hopelessness. Then . . .

SHERIFF

.I don't know. I don't have anybody to blame but myself.
            (*leans toward Dennis . . .*)
I mean, right from the start it was a painful and unsatisfy-
ing relationship!

Dennis is at a loss.

DENNIS
(*carefully*)

I'm sorry.

The sheriff falls back in his chair and sighs tragically. Finally . . .

SHERIFF
(*slowly*)

Life . . . is sad.

EXT. BAR — MOMENTS LATER

Kate pulls into the parking lot and gets out of her car as . . .

Jack pulls up alongside of her. He gets out, but stands there by the car with the engine still running.

She comes over to him, tired and angry.

> JACK
>
> Thanks for breakfast.

> KATE
>
> It's OK.

> JACK
>
> Take care of yourself.

> KATE
>
> I will.

Jack gets back in the car and she watches as he drives off up the road.

Finally, she turns to enter the bar.

Bill comes out on to the porch as she ascends the steps.

> BILL
>
> What happened?

She shoves him out of the way and goes inside. Bill is worried. He follows her in.

INT. BAR — SAME TIME

Kate collapses at a table.

> KATE
> *(screams)*
> Why are all the MEN in my life CRIMINAL?

This stops Bill dead. He pauses, then glances back out at the road. He steps a little closer.

                          BILL

Where's Dennis?

                          KATE

He's been arrested.

Bill is shocked.

                          BILL

For what?

                          KATE
                        (sits up)
For your crimes, no doubt!

Bill is at a loss, stunned. He sits down to think. Kate sits back, exhausted.

                          BILL

Kate, I was going to tell you everything.

                          KATE

Yeah, when?

                          BILL

In time.

                          KATE

You lied to me.

                          BILL

I never lied to you.

                          KATE

You should leave now. The cops will be here soon.

                          BILL

I don't want to leave.

                          KATE

Your father is at Martin's boat. Dennis said they'll take you with him.

                          BILL

Take me where?

KATE

I don't know.

Bill starts to get up.

BILL

I have to go get Dennis!

Kate stops him. She gets up and closes the door.

KATE

He said not to!

Bill turns to her.

He wants you to go with your father.

Bill looks around the room, feeling helpless and guilty.

BILL

Kate, they've got nothing on me if you tell them I've been here for the past three days.

She looks up and stares at him a moment, then turns away.

KATE

You want me to lie for you.

BILL

Yes.

KATE

I won't lie for you.

BILL

I thought you wanted me to stay.

KATE

I do, I really do. But I won't lie for you. I'm sorry.

He looks away, resigned.

BILL

Don't be.

EXT. PORCH — MOMENTS LATER

The sheriff and a deputy come up on to the porch and knock at the door.

A moment later Kate appears at the window. She doesn't open the door.

> SHERIFF
>
> Hello, Kate.

> KATE
>
> Hello, sheriff.

> SHERIFF
>
> Kate, I understand you know this young man we're hold-ing over at Vic's garage.

> KATE
>
> Yes.

> SHERIFF
>
> How long have you known him?

> KATE
>
> Since yesterday.

> SHERIFF
>
> We believe he's traveling with another man.

Kate doesn't respond. The sheriff waits, then . . .

> Have you seen him with another man?

> KATE
>
> Yes.

> SHERIFF
>
> When?

> KATE
>
> Early this morning.

> SHERIFF
>
> Where?

*Kate's gaze wanders out across nowhere and she sighs wearily.
Then . . .*

                    KATE
Nearby.

*The sheriff looks at the deputy, and the deputy just looks away and
moves his hat back further on his head. The sheriff looks back at
Kate.*

                    SHERIFF
Can you be a little more specific?

                    KATE
Yes.

*They wait, but she doesn't continue. Now the sheriff is getting irri-
tated.*

                    SHERIFF
Kate, this man we're dealing with is quite possibly a dangerous criminal.

                    KATE
How do you know?

                    SHERIFF
What do you mean, how do I know?

                    KATE
What is it that makes a man dangerous, anyway?

                    SHERIFF
Look, I'm asking the questions here, OK!

                    KATE
Well, I guess I don't have any choice, do I?

                    SHERIFF
That's right, you don't!

The sheriff heaves a big sigh, hitches up his trousers, and sits.

Now look, where exactly did you see these two men
together last?

                          KATE
In the street.

                        SHERIFF
This street?

                          KATE
Yes.

                        SHERIFF
Do you know where this other man is now?

Kate steels herself and looks right at him.

                          KATE
No.

                        SHERIFF
Where's Jack?

                          KATE
He left.

                        SHERIFF
Where'd he go?

                          KATE
Florida.

                        SHERIFF
Has this other man gone with him?

                          KATE
No.

                        SHERIFF
Do you mind if we search the premises?

She pauses, then . . .

                          KATE
You'll have to get a warrant.

INT. BAR — TEN MINUTES LATER

Bill comes in the back door, ready but reluctant to leave.

Kate sits at a table, sad and quiet.

Finally . . .

> KATE
>
> Now what?

> BILL
>
> Can I have your car keys?

She hesitates, but then reaches into her pocket and removes her keys. She crosses the room and hands them to him. He watches her as he takes them, but she keeps her face averted.

> KATE
>
> Maybe they won't come back?

> BILL
>
> They'll be back.

She turns to him.

> KATE
>
> Maybe they won't ask questions.

> BILL
>
> They'll ask questions.

Beaten and sad, she leans against him. They kiss.

EXT. PARKING LOT — MOMENTS LATER

Bill peels out of the parking lot, swerves out on to the pavement, and speeds away down the road.

Kate stands on the porch, watching him go. She looks up the road in the opposite direction and sees . . .

The sheriff approaching.

Kate leans back against the front of the bar. She folds her arms, looks at the floor, and waits.

The sheriff and his deputy pull up and get out. They stomp up on to the porch and wave the warrant at Kate. She ignores it and lets them begin their search.

ON THE ROAD . . .

Bill speeds along and passes . . .

THE GAS STATION . . .

Inside, Dennis watches him roar by and smiles to himself.

BACK AT THE BAR . . .

Kate sits silently on the porch as the cops pull the place apart.

AT THE BOAT . . .

Martin and Dad are untying ropes and preparing to disembark when . . .

Bill skids to a stop at the far end of the pier.

Dad looks up from what he's doing and stops.

Bill just sits there, staring at the wheel. Then he sighs and looks out at . . .

Dad, as he steps up on to the pier, watching and waiting curiously.

Bill gets out slowly and stands by the car.

The two men stand there, fifty yards apart, watching each other and waiting.

Elina comes up beside Dad and watches Bill as well.

Bill steps aside and runs his hand through his hair, unable to decide. He hangs his head, distraught, and sighs. Once more, he looks out at . . .

Dad and Elina, waiting.

But Bill just turns and goes back to the car.

Dad and Elina watch him drive off.

EXT. BAR — SAME TIME

Kate sits on the porch steps with her knees drawn up to her chin and her arms wrapped tightly around them. She broods, staring out at the road. She's ignoring the sheriff, who is sitting on the porch sermonizing.

> SHERIFF
>
> Kate, look, I know life's just one big endless quagmire of futility, broken dreams, and smashed hopes! You're not doing yourself any good covering up for this guy! You give your heart and soul to people and they just stomp it to pieces!

But she has seen something approaching up the road. She lifts her head.

In the distance, Bill is speeding toward her.

She lowers her knees and rises slowly from the steps.

The sheriff is exhorting passionately, at this point oblivious to Kate . . .

> Love! Affection! Consideration! These things are myths! Myths invented in a torture chamber! A torture chamber in hell!

Bill plows ahead, closer and closer.

Kate wanders out toward the road, never taking her eyes from . . .

Bill coming nearer and nearer.

> SHERIFF
> (off)
> What can we ever really know about another person anyway! They have their own needs and wants! Their own passionate and perverse dreams! Falling in love is like sticking an ice pick in your forehead . . . But we keep doing it! We hurl ourselves into the cauldron of passion! The bottomless pit of desire . . .

The sheriff's fit fades away as . . .

Kate stands there in the parking lot, waiting.

Bill comes skidding into the parking lot, with a cloud of dust and screeching of tires. He jumps from the car and throws off two deputies as he makes his way to Kate. He stops before her.

She simply waits for him to do something.

He braces himself.

She waits. Then . . .

Bill lowers his head and lays it on her shoulder. She raises her hand and holds him to herself. She holds her cheek to his head.

He closes his eyes.

                    SHERIFF
                    (*off*)

Don't move.

CUT TO BLACK.